# In the Light of the Night and the Dark of the Day

MIDNIGHT SUN

MIDDAY MOON

## Tales of Alaskans at Work and Play

COMPILED BY JANET BOYLAN
EDITED BY JEAN PAAL
ILLUSTRATED BY ROBERT GILMORE
FOREWORD BY GEORGE SULLIVAN

Publication Consultants
Since 1978

PO Box 221974 Anchorage, Alaska 99522-1974
books@publicationconsultants.com — www.publicationconsultants.com

ISBN 978-1-59433-052-0

Library of Congress Catalog Card Number: 2006935283

Copyright 2006
Anchor-Age Center
1300 East 19th Avenue
Anchorage, AK 99501
(907) 258-7823
FAX (907) 278-2454
Website: www.anchorageseniorcenter.org
E-Mail: asc-admin@ak.net

First Edition

Front cover art, pen and ink with watercolor
wash by Robert F. Gilmore, is designed to show
the two seasons in Alaska, as expressed in the title.

Manufactured in the United States of America.

# In Memoriam


Robert J. Cacy

Darryl L. Gremban

Dorothy H. Kruger

# Our Gratitude

A great big thank you for

all those who have helped put this book together.

First of all, thanks to those brave souls who have

trusted us with their stories.

To all those people who called and sent fliers and letters

to friends soliciting stories we owe a debt of gratitude.

A special thank you to the staff of *the Senior Voice*

for helping us get the word out.

The staff and volunteers at the Anchorage Senior Activity Center were

a great help in getting the word out to people who came to the center,

and in making sure the stories got to us.

We appreciate the expert advice

of Evan Swensen of Publication Consultants.

Thank you Dolores Roguszka for your special expertise.

Each of you has been a great help,

and without you this book could not be published.

We apologize for any errors, they are ours alone.

*Janet Boylan*
*Jean Paal*
*Robert Gilmore*

# Contents

## Flying Alaska

## Animal Encounters

## Life in the Bush

# Foreword
## George Sullivan

Looks like she's done it again! First a collection of stories from survivors of the 1964 Alaska earthquake, and now Janet Boylan has managed to collect another fascinating group of stories that help tell how Alaskans are unique. Having 84 years of residency in our great state, I can vouch as to the authenticity or the possibility of most of the stories.

Where else on earth do people suffer from so many different natural disasters? Everything from earthquakes, tidal waves, wind storms, extreme weather conditions, floods, and even volcanic eruptions plague the state.

No other state can boast of an area so huge, larger than twice the size of Texas. Hunting and fishing can almost always guarantee a bounty, and still leave the sportsman wanting to come back again and again just to look and enjoy our the scenery.

Since more than three fourths of the state is inaccessible except by airplane, Alaskans fly more than any other group of people on earth, and hence suffer more crashes, some more serious than others. However, the mishap always offers an extreme challenge to survive, even if the pilot and passengers are lucky enough to live through the crash.

Recreational opportunities are so varied there is no place on earth where so much is possible. Because there are two major seasons, outdoor enthusiasts can enjoy both summer and winter activities in turn, and observe everything from the level of the ocean to Denali, the tallest mountain in North America. Life never gets monotonous.

Alaska, as a state, is so young, people can still remember "territorial days" where the only meaningful law was the federal marshals. The stories in this book help to portray some of that early spirit of the pioneer in the wilderness.

As a collection, the stories in this book portray the uniqueness of the land and its people, as varied and different as the "Great Land" itself and is a must read. I would highly recommend this book to anyone still hoping to live out their dreams of a true Alaska adventure, or anyone who has had an adventure of their own.

*George Sullivan: Mayor of City of Anchorage October, 1967–September, 1975. Mayor of Municipality (after unification of our two local governments) until January 1982.*

# Preface
## Jan Boylan

This book was conceived for two purposes. First, it is a way to preserve some unique Alaska experiences, which others should have an opportunity to enjoy before they are lost forever. People in the public eye have chances to tell their stories, but the stories of less visible people are seldom heard. At the Anchorage Senior Activity Center we have a ready pool of people willing to share their true stories, and we are pleased to provide a forum for them.

The second purpose is to make money for the Anchor-Age Center, a nonprofit corporation. We provide services through the Anchorage Senior Activity Center, an activities, educational, and recreational center for anyone over age fifty-five. It is our hope that one day we will not need to draw on the ever decreasing pool of public money, and can be self-supporting.

# Hunting, Fishing, and Trapping Alaska

# White Fishing—Alaska Style
## Don Boylan

Fishing in Alaska is not quite the same as it was forty years ago. I don't know if what we did was against the law or not, but I don't think so.

The first thing we had to do was build our three pronged spears, which we called "gigs." We put aluminum foil on one side of a Coleman lantern so the light would only show out of the other side. Then we dressed warmly in what was available at the time. First we donned down underwear, then flight pants, which had a thick layer of wool inside and a nylon lining. Down underwear on top went on next, and a heavy down parka. We put bunny boots on our feet over wool socks, cotton monkey-faced gloves on our hands, and a good stocking cap. Most of the time the temperature at that time of year was between twenty and thirty degrees below zero.

The white fish were running in the river around Thanksgiving time, and we could get time off work, so we met at the cabin, and prepared our supplies, snowmachines, sleds, and ourselves for the short trip to the river. We liked to be ready as soon as it got dark.

Fishing was a three person operation, one person in the middle with the lantern shining toward the front. Then one person on either side took their positions. We waded up stream in the middle of the shallow river. In most places it wasn't over knee deep. Because of the light we could see the fish well enough to spear them. Then we threw them up on the river bank and speared the next one. We changed lantern carriers often so we could warm our hands on the lantern before we went back to "fishing." When we had all the fish we wanted, we gathered the frozen fish into gunny sacks, put them on the sled, and rode the snowmachines back to the cabin.

Once my friend, Mutt, slipped on the rocks and sat down in the river. By the time we rode back to the cabin his clothes were frozen in position. Jack and I started for the cabin, and Mutt yelled at us, "Wait a minute, I can't get up."

We pried his hands off the handle bars, all the time laughing at him, carried him into the cabin and sat him in a chair until his clothes thawed out. He sure looked silly, and boy was he mouthy.

After my wife and I got married I was telling her uncle in Idaho about white fishing in Alaska, and he kept saying things like, "Doesn't the water freeze when it's that cold."

"No, the water is running fast enough that it doesn't freeze."

It was obvious he really didn't believe anything I was saying, he kept questioning, "What kind of waders did you wear?"

"We don't wear waders."

"Don't your feet get wet?"

"Yes, but they stay warm in our boots."

"What kind of boots do you wear?" He looked very skeptical. He didn't believe a thing I was saying.

"Bunny boots."

"Bunny boots?" Now he just knew this was a tall tale.

So I decided to oblige him, and I said, "Yeah, you really got to run to catch them bunnies."

The funny thing was that everything I had said to that point was the truth.

After we returned to Alaska word got back to us that he was going around the family saying that, "Finally there is someone in the family that is a bigger liar than I am."

# One Tough Salmon
## Bill Held

On a beautiful slow fishing day in Valdez I was trying to catch my silver limit. I threw my line in the water and slowly reeled in. Suddenly, the beauty of Valdez Bay disappeared from view as water splashed and a huge silver leaped five feet out of the water close to shore. I fought him as he ran away until he suddenly seemed to try a new tactic. The line stopped jerking and he began a slow even retreat. I thought, "This fish isn't that big! Why can't I stop him?" I tried everything. I put my pole tip in the water, turned my pole on its side, but nothing worked. My line steadily made its way out into the bay. Slowly a dark sleek head began to emerge. A seal! The seal had my fish in his mouth; my lure flashed in the salmon's mouth.

When the seal got a look at me glaring at him and at the people now pointing and laughing, he seemed to be so shocked he dropped the fish. I began to reel frantically before the seal could recover but I was not quick enough. The seal grabbed the fish again and I bent double with the weight.

I'm sure the fish was so traumatized by this time I doubt he cared who won. The fight was on. The seal and I glared at each other. I would gain a few yards and then the seal would bear down and out the poor fish would go. Working hard I pulled the seal within fifteen yards of shore. With a fish in his mouth he couldn't swim backwards with force. It was finally more than he could take. He let go. The people on the beach erupted in cheers. I held the wounded fish high and took a bow as the seal swam away.

# Fishing the Talachulitna
## Dr. Darryl Gremban

This was my first trip to Alaska, and I was sort of a flat-lander from the Lower 48. My brother-in-law, Jon Kolbeck, did not understand that I actually did know how to fish. I talked to him and his wife, Eileen, on the phone and asked him to arrange a fishing trip for us when I got up there. He said, "I'll work on it."

Sure enough, he and his friend, Gene Johnson, had a trip organized to float the Talachulitna. He had arranged for a bush pilot to fly us in and supposedly pick us up. (At that time it was always "supposedly" because you never knew if they would show up or not.) We flew in to a little lake, and unloaded all our gear–an inflatable raft, grub, change of clothes, and fishing pole. You didn't want to go in very heavy, so we only had one change of clothes in case we got wet. We could dry out our clothes at night.

When we landed and inflated the raft, Jon said we shouldn't put anything on the floor. Things on the floor cause rafts to scrape as they go over rocks, causing abrasion and tears. So we built a little rack and put some sticks across the pontoons, secured the sticks to the raft, put the gear up on the sticks and off we went. One guy was on the front paddle, one guy on the back paddle, and the third guy sat on the gear and fished as we floated down the stream.

We could see the fish just scurrying out in front from underneath the raft in the crystal clear water, so we would get to a hole, pull ashore and fish for ten to fifteen minutes. Then someone would say, "We've got to make some tracks." and we'd get going, again, changing positions so everybody had a chance to sit on the gear and fish.

It happened that I was up front paddling, Jon was in back paddling and Gene was sitting up on top of the gear, talking pretty smart, "Ha, ha, you're paddling and I'm fishing," when we came around a corner and saw a tree had fallen across the river. There was probably a foot or a foot and a half clearance underneath it. We looked at the situation. The current was pretty fast; we were making hay to get to the tree quicker than we wanted. While we were trying to figure out how to slow up and get around the tree, we banged into it, and swung around parallel to it. The raft was working its way underneath the tree, the water just pushing it, with everybody shouting "What are we going to do?" when it just went. We ducked into the raft bottom, underneath the pontoons as best we could.

We took on some water as we went underneath but we popped up on the other side and were swept on down the river. But only Jon and I were onboard! We looked back and there was Gene, hanging onto the tree with two arms over the top, his legs underneath, and his hip boots filling with water. As Jon and I were trying to figure out how to get the raft stopped and get to shore, Gene was thinking, "Gee, these guys are never going to get stopped. I'm going to have to get to shore and walk," so he just let go. He bopped up on the down-stream side of the tree, buoyed by his life jacket. Then, suddenly, here he was floating alongside the raft. We grabbed him and pulled him in.

Of course he had a few choice words about the situation. He was cold and wet, so we had to stop and get his dry clothes out. Naturally we kept on fishing; it was still early in the day! We started going again.

Now Gene was in front, Jon was in back, and I was sitting on a bunch of gear fishing. As we came around a bend in the river there was a really nice hole. We could just see the fish down in there. I turned around and threw back the line, let it float down, and I had one on. There were fish all over this place. Gene and Jon were trying to get the raft to shore so they could get their poles and fish. Jon says, "Right over there, right over there." They paddled over there, and we said to Gene, "Jump out, jump out and pull us to shore," It didn't look very deep, so he did. Except when he jumped out he was shoulder deep. Now he had both sets of clothes wet, so we decided we really had to stop for the night.

We found a spot on a sand bar, parked our raft there, set up our tent, and got a fire going. Gene was huddled by the fire, cold and trying to dry his clothes. Jon had left home not feeling good, so he crawled into his sleeping bag. I grabbed my pole and went down to the river to fish.

Now, as you will recall, I was the flatlander who needed them to bait my hook, and take care of me, but here I was, down at the river fishing, and yelling out, "Hey, I got one on." Then "Hey I got another one on." The third time I said it they both come tearing down. "We aren't going to let you fish here by yourself."

So that's how I proved myself, showed them I knew how to take care of myself, and I knew how to fish. Then they said, "You can come along fishing with us, anytime."

# A Different Black Bear Hunt
## Lee Miller

The date was September 17, 1971. I was living a few miles south of Anchorage in the Rabbit Creek area. The weather had been really cloudy for several days, then a big high came in from the Alaska Range and cleared the air around South Central Alaska. Sunny days, and it got warm during the middle of the day, 40-50 degrees.

I had been promising to take my boys, Mike 5, and Lynn 7, black bear hunting. On this particular Friday night I told the boys, "It looks like it's gonna be good tomorrow. Let's go for the blackie." I wanted to go up high on the Kenai Peninsula and get one feeding on berries. There was a trail that I learned of while working for the U. S. Forest Service in the late 1950s, while checking out old gold mines. I thought we would go climb up the old trail to the top and glass around for a blackie. I didn't take much gear because it was going to get warm during the day and I didn't want to have to pack a bunch of coats, hats and gloves along with the bear meat if we got one. All the boys had were their sweaters. I had on a light windbreaker and was carrying cheese cloth meat sacks to keep the meat clean.

We finally got on the trail about 8 a.m. When we got up to where the old cabin used to be, we found it dilapidated, as the miner had been gone for years. The lower areas of the mountains on the Kenai Peninsula are covered with alders, willows, and devil's club and are sometimes tough to get through. That's why I like to stay on these old trails. This one had grown over, but we did manage to follow it up through the lower part of the timber and brush and finally break out into the open. That is when we hit the wind, 10 to 15 knots right out of the north, and very cold.

As we climbed up, I noticed the boy's hands were starting to get a little blue. The only other thing we had, besides what we were wearing, were the meat sacks, so I took those out and wrapped them around their heads to keep their heads and ears warm. After another 45 minutes, almost at the top of the ridge, I told the boys that maybe we'd better turn around because they were really cold.

I put them behind some big rocks and said, "You guys stay there, out of the wind, and I'll climb to the top and look around. There might be a blackie right over the top of this ridge."

So they snuggled down behind the rocks and I went to the top and glassed around. I didn't see anything close by, but happened to glance across the valley and saw a couple of white spots which I recognized as sheep. I put the glasses on them and saw there were four of them lying on the top, on the rocky ledges. They looked like rams. Although I couldn't tell how big, you can kind of see those horns, even at a great distance.

So I yelled at the boys, "Come on up and take a look over here. I want to show you something before we go back!

They climbed up and I pointed out the sheep to them. They got all excited and I said, "You know, it is sheep season and I do have a sheep harvest ticket. I think those are all rams. Wouldn't it be something if we could go get one of those sheep? It's too bad it's so cold."

They wanted to go after the sheep, although it was a long walk. I said, "It's up to you guys."

They said, "Well, let's go." All of a sudden they were a little bit warmer.

I said, "Okay, we'll give her a try. If it gets too bad, we'll turn back."

We dropped back down below the ridge and paralleled it for approximately three quarters of a mile to the mouth of the valley. There was a glacial moraine going across the mouth and we worked our way below the little lip of the moraine so the sheep couldn't spot us. You had to watch very carefully where you stepped, so you wouldn't fall in the loose rock and make a lot of noise.

One thing in our favor was the wind coming down the valley, away from the sheep. We got on the other side and worked our way around the corner of the entrance to the valley, keeping behind the rocks, and got within five or six hundred yards of where the four sheep were lying. They were up the valley and above us; there was no cover except hummocks, grass and moss covered mounds. I told the boys there was no way to go except right up the valley in the open. Sometimes sheep, if they haven't been spooked or hunted hard, will stand and observe before leaving. I was very familiar with this area and had never seen sheep near here, so I thought maybe they hadn't ever been hunted. It was not a valley one would expect to find sheep.

We had to decide how to advance (none of us had proper footwear for the terrain). The boys had worked up kind of a sweat and forgotten about their cold walk across the moraine. I said, "There's only one thing we can do. Sometimes these sheep are curious enough if they haven't been hunted hard, that they don't know what to do. It's not that they don't see you, but they'll just lay there and watch you for a while. You guys get down between these hummocks out of the wind, and I'm going to go right up the valley floor and see how close I can get."

I had my old 270 cal. Winchester model 70 with 150 gr. bullets, which I found to be the best for long range shooting, and zeroed in for about 250 yards. It's pretty accurate at even 350 yards, so I started up the valley floor, in the wide open, with the wind coming down in my favor. I got part way up and sat down. Glassing them over, I checked that they were all four rams and looked like they were legal. They stayed lying down as I studied them, so I kept going up. Then the whistler marmot started howling (whistling) giving the alarm.

At the sound of the whistle, two of the sheep stood up and started moving off but the others remained lying down. I got within 350 to 400 yards and they stood up. I lay down on one of those hummocks and took a good look. I picked out the largest one, horn-wise, and thought, "This is it. I can't get any closer." I knew I was within range, and I sighted and fired. I hit him. The other three took off over the top.

I stood up and waved for the boys and they came running up. We were within 200 yards when the wounded sheep stood up. I sat down and put a finishing shot into him. We then climbed up to where he fell, part way down the base of the cliff and dragged him down to the flat part of the upper valley in the grassy area. The boys were all excited. We took a few pictures.

I started boning the sheep out. I hadn't really planned on packing a sheep out. I had to really do some close boning. After I salvaged all the meat I could we cut the horns off. He was a nice young sheep, certainly no trophy, but legal.

I took the meat sacks off the boys and loaded up all the meat on the pack. I also took the horns, as required by law as proof of size, and the skull plate.

It was getting into the late afternoon when we started back down the valley. By the time we got about halfway back, I was really starting to wear down, but the boys were recuperating now. We hit a few berry patches on the way down and enjoyed a meal of blueberries and bearberries. Further down, we found some smooth slopes where the boys were able to roll down. After a while, I talked Lynn into carrying my rifle so I at least had that much less weight.

We got back to the truck just as it was getting dark and loaded up all our gear. That's how our black bear hunt ended that day. Out of the eight sheep I've killed, this one was the most memorable. I certainly won't forget, it, and I'm sure the boys won't either. They were probably the youngest sheep hunters in the state that year.

# The Ghost Caribou
## Robert J. Cacy

I had been on a business trip to Valdez, and returning to Fairbanks I stopped in at Paxson Lodge near Summit Lake for lunch. While visiting I learned large Woodland Caribou were still crossing the road about forty miles down the Denali Highway. Even though I was by myself, I decided to drive down that gravel side-road to see if any could be seen. I always carried my rifle while traveling during hunting season. My 30/40 Krag was in a black suitcase type carrier with my hunting knife, binoculars—everything necessary.

In September the light does not last long, so I finished my lunch and set out. It was mid week; there was no other traffic on the road. Right at forty miles, off in the distance I saw one lone caribou. Opening my case, I grabbed my rifle, opened the lever action and reached for a box of ammunition. I couldn't believe my eyes. I always carried extra ammunition, but no box was to be seen. Totally emptying the case I found three shells. I had carried this rifle more than twenty years, and most years, one shot was enough to down my game. With confidence I marched away from the pickup on this overcast day and walked toward what I considered to be my caribou.

There aren't many trees in this area, just occasional willows, but the tundra has a rolling shape, so that sometimes I would be two or three feet below the horizon. Finally, quite a distance from the road, I located the caribou again, walking away from me. The distance was great, but with confidence I pulled the trigger. My caribou took a few more steps. I pulled the trigger again, and it took a few more. I must get closer. I only had one bullet left. The caribou moved away. Finally there appeared to be a good shot. I fired my last shell. I heard it hit my caribou. I waited and waited, probably ten minutes. Then I realized this caribou would not lie down.

I returned to the highway, and had to make a decision. I could return to Paxson to locate ammunition or I could stop the first car and ask if they had a rifle. But there had been no traffic. Then I remembered a small lodge within ten miles, but how likely was it that they would have ammunition for my ancient rifle?

They did! With many thanks I literally ran out the door to my pickup. The overcast had now descended, bringing snow–so much snow that it was difficult to tell where I'd been parked. Making a best guess I started in the direction where I had last seen my caribou. I could only see about fifty feet and the ground was now snow-covered. I became cautious, looking at brush and rocks for markers to my return.

Suddenly right in front of me, the caribou jumped to its feet, almost like dancing and ran off into the snowstorm. I wasn't ready, and it was gone. Looking at the ground, I could see the sign that he was wounded. Now I must finish what I had started. The snow started to let up, and in the distance I could see him entering an opening in some trees. I took my direction and started toward that opening in a sudden squall which stopped as I arrived at the opening through the trees. There was a caribou track!

I walked slowly and quietly; from the sign of the track my caribou was slowing down, but so was I. I was tired, and beginning to get cold. As I walked through the trees without any landmark, I had a feeling I should turn to the left. I also imagined meeting the caribou face to face, he with his huge antlers, and I with only a gun. It was scary and I was hallucinating. I looked around, then behind me. What I saw scared the hell out of me. There was the caribou ghost, covered with snow, following me.

It was one of the most difficult shots of my life.

I cleaned my caribou, placed one hindquarter on my shoulder and with the gun in my hand began walking through the snow in what I hoped was the direction of my pickup. The snow was continuing; visibility was poor. I found the pickup, left my gun, and started across the tundra following my tracks from minutes before, but, as I progressed, they disappeared in the snow and increasing darkness. Nevertheless, I found the caribou again, but I began to realize this was my last trip. I took the two front quarters and tied them in a tree, put the remaining hind-quarter on my shoulder and started back to my pickup again. I was tired. I finally conceded the loss of my front quarters of caribou. This probably was the only intelligent thinking that I had done that day.

The following day I was still exhausted. My two teenage boys, who were anxious to go hunting, volunteered to go and retrieve the two front quarters. One day later they returned with the meat.

This story is really about how these boys, Rob and Brooke, were able bring home the bacon. Without firing a shot, and searching practically without landmarks, working from a description of what I saw when I was 90% lost, I don't see how they found that caribou.

# A Packer's Bonus
## Caleb Coleman

My Grandma was bugging me about getting a job and I was at her house looking in the paper for a job. There was an ad in the classified section for a packer, a job which paid $50 a day plus room and board. I made a call, contacted Sam and rode my bike over to meet him at McDonald's in Spenard.

We had a short interview and he bought me a cup of coffee, even though I don't drink it. He asked me if I ever did any hunting or been in the woods. I told him, "Yes, lots."

He asked if I had a gun and I said, "Yes." He said I could bring it with me but my job would be packing moose out for the hunters. He didn't seem very nice, but I took the job anyway.

I went home and packed some things and took the 12 gauge that I had. My grandma hoards old crap, and there I found a pack-board to use. The next thing I knew I was in Cordova. We spent two nights there because the weather was so bad planes couldn't fly. I had to do dishes at the lodge where we stayed. Not much fun!! After two days the weather finally lifted and we were flown out to Tsui Lodge east of Cordova.

As soon as I got to the lodge I was told to go help a hunting party, so I boarded a super cub and was flown straight out to the Bering Glacier Drainage, a terrible place to be. I met Doug who was the guide for the trip. I had no idea what I was doing. Doug told me there was a moose they had killed only one half mile away. So I excitedly said, "Let's go get it." I wouldn't have been so anxious if I had known what I was getting myself into.

As I started packing the moose out, I realized that as far as I could see there was knee deep swamp, and head high brush–pretty difficult trying to hike through with 150 pounds of moose on my back. I had never been more tired in my life, and then, about half way back to camp, that old pack-board started to break apart, which made it darn hard to pack the moose.

I made it all the way back, but it was terrible. When I got back to camp my legs locked up with "Charlie-horses" and I couldn't move them for a while. I was only 21 years old and thought I was in good physical shape before I got to camp (I was a runner and rode my bike all the time) but that didn't help me on that day. Furthermore, and unfortunately for me, Doug had an extra pack, so they gave me that to use, which meant I got to hike back out to retrieve the rest of the moose. Retrieve it I did, and I was hurting the entire time. The next plane with supplies brought a good back pack for me.

A big down-side to being in the bush is that I only had two sets of clothes. The clothes you wear in the woods get wet, so you are supposed to hang your wet ones up at night and sleep in your dry set. The next day you're supposed to put your wet clothes back on, since when you are moving so much in the woods you get hot and sweaty and can stay warm. I told my stupid self, "Screw that!" I didn't want to get into wet clothes. I went out in the dry clothes and left the wet ones hanging in camp. After we had hiked to the kill site and packed in the rest of the moose, of course, I had two sets of wet clothes.

All the moose was out of the woods and we had to wait for the super cub to come and pick us up. Normally they fly the client out first, but this time they took me first, because I was so wet and cold and shivering they were worried about my health. I have never shivered more in my entire life.

I had only been there two days and I had three months left. The boss asked me if I wanted to quit. I said, "No! Quitting is for wimps."

He said, "Good, since you made it through the past two days you can make it all summer."

The guides are only allowed to take two moose from the Bering Glacier Drainage and I happened to be the unlucky greenhorn packer who was sent there with that piece of crap backpack. Honestly after making it through that I, too, felt I could make it, because I learned a lot from my mistakes. I went on more packs and things got a lot better from then on.

When you are a packer at a lodge, you always have to do a bunch of chores. We needed to dig a new leach field for the restrooms there. It was a large leach field. I came in from packing one night, a much easier pack than the first one. The cook wanted me to help her do dishes. I told her, "No," because I'm stubborn. When I said I wouldn't do dishes the boss told me I could start digging for the new cesspool and leach field. I went outside and grabbed a shovel and started digging. I dug ten to twelve hours a day for the next seven days. The first three days people told me I was stupid and I should have listened, but I was pig-headed and wouldn't give in and wash those dishes. After digging alone for three days others started to help me. The "cess" pool was about 12x14 and 12 feet deep. Fortunately it was sandy and easy digging, but sometimes the sides would fall in. When I finally got it deep enough we cut trees and lined the inside of the pit with logs and wrapped it with burlap to hold the walls.

When that was all done I never had to do dishes, although everyone else had to take a turn. I won my point, but it would have been much easier just to do the dishes.

We came to the end of the season, and the boss told me I could go hunting for a black bear, something I wanted to do. I was fleshing out the hides (scraping the fat from them) when one of the planes landed and Desmond, the pilot, told me to grab my gear and get on the plane. I had only five minutes to get ready before I got left. I immediately dropped everything because I finally got to do something fun. I gathered my gear and extra food and ran to the plane.

I got dropped off in the Suckling Hills, and set up camp late in the evening. I felt a little concerned because I was all alone in the woods; I had never been hunting alone before. From in my tent I could hear the animals all around me. I had a borrowed 300 Winmag rifle, which I grabbed and stepped out. I could not see any critters, but I could sure hear them. There was a full moon and the air was crystal clear. Beautiful! I could look out and see the coastline of Cape Suckling. I fired a few shots in the air, and then went in and slept for a couple of hours.

The next morning when the sun rose I woke up and grabbed my rifle. I came out of the tent and made some oatmeal and raisins for chow and started my hunt. In the span of the first four hours, I counted thirty eight bear; it's a real pick-and-shoot area. I was hiking up the ridge and as I came over the top I saw a nice bear with his head down after a ground squirrel. There was a little ledge beneath him, which I hoped he would stay on. I took aim at the bear and fired one shot. It was a perfect shot. The bear dropped and rolled down the hill. The ledge didn't stop him. He rolled into a tiny stream and wedged under a bush. I hiked my sorry butt down there. As I was going down a good incline, I slipped and started to slide. I suddenly realized I was going to slide right into that bear, and I couldn't stop. I managed to chamber another round, scared to death that it was still alive. My two feet hit the bear and stopped me. I scrambled back as fast as I could move. Luckily for me the first shot did the job and the bear was dead.

The work started as I dragged the carcass from under the bush and out of the creek where I could get at it to skin it. I then realized that in my excitement and haste to leave camp I had left my skinning knife where I had been using it to flesh hides. I began to think I was in a pretty bad position. I was in a gully alone, and I had seen thirty eight bears in the vicinity; I had listened to them all night. I was more than a little scared.

The only knife I had on me was a Swiss Army knife that my grandma had bought me. I had to skin the bear and get out of there. To my knowledge I am the only person ever to skin a bear using a Swiss Army knife.

It makes a boring story, but, with so many bears around, not one came over the ridge toward me. I took the hide and skull and the next day I got picked up by the plane with my prized bear and a great story to tell back at camp.

This all happened quite a few years ago, but I have relived every minute of the adventure while relating this story. Some of the memories are good and some are not, but it was a summer when I learned so much and will never forget.

# Trapping With My Dad
## Gladys Markley Jones

Dad's trap line on Judd Lake was located 90 air miles west of Anchorage; just past Mt. Susitna and was accessible only by bush plane. Dad usually used Toivo Aho or Haakon Christensen to fly us over. No matter what the weather was they were almost always able to find the trap line without navigational aids of any type. The trap line had five cabins, about five miles apart.

The minute we stepped out of the plane you could feel the wonder of the area. It was unbelievably beautiful. The white of the snow was translucent. It was almost surreal; like being on another planet. I could see why dad loved it so much. It was very still and quiet, except for the wolves at night.

Our days were spent on snowshoes going from cabin to cabin inspecting and resetting the traps along the way. When we got back to the main cabin, dad dried the skins and stretched them on the cabin walls and ceiling.

At that time you were allowed to trap as many mink, martin, wolverine, ermine and fox as you wanted, but the Federal Fish and Wildlife required that you "tag" a limit of only 10 beaver. To support a family of seven, you needed to "tag" as many limits as possible. So, for one week each year Dad would take me, my brother, Bill, and my mom to the trap line so we could each trap a limit of beaver.

The year I was 16 and my brother was 12, Dad made us roll the beaver hides, tie them with a rope, strap them to our backs and walk in shoepacs from our home on Fifteenth and H to the Federal Building on Fourth - a distance of twelve awful blocks right past our school where hundreds of eyes were staring at that strange sight. When I was a child, Dad would always tell me if I stepped into a hole, I would drop down to China, and right then I was wishing I could find that hole. Instead, unfortunately, we kept going past the school–all my classmates, my teachers, all the boys that I idolized. I could feel a hundred eyes on me.

Worse was yet to come.

Before going in, dad had warned us to just speak when spoken to, only answer the questions asked and not to volunteer any information unnecessarily. When we entered the office, they recognized Dad and knew that he'd probably caught the majority of the furs. So, they scoffed at us and began to quiz us kids on how we caught these. I rose to my dad's defense, "My dad taught me how to set a trap, I know how to shoot an animal, I can 'mark' the trail, I can snowshoe all day with my dad." Finally, I could hear dad shushing me in the background and I shut up. The agents finally relented and tagged our beaver.

One-quarter of a mile from the Judd Lake Cabin there was later a world-class hunting and fishing lodge.

Early Anchorage

# Money for School Clothes
## Colleen Markley Rutledge

Starting in the mid 30s my father, Bill Markley, and his brother, Jake, had a five-cabin trapline in the Judd Lake-Talchulitna area. They bought the trapline from "old man Judd." When I was six and starting first grade, dad gave me a wolverine hide. When it was time to sell the furs I bargained with the old fur buyer that came to our house for money for my wolverine. With the proceeds I could buy school clothes. I think I got $25 and that went a long way for clothing in that day and age.

Summers we had set-net sites at Granite Point in Trading Bay, Cook Inlet. Dad and my brother, Bill, would "pick" the fish out of the nets at high tide using a dory. There would always be a few fish caught on the ebb that they couldn't get back to with the dory. At the start of my freshman year, Dad gave me all the Kings that were caught on the ebb from one beach site. So, without benefit of water to help ease the fish out of the net, I would manage to get them loose, then attach them securely to a gaff hook and slip-sliding away (falling in the mud many times) I would head for the beach dragging my fish behind me. Depending on how many fish were caught that day, I may have had to make that trip several times. The money I earned, I could spend on school clothes when I started high school. At the time, the cannery paid $5 for each King and once again was a nice payoff for me.

I always admired my dad because he did what made him happy (hunting, fishing and trapping), and managed to support five kids while doing it. Mom was a partner in his adventures and did the really hard work in making ends meet between two paydays a year–one in the fall after fishing and one in the in the spring after trapping.

# Alaskan Hospitality
## Arlene R. Cross

In a hot, sticky, non-air-conditioned college classroom at Pennsylvania Museum and School of Industrial Arts (P.M.S.I.A.) Philadelphia I made a passing remark that I was going to Alaska some day to escape this heat.

The student next to me said, "You are? I've already sent to Delegate Bartlett for information on homesteading in Alaska using my GI bill."

Bob and I spent the rest of the year planning our trip and by March, 1947 we had left our classes and jobs, bought a surplus army jeep and trailer, gathered our gear for homesteading, and talked my brother into going along with us. We were married March 16 and left for Alaska on April 16. On the road about everything imaginable on that jeep gave out or had to be replaced. The clutch and transmission left us in debt in Canada, and we arrived in Alaska on June 7 broke, but with a practically new jeep.

My brother got a job with the Alaska Railroad the second day here and left for Ferry, a section house north of Healy. Bob was hired as a draftsman under Art Reinikka at Fort Richardson, but he didn't start work until August. Instead he went to the Army Hospital with an appendicle abscess. The head nurse, Tina Rozell, took me home with her. She said I couldn't stay in our tent down by Ship Creek by myself. She put me to work cleaning up after the wedding reception she just had for her brother and sister-in-law, Rusty and Viola Halverson. Then she recommended me for a job at Post Signal as a telephone operator. I was able to get into married quarters on the Post, but the Rozell's stored our jeep and trailer in their back yard until Bob got out of the hospital.

The Army Hospital was located in a row of barracks out near where the weigh station is now located on Glen Highway. It was a very dry summer and they nearly had to evacuate the hospital due to forest fires along the Chugach Mountains. The military managed to control that fire, but forest fires burned out of control east of Sterling on the Kenai Peninsula. The winds were blowing north and kept Anchorage smoky all that first summer in Alaska.

Bob went to work, but Labor Day week end he was back in the Army hospital with a ruptured appendix. I've never been sorry I made that comment about getting out of the heat back in Philadelphia. This truly is God's country. He has transplanted some of the most wonderful caring people in the world to this area and I thank God daily I've been here among them.

# Coming to Alaska
## Micki Nelson McGhuey

As a boy my dad heard all about Alaska from his father, who had come up to work on the "Iron Trail" in about 1920. He learned about the beauty of the place, and how much his dad wanted to come back. Unfortunately, when Dad was nine he lost his father, so the dream was never realized. That is, not until Dad, Clarence Nelson, left his family outside and came to the far north with nothing but his ticket.

Dad's journey began in the spring of 1937. He left Seattle by steamship in search of his future. When he arrived in Seward, he had very little money in his pockets. He took the train to the first stop, Moose Pass, got off the train and worked there until he had enough money to continue on to Anchorage. Work was very scarce, but he did many odd jobs before he found the job he wanted. He worked on the railroad, a gold dredge in Money, helped out in a local hotel, worked at Piggly Wiggly grocery store, and for George Vera at the Pepsi Cola Bottling Company. By the time the termination dust hit the mountains in the fall he knew he needed to go home, and come back later with a bigger stake. He left Alaska by ship that fall.

In 1942, he finally came back determined this time to make it. He returned to a job at the Pepsi Cola Bottling Company at the corner of 5th and I Street. Later he and a friend, Earl Stenehjem started the first potato chip company in Alaska, "Alaskan Made Potato Chips."

Houses were very scarce then, and you were happy to find what you could, but Dad was anxious to send for his family. In the summer of 1944 he found a house that was in his price range at 12th and E Street. The family was soon on our way from Tacoma, Washington.

It was August by the time Mom had sold our large farm type house, boxed up all our worldly goods and shipped them off to Alaska. She said her goodbyes to all her brothers and sisters, whom she knew she would not see again for a long time. With ticket in hand, she took my brother Andy 5, and me, 8 together with our bag and baggage, and went to Seattle to board the steamship. No one told her she needed reservations. The last ship to leave Seattle for the year, the Nome Boat, would take the outside route (open sea) all the way to Seward, then on to Nome to deliver food and supplies to keep them over for the winter.

We arrived at the docks in Seattle, ready to go, only to find a full ship. My mom begged the Captain not to leave us behind, no matter what; we had to get on that ship. She did not want to have to spend the winter with her mother in law until the next spring, and she was determined to get on the ship. She was packed and ready to go. The Captain finally felt sorry for this crying woman with two kids in tow, but the problem was the ship was already over booked. Even the Captain's Quarter's on the top of the ship was housing extra women, but they did have one bunk available. I got that one in his stateroom, Mom got a bunk on the mid deck, and my five hear old brother was given a bunk in the hold with five grown men that promised to watch this active boy and keep him out of trouble.

The seas were very rough, and nearly everyone was very seasick for several days, but one active five year old had free run of the ship. After we recovered, Mom was playing bingo one evening, when a little girl came up to her mother and said, "That's the mother of the little boy, that slid all the way down the outside of the ship when everyone was so sick." My mother went right down to the men that were supposed to be taking care of her son, grabbed her little boy, and the rest of the trip he slept with her, even though the Captain was not too happy with a boy in with the women.

On board the ship were a lot of kids coming home for school, which started in September, just after we arrived. They had been outside visiting their grandparents or family for the summer. One I remember was Corkey Kellogg, who played the piano to entertain us. Most of the kids came to Anchorage and we were friends all the way through school.

Other things we did besides run all over the ship was to play blackjack. We played for pennies, and when the losers ran out of pennies we begged pennies from the other passengers. By the time the ship landed we had every penny that was available on the ship.

Mom must have been very disappointed when she saw our house. She had left a big house, a big family, and our house was so tiny we had to climb over the bed in the master bedroom to get to the bathroom. There was one bedroom, living room with room for a small table, an oil heater sat in the middle of the floor, and there was a small kitchen barely large enough to turn around in. Many of the things she had shipped up had to stay in boxes for many years.

The laundry room sported a stationary tub, a set of bunks for my brother and me, a few shelves for groceries and a wringer washing machine. Clothes were hung out and left to freeze dry. When they came in they stood up on the floor until they thawed so they could be folded and put away. Because wet clothes were carried outside, water dripped onto the floor in the doorway and froze solid. Often the door would not close all the way. But, no matter, it would be our home for a few years.

Many people who came to Alaska arrived without a job or a place to live. Housing was scarce so they would knock on doors. People came to our house looking for a room. We had a garage available with a car work pit in it that we ended up renting out to a couple so they would have shelter for the winter. They had no trouble finding a job, as they were entertainers and wanted a job in a bar. There were lots of bars.

In those early years many people lived below ground. The first thing they had to do was purchase a piece of land or if they were lucky, qualify for a homestead or home sight, and clear some land. Then they would build a home. Many would start with the basement first, live in that until they had money to build the next floor, and when the house was finished it was paid for. During the winter when we walked around town, on some lots all we could see was a small building that looked like an out house with a floor and behind that was a stove pipe coming out of the ground. The small house was the entrance to very steep steps going almost straight down into the living quarters of the house, and the chimney kept the smoke out.

Where we lived was near the outskirts of town, since it didn't go much past what is now Fifteenth Avenue. Chester Creek was through the woods. My brother, Andy, loved to go fishing at the creek. I would tag along with him and sit on the rocks by the creek and watch him fish all day. He didn't like me going along, because when he would catch a fish I always wanted to hold it, and as soon as he would hand it to me, it would slip right out of my fingers, and back into the water. He would get so mad at me, he would stomp all the way home so he could tell what I did. But still, the next time he would let me go with him.

One day we were fishing and heard a lot of noise in the woods. A bunch of dogs were barking, natural curiosity got the best of us and we had to go see why all the commotion. Someone had left all those poor dogs locked up, and they were crying and howling to get out. We felt very sorry for them, all locked up and no one to play with. We had a lot of fun that day, running and playing, and jumping. Later we found that all those lonely, sad puppies were at the city dog pound.

My dad was delivering Pepsi Cola down town that day, and when he came home from work that night he said no one could figure out why the whole town was suddenly over run with stray dogs. There were a lot of them hanging around our house, almost like they were waiting for someone to come out and play with them. They hung around for a couple of days and we did get to keep one of them. We hoped others found a new home before they were caught again.

We had many more adventures, as we grew up in Alaska. It is too bad my grandfather was never able to return to see what had become of the land he loved and dreamed about.

# Tenting on Our Road
## Phyllis Chamberlin

In the spring of 1951 my husband, Bill, and I moved out to the Hillside from East Anchorage where we had lived for four years, and settled on five acres of land we received, through the auspices of the Bureau of Land Management, from a soldier who relinquished it to us for a small fee.

Guided by BLM rules, we had the choice of designating the property as either (1) a home site, (2) a cabin site, or (3) a trade and manufacturing site. We opted for a cabin site, leaving the other two categories in case we wanted to use them later.

Before moving we dug a pit for an outhouse–a requirement to proving up on the property.

Our neighbors in town, Charlie and Ruth Cannon, acquired the five acres next to us, so we all moved out at the same time, using our four-yard dump truck to accommodate our belongings, including about 40 sled dogs, theirs and ours, and accompanying dog houses, dog food and gear.

Moving onto the property was a laborious affair. The weather was rainy for days and the half-mile from O'Malley Road to our property was a morass of mud. In order to negotiate it we had to move the wheels of our vehicle over about a foot each time we used the road, often winding up on the berm to escape getting really stuck. If the road was too bad, we walked, carrying everything we absolutely had to have. I was about four months pregnant so it was not easy for me. We also had a three-year old son, Robert, a cute, funny little boy.

We lived in a tent the first year. Before we began bringing our belongings and building supplies, we hired George McCullough and his TD24 Caterpillar bulldozer to clear a building site for the house and, a hundred or so feet away, a site to pitch our two tents, in which we would live while we built the house.

To begin with we put up two separate tents: The first was an 8 x 10-foot cooking tent, with a wood floor and four-foot sidewalls. On one wall inside we installed cupboards made up of empty Blazo boxes, (at a premium with homesteaders) which made excellent shelves for foodstuffs, etc. Across the top we nailed a ¾ inch sheet of plywood for the work counter.

At the end of the counter we put a five-gallon wooden barrel for water. Bill put a spigot at the bottom. We installed a new, galvanized 50-gallon garbage can in the corner behind the stove and hauled water every day from the creek a half mile away. When the little barrel on the counter ran out we had plenty in the big can. We needed a lot of water. In addition to the family's needs, we cooked a huge pot of dog food every day. We were told part of the Hillside was a glacial moraine and getting water would be an iffy prospect. Ultimately, much later, Bill "witched" our well and found water at about 83 feet—fine, good water. But until then, we hauled water. That chore, along with cutting and splitting wood for the stove kept Bill busy.

On either side of the tent we installed a wood Yukon stove with a flat cooking top and a small oven, which was also our heat, winter and summer. There was just room to put a card table, two chairs and a stool.

Cooking on a wood stove was a lesson in patience. It was often too hot or too cold. And trying to cook frozen eggs was the funniest. We always had scrambled eggs because we discovered when eggs froze the yolks broke. I was glad I had some experience cooking on a wood stove a couple of years earlier when we went trapping up north.

The second tent was a 16 x 20 foot tarp flung over a tent frame. In this tent we piled our belongings on wood pallets; in the front part we put our double bed on top of many boxes. Robert's crib was in the corner. This "sleeping tent" was about ten feet from the cooking tent. The dogs, about twenty of them, we tied to trees on the property - not too close to our living area.

Before it got really cold, Bill and I built a 16 x 16-foot addition to the cooking tent, with a wood floor and four-foot side walls. We moved our bed and Robert's crib into the new addition, put a rug on the floor and life was much more confortable. Although, at night, when it was 30 degrees below zero outside, it was 30 below zero inside. When it got really cold Robert slept with us.

Every so often the dogs would begin a huge uproar and we would discover a moose had invaded their space. We always got a kick out of watching our dogs and the visiting animals. We saw a fox, lots of moose, and the most curious was the neighborhood lynx who spent the winter nights up on Birch Road on Fenwick's basement roof, curled around their stovepipe. We saw lots of birds and one day a flock of tiny owls landed in the trees in the yard. They made high, piercing whistles. They stayed for about an hour and we were delighted to see them.

Our winter days were routine. In the morning our blankets were covered with dew from condensation from our breath. I was working for the Office of Rent Stabilization as assistant to the attorney and Bill worked at Ft. Richardson in Roads and Grounds. Every morning we watered the dogs, got ourselves and Robert dressed and fed and set out for town, dropping Robert at the baby sitter on the way.

We had no electricity until very late in the fall, just before it got really cold. There was no telephone service yet, so we and other neighbors on Our Road, and even the two families across O'Malley Road on Our Road North hooked up field telephones.

We had many fun adventures in the coming year, during which we began building our log house.

Getting building materials to the site was difficult because the mud was so bad on the road. Construction firms charged a delivery fee of at least $10.00 to deliver anything on the hillside area. They said we were nuts for trying to live in the "boondocks." We just laughed.

We poured cement footings for our house on a bitterly cold day in October. In those days the cement firms did not have insulated trucks–they just mixed with hot water, hoping they could make the delivery and pour before the cement froze. They didn't quite make it soon enough to our place and at the last of the pour we helped the driver knock freezing cement out of the mixer. Then Bill and I worked madly to cover the cement with heavy roofing paper and then shovel cold-frozen dirt over the top to keep the cement from cooling too rapidly.

Our Road was not called Our Road early on–it was called Canberlin Road, for Chamberlin and Cannon, the first residents. Later it officially became Our Road when a neighbor penciled the name in an area map he made for the City Telephone directory. We all called it Our Road anyway so the name suited all of us.

I still live on our property on Our Road–in 2006, 55 years later.

# True Adventures of
# Mr. Polar Bear
## Janice Johnstone

In the spring of 1967 my husband came home from work one day and asked me if I'd like to move to Alaska! As soon as I found a map and had a dim view of where Alaska was and that, yes, there was a road through Canada, I truly felt we could make this move.

We arrived in Anchorage on the last day of June 1967, and I was glad to have a long holiday weekend to house hunt and get my bearings. Little did I know that a good many houses being built at this time already were covered by "options to buy" from the oil companies.

We did know one couple in Anchorage and we had an invitation to come to their house for lunch as soon as we arrived. Our friends lived in Scenic Park; way out at the end of Tudor Road. When we drove around the subdivision we saw a house for sale and I made a call to the realtor to meet us at four that afternoon. We had been in Anchorage less than twenty four hours and I had a vacant house to look at. Having four kids in a tent would never have been my idea of a good move.

The house was wonderful, big yard, nice subdivision, and it was vacant; but there was one small detail–or should I say one really big detail.

The man selling the house was moving to Kenai, and he did not want to take anything with him. Not the furniture and definitely not the standing mount polar bear in the family room. Yep! If I wanted the house I would have to keep the polar bear.

I wanted the house, but I soon found out this was no ordinary polar bear. He had a name, and had been to court twice.

Shorty was a Guinness Book record size bear and so Jan Koslosky, who shot him, decided to have a standing mount done instead of a rug. However, the taxidermist turned the job over to a young man working for him and the young man cut the bear hide down to fit a pre-made plaster form. The bear was cut around the middle and its legs were shortened so "Shorty" was no longer an award-winning bear.

Mr. Koslosky took the taxidermist to court, suing him for damages. The taxidermist had to pay an undisclosed amount for the mistake and he got to keep the bear.

The taxidermist gave the bear to the First National Bank to put in the lobby of the downtown branch. The Vice President of the bank loved the bear and named him, so when the Vice President left to go into business for himself, the bank gave him the bear.

Next the taxidermist sued the bank for giving away the bear. He had intended for the bank to keep the bear in the lobby as advertising. The judge ruled that the taxidermist gave the bear to the bank and therefore the bank could give it away.

So Shorty was moved to the family room in the Scenic Park home of the ex-Vice President, and hence came to us.

To Mr. Bear's credit he did not stand in a corner ignored for the thirty eight years I lived in the house. He got some revenge of his own. One woman ended up with four stitches in her head when she stood up under the outstretched paws. He withstood an attack by a dog. Once, he terrified a small child who went down the stairs to play. When she saw the bear, she screamed, "Big dog!" It took a full year to get her back in the basement. I learned that you should not put a pool table too close to a bear as a really good shot can be ruined with one swipe of his paw. I rose up and cut my shoulder on the claws. The bear may be stuffed, but the claws are real.

Now the bear is going to a new home. I have sold the house and am moving to a town house, which has no room for Mr. Bear, so my son is moving Shorty to his home to reside in his family room and reign over his four children.

# Life in Wonder Park
## Vicki Rearick

In 1951 Jim, my husband, came home from Korea. He had no work so we decided to travel the Alcan to Anchorage. With one child, we arrived in Anchorage and moved into my brother's two room house. It was unfinished with no bathroom. The Mexicans next door, who didn't speak English, let us share their outhouse. We put up sheet rock on the walls and filled the cracks in the floor with rags and old socks and spent the winter there.

Jim got a job with Gilman's Bakery on Cordova Street between Fifth and Sixth Avenues. Pappy Gilman owned it. At the same time Grover Fireoved subdivided his homestead between what is now McCarry Street and Boniface Parkway. We bought one of those lots on Kobuk and Bunnell, then the only street in the subdivision.

We started clearing and planned the house. Work was seasonal and Jim was laid off after we had already started the stud flooring on the house. While clearing the brush, I learned more about Alaska. I noticed all of the little stone piles on the lot. I thought maybe the cute little squirrels had piled them there. They were actually moose droppings.

Jim got a call from the Union to work construction in Valdez. It was lonely without him, but I had a car, although I didn't drive it much because I was very large with my second pregnancy. Jim would come home every week or two to see me. It was a long drive. He would leave Valdez on Saturday night and get home about two in the morning. Then he had to start back at four Sunday afternoon.

Our son was born on Friday, October 3, 1952 at Providence Hospital on L Street. My Mom came to stay with me when I came home the next morning. Jim came home that night.

I said, "We'll have to sleep on the floor. Mom is here."

He said, "Okay."

We laid out the sleeping bags. I said, "Hey, aren't you even going to look at the new baby?"

He was surprised, he hadn't known. So of course, he took a peek at the baby who was asleep in a cardboard box.

Jim was laid off a few weeks later and wanted to go back to Minnesota. I could not leave until the baby was six weeks old. After the doctor said it was okay to travel, we went back down the Alcan, only to find no work in Minnesota except for two weeks at Christmas delivering mail. It was the worst eight months of our marriage. In May, we borrowed money and headed back to Alaska.

When we arrived, we lived next door to our lot with my sister. I was pregnant again. Jim went to work for a construction company on Elmendorf Air Force Base. Every bit of extra time was used to build on our house. He worked nine or ten hour days and then came home and we worked on the house, sawing and hammering until midnight. Everyone in the neighborhood was building. It seemed the pounding never stopped because it was light all night.

We finally moved into our house on Thanksgiving, 1953, although it was far from finished. We had no toilet, but we did have a pipe with running water. Our second son was born two weeks later. Even though we had more work to do, we were finally in a house to call our own. It had two bedrooms and was tiny. Even later, when we added a small addition it was still small, but we lived out our marriage and raised seven children in it

Grover and Althea Fireoved owned the original homestead and lived two blocks from us. Part of their land was on a hill next to Boniface Parkway. Before World War II Mr. Fireoved was approached by the military who wanted to buy his land. They needed it for underground storage and a place for bunkers as a fall-back spot. Mr. Fireoved told them he wouldn't sell his land, but they could use it. If we won the war he wanted his land back and if we lost then he guessed he wouldn't give a damn.

My kids loved to explore. Mr. Fireoved designated them as keepers of the land. They were even allowed to cut Christmas trees. There were many dangerous drainage ditches. My kids weren't supposed to play in them but of course they did and even fished in them. In the woods on the hill were the remains of the Army camp, which, of course, the kids started exploring. They dragged home helmets, canteens and various other army items and I worried about live ammunition. Nevertheless, they spent many happy hours there and parading around in the treasures they dragged home.

Mr. Fireoved was proud of his subdivision–our Wonder Park. More people built and he would have a picnic each summer with hot dogs and goodies. The kids would have a ride on the skid behind his tractor.

Eventually Grover died and Mrs. Fireoved tried to continue on, even having the picnics. But life goes on. She sold most of the land and moved away. More houses sprang up. The woods disappeared as condos and apartments took their place. A school was built. Wonder Park grew. I still live there, now alone, in our own house. Wonder Park seems like the right place for me.

# Life in a Tent in Anchorage
## Barbara Maxwell

Les and I had married in September of 1948 in our hometown of Fort Collins, Colorado. On March 21, 1949, Les and I, and Don Rohbecker, set out for a trip to Alaska in our '48 Ford club coupe, Thomas Todd (Todd), Jack Dexter and Paul Nelson joined us in Paul's Ford car.

We went a back way through Montana and when we got to the Canadian border their customs was closed for the winter. The US Customs checked us through and off we went. The road at that time went up around the Lesser Slave Lake, which added about 200 miles to the 3200 mile route. Service stations and restaurants were very few, very rustic, without modern conveniences and a long way apart. We arrived at the Little Smoky River, close to Grand Prairie about midnight. The bridge across the river hadn't been finished at that time. One crossed in the summer by ferry and in winter by driving on the ice. It was beginning to thaw, and the car tracks were deep in water. With the ferry keeper walking ahead of us in hip boots to show us where to drive, the water still came up almost to the car door. Before we got across I was scared to death, sure we would float down the river.

When we got to Teslin Lake we saw beautiful northern lights.

The Alaska Border Station at Snag was closed for the night when we got there. There was a campground but no place to park, so we left the cars in the road. No one else could get through anyway. We waded through snow several feet deep to get to the small, closed-in shelter. Luckily there was wood there. It was a restless night. Paul was sleeping on the picnic table and kept falling off. When we checked in at the border in the morning, they had a fit as we weren't properly entered into Canada, but they finally let us through.

When we arrived in Anchorage a week later, we parked on 4th Avenue, the only paved street in town, in front of the Union Club bar. The bouncer from the bar, who was from Wyoming, saw our Colorado license plates and came out to greet us. It turned out he knew people we knew and so he invited us in for a drink. I had coke. After a little while the bartender wanted to know my age. When I told him I was 18, he said I had to get out. He had been shut down for two weeks for having a minor in his place. It didn't matter that I wasn't drinking. We all left right away.

We drove out Gambell toward the end at Fifteenth Avenue and found a motel at Thirteenth Avenue in the alley. There was no room at the inn except a ten by ten foot storage wall-tent. The tent had plywood up four feet on the sides and a wooden floor. It had an extension cord with a light hanging from the ceiling, an open cupboard with a counter on top about three feet long, one double bed and a small oil fired heater. Bathroom, shower and laundry were across the way. All this luxury for $96.00 a month! Since economical living accommodations were few and far between and no one had any money to speak of, we decided to take it. Carr's was located where it is now, just half a block from our tent, but was mainly a hardware store. There was a small grocery store in the middle of the block on Twelfth Avenue where we traded.

We settled into our new "home." Les and I got the bed. The fellows put their sleeping bags on the floor. We used our Coleman camp stove on the counter to cook, and later, got a Dutch-oven to put on top of the burner to bake biscuits. Not long after that, we ran into several others from home that needed a place to stay. "Okay, if you can find a place to put your sleeping bag on the floor." The last one in at night had to knock on the door so the person sleeping next to it could move out of the way. Les had bought a new pair of boots just before leaving Colorado. He reached out of bed one morning, turned the oil heater up a little and put his boots on top to get dry. We went back to sleep for a few minutes and when we woke up the boots were ruined.

There were only a few inches of snow when we arrived and it should have been getting along toward spring but instead we had a record amount of snow. It would snow, melt some and the next night drop below zero and freeze into ice.

The fellows all went to work within a day or two, driving for the bus line. That was an experience of its own. The buses were in bad need of repair, which frequently had to be done on the road by the drivers who had to get down and under. The roads during break-up were in very bad shape, deep ruts, water standing everywhere. There were no storm drains and mud you would not believe. All this fun for $1.50 per hour, but Todd and Paul kept driving for about a year. One route went to Potter, where the highway ended at a home-stead up on the hill. The only way to get there was to take Spenard Road, turn onto Potter Road (which followed parts of present day Arctic, Dowling and Old Seward).

I got a job at the Headquarters Building at the base, which was Army and Air Force together at that time. I worked in the communications room in the basement with the teletype machines. It was a high security job and like a dungeon down there. Being the new one on the job, I had the late shift, getting off at 11 p.m. They provided the late shift with a ride home, but during the worst of the breakup I still had to walk a couple of blocks as the mud was too deep to drive in. When I got on the day shift, I rode the bus most of the time.

Les drove to Goat Creek early in the mornings to pick up the school kids and take the elementary ones to Denali the only grade school. The junior and senior high were in the middle of town where the Performing Arts Center is now. He was off then 'till 3 p.m. when he took the school kids to Potter and then drove around the city till 10:30 p.m.. Somehow he also got all the weekend routes. This did not match my schedule very well.

One day when I was off I went with him. On the return trip from Goat Creek the bus overheated. A jeep came along, hooked a cable to us and pulled us up the hill to Mirror Lake, where we got some water in a small container from a creek beside the road. That was quite a sight–a jeep pulling a large bus. When we stopped for water, the kids all piled off the bus and climbed to the top of the high snow banks along side of the road and slid down. They thought it was great fun.

One Sunday Les decided he had had enough and told all the people getting on the bus that it was a free day and they didn't have to pay. At the end of the run at the bus depot he walked off and told the boss he quit. His boss tried to garnishee his wages but in the end he collected all of them. He immediately got a job on the base where they were building the 500 man barracks.

Todd and Les went rabbit hunting one day. They got several rabbits, dressed them and put them outside to keep cool. The neighbor's cat took advantage of the opportunity for a free meal. Fortunately it couldn't eat them all. Les cut away the cat eaten parts and never did tell Todd.

After a couple of months in the tent, Todd, Paul, Les and I moved into one of the motel units. Oh, luxury! It consisted of one room, one bed and a couch that made into a bed, a small kitchenette and a very small toilet room. We still had to take showers at the washhouse.

When we had a weekend or evening off together we went salmon fishing. The owner of the motel, Arnold Cloe, had a fish net and we would go with him down over the bluff at the end of Northern Lights Blvd, which was a narrow one way dirt road. He had attached a rope to a tree at the top, which we would hang on to get up and down. We caught lots of salmon that we really enjoyed eating, as it was fresh. That was the only thing we had that was fresh. Food was extremely high priced. Everything was shipped up by boat which took at least a couple of weeks. There were no refrigerated containers or air-fresh food at that time. One egg would fill a 10" skillet and usually turn green.

When August came along we decided it was time to leave and go back to Colorado so Les could finish his last year of college. We didn't intend to return, but a few months after he graduated, in August of 1951 we decided to see what the future would bring for us in that far country. Linda was 18 months old. We loaded up an eighteen foot house trailer behind our 1950 Ford car and off we went. But that starts another whole chapter of our lives.

# Natural Disasters

# One Family's Heartbreak
## Dorothy E. Emerton

Like many Alaskans we had a summer cabin on the Kenai River. In 1959 we had applied to BLM for a "recreation site," and to prove up on it we had built a 20 x 15 foot cabin. We later received title and patent to the land. Every year we made improvements, like adding two bedrooms, large windows, hand water pump inside, and an oil heater. There were even three swings of heavy rope for the kids. The boys and I would spend all summer there, with Howard coming down on weekends. We all learned to operate the boat and motor so we could go to Moose River, a quarter mile away upriver, to the grocery store, or to pick up Howard when he arrived.

January 18, 1969. A date to remember! That is the day the Kenai River went crazy! Our cabin along with many summer homes, cabins, and year round homes were destroyed by a quirk of Mother Nature.

The glacier at Skilak Lake was being monitored by the Corps of Engineers, as they had observed a crack in and across the glacier. There was an inversion under the ice, and the melting ice was causing a large body of water to build up. The infra-red photos taken a few days before were mis-read, and the ominous crack across the glacier was overlooked on the photos. There was no urgent warning; they did not think it would break soon.

About 4 a.m. I was home in Anchorage listening to the radio. Suddenly I had the strangest feeling I should turn the dial to the Soldotna/Kenai radio station. As I dialed the station, a news bulletin came on from the Civil Defense officer. He said the glacier at Skilak Lake had broken, and the lake was fast rising, with water and ice heading down the Kenai River. Everyone near the river was urged to leave.

I called a local radio station and told them of the news bulletin I had just heard. The fellow laughed and said I must be mistaken, he hadn't heard anything about it. I suggested he call Laura Pedersen at the Moose River Resort and confirm it, or call KSRM radio at Soldotna. When I turned back to the Anchorage station about twenty minutes later I heard his news flash. He had Laura on the line telling of the apparent devastation happening along the river, as she was looking down on the river from her house on the hill. She confirmed what I had reported.

I called Laura, asking if she could see as far as our cabin downriver. She said, "Dorothy, it looks like your cabin is a "gonner" there is ice piled up all around it. I suggest you folks come down as soon as you can to check it out."

Howard, son Steve (16), and friend Tom, loaded the Skidoos on the trailer behind the pick-up and headed for Soldotna the next morning. To reach our place by road, they followed Funny River Road to its end and rode the Skidoos the remaining five plus miles over trails. They all were shocked by the sight greeting them from the hill overlooking the cabin. Later, Steve said he cried at the sight, as he had spent twelve summers of his young life there at our summer place. They found it hard to believe such destruction of the cabin and the storage shed. Huge ice chunks six to ten feet high were everywhere, even back in the trees fifty feet or more from the river. Climbing very carefully over the ice to get inside, Steve said he found bent propane lights, broken dining chairs, table, and dishes in the cupboard, except for one shelf, which still had cups hanging on the cup hooks.

The oil heater was buried under ice, as was the new Franklin fireplace stove which was to be installed in the spring.

Steve took pictures, both color and black and white, as he knew the family would want to see what was left of the place.

On the way back to the truck and trailer, they stopped at some of the homes and talked to the folks living in the area. They said the noise of the rushing water and ice coming downriver was deafening. They could see chunks of ice flying through the air in all directions as the tremendous pressure pushed tons of water and ice downriver. Some were fortunate and didn't suffer any damage, as they were back from the river, or on higher ground. Others lost everything, as we did.

# Ice Dam on the Klutina River
## Patricia McClure

After the 1964 earthquake, we moved to Copper Center, 100 miles north of Valdez. There, we were able to rent a log cabin from George Ashby, owner of the historic Copper Center Roadhouse. My husband's trucking job with Bayless & Roberts resumed a normal routine and the summer progressed very nicely. Winter arrived with lower temperatures than usual for December.

About two weeks before Christmas in 1964, it dropped into the minus sixties. On the morning of December 16th, after I checked on the school closures and crawled back into the bed, I heard a sound like a tremendous windstorm. Our bedroom window faced the Klutina River, and when I looked out I saw a huge white wall rushing toward the cabin. I woke my husband, grabbed our twenty-two month old daughter, and was about to wake up our son when the noise stopped. When I looked out the window again, I saw that a wall of ice was about one foot from the corner of our cabin. It then became apparent that the Klutina River had frozen more than usual, and the restricted flow of water had built up and created pressure that released a huge ice jam.

About 10 a.m. we noticed the water that was coming into our dugout basement had reached our heating system. I decided to take the two children to the lodge for warmth while Earl did what he could to stop the flow. Unfortunately the water began to flow around the buildings. Some friends arrived to help us move our vehicles. George Ashby opened the lodge to others in the area, who also had to vacate their homes.

Early the next morning, George contacted Governor Bill Egan for help. Soon, all of us had to leave the lodge because of the rising water. We left on a Department of Highways road grader because its axle was above the flood level. My children and I joined two other families, including all our pets, at the home of Howard and Alice Bayless, which was on higher ground.

Bayless & Roberts plant employees and personnel from the Anchorage Standard Oil Company stayed busy non-stop with sandbagging the fuel storage tanks at the bulk plant. I remember that thirty people ate dinner at the Bayless home one day. I was told the sump pump in the basement was close to its pumping capacity due to the rising water level. Fortunately, electrical power remained on. In the darkness, the streetlights toward the lodge cast an eerie light due to the heavy vapor from the cold and the water.

The water was flowing through the lower triangular area where the Copper Center Roadhouse, our cabin and the Copper Center Bar was located. Dick Roberts decided he would attempt getting much of my family's belongings from our cabin using Neil Huddleston's D8 Caterpillar and a boat. It was a harrowing ordeal because the water current was extremely strong by that time. Dick would use the boat to enter the house, load it and then transfer the items onto the D8 blade. At that point, the water had risen to the top of the kitchen cabinets and the washer and dryer. However, our deep freeze floated. With a large flashlight, Dick salvaged as much as he could see above water.

Eleanor and Bill Rosent, owners of Rosent's café, sent word that they could house my family and my sister's in an adjacent room of their café. The two families included my sister, her four children, me, my two children, and the family's two dogs. All of us slept on mattresses on the floor and my sister and I tried keeping the kids content in one large room. Our husbands napped at Copper Center when they had a chance. I remember that every morning and evening, Bill Rosent would use a blow torch to thaw the water pipes in the bathroom next to our room so that we could use the toilet and sink.

Meanwhile Governor Bill Egan had contacted the Civil Defense who sent a couple of hydrologists to study the situation. They decided to bomb the river channel so the water would return to its correct course. Louie Lincoln, an older local Alaska Native, had mentioned several times he knew where the problem was. Louie was born and raised in the area and remembered the flood in 1934 when Mrs. Florence Barnes (Ma Barnes) owned the roadhouse. Unfortunately,

Louie's advice was ignored and the bomber was sent from the Kodiak Naval Station. It released its payload but accomplished nothing except shattering windows. Ralph Lane, another local resident, then helped Louie load some dynamite on his dog sled and ventured out to the spot where Louie said the river's channel was. They set off the charges and that did the trick! Of course, the water that had covered the area froze in place until the spring thaw, but no additional water flowed out of the channel.

When school closed for the Christmas holidays, the Glennallen 6th grade class donated their classroom's Christmas tree for our kids. It was delivered to Rosent's on the 20th and gifts were quickly ordered from Fairbanks for Santa to deliver. On Christmas day Bill and Eleanor put a closed sign on their café door and treated our families to a wonderful dinner.

Soon after the first of January 1965, the American Red Cross sent out mobile homes for those planning to stay in the area. They were located in the Department of Highways camp at Glennallen until early summer. By that time three families made other living arrangements. We purchased land and remained in Copper Center until moving to Anchorage in June 1970 with our three children.

# Alaska–For Better or For Worse
## Robert Ferrin Gilmore

My Alaska adventure began one June day in 1962 in Tulsa, Oklahoma where I was a Senior Map Draftsman/Illustrator for Sinclair Oil and Gas Co. A map draftsman from the Exploration Department came by and said he was really scared that they were going to transfer him to Anchorage. He didn't want to go to that frozen land to the north and was wondering how to avoid it. Alaska had always been a dream for me, so I went to his boss and volunteered for the assignment. Within a week my family and I were packed and on our way to Alaska. I became the Chief Map Draftsman for the Alaska District.

Of course, the most significant experience was the March 27, 1964 earthquake, which has been told in another story. Compared to that experience, nothing seems too impressive, but I have had some milder adventures, not white-knuckle types, fighting off bears (although we've come face-to-face) or being swallowed by a glacier. Ours have been an everyday kind of Alaska adventure we could have never gotten anywhere else.

For example, in 1984, my wife Lisa and I purchased a house east of Muldoon near the Ft. Rich Military land. Little did we know this was "Williwaw Alley"! We decided to build a 6 ft. high cedar-board fence to keep out the stray dogs and moose wandering the new neighborhood, but a couple of years later a "white tornado" came ripping through the bog and scattered the boards everywhere, driving two-by-fours through the back of the house. Shingles and debris flew through the neighborhood! Later, gathering up the boards, we decided we would just use them for a twelve by sixteen foot cabin we had started on fifty acres we owned a few miles this side of the Matanuska Glacier. The destruction of the fence was a godsend. The cedar boards were just enough to side the cabin and also our outhouse. So, there you go—everything seemed to be for the better.

Lisa and I also enjoyed sailing, so one week while my sister was visiting from California, we bare-boat chartered a small sloop "The Northern Spirit" and headed out of Resurrection Bay near Seward. We were having a great old time until the afternoon breezes started. Pretty soon we were bouncing around in whitecaps and things were getting stirred up. We were in the middle of the bay heading for Humpy Cove when I decided to reef the main and sail with the jib. We made it into Humpy Cove and were caught in an eddy behind the mountains where we were just sailing in circles and getting closer and closer to the rocky shore.

We tried the motor but the fuel filter was fouled with sediment sloshing from the waves. Even though I struggled below cleaning the filter, the engine would only run for a short period until it clogged again. All this time, with gale force winds, Lisa was trying to keep us off the rocks. With Lisa's sailing skill, we finally made it to calmer waters and got a tow into Thumb Cove where we could anchor for the night. My sister never asked to go sailing with us again.

# Volcanic Ash
## Phyllis Holliday Ondra

Mt. Redoubt Volcano is situated across Cook Inlet from Kenai, Alaska. On December 14, 1989 the 10,197 foot mountain exploded sending off ash-rich emissions which seriously affected the Cook Inlet region and air traffic as far away as Texas.

My husband, Terry Holliday, and I lived in Nikiski, about twenty miles north of Kenai, having just moved from Anchorage a month earlier.

On the morning of the eruption we were headed into Kenai for groceries. As we left home we did not notice anything unusual other than a large, high black area in the sky. Turning on the radio we found out about the explosion. It looked distant, but it was coming our way. We decided to pick up some groceries, check on an absent friend's house in Sterling, and head back home.

What we did not know was that the ash cloud was traveling toward our area at 50-70 mph.

The first indicator of trouble was the darkness that was descending on us as we headed to Sterling. The sun was blotted out completely. The headlights did not help and it was hard to see the road. About three inches of ash had fallen.

We reached our friend's house and rushed inside. We were coughing and our eyes were burning. By now it was dark and it was noon. The ash was bouncing about on the snow. We needed to get home to our dog and horse to protect them. We could not attempt the thirty mile drive until morning because of visibility, and the radio announcer said it would ruin the engine in the automobiles. "Don't drive!"

In the morning we could see the road to drive so headed off for home. The dog was fine, the horse was nervous and pacy, but was somewhat protected in the barn. We washed her eyes, ears and nostrils. I had never heard a horse cough before, but it was happening.

In the weeks to come you could tell how often the ash had passed over the house. It was layered. First snow, then ash alternated into black and white, horizontal bands.

We had major, constant clean-ups for many weeks–house, yard, car, everything. We could not get rid of the ash. We both had a cough for months. This event was not as scary as the '64 earthquake experienced in Anchorage, but it made us ask, "What's next?"

# Excerpts From June 10, 1964 Letter
## Mary Ellen Segelhorst

Dear Relatives and Friends:

It is with thankful hearts that we can say we have survived the earthquake and, although we did loose a lot of our treasured items and sustained some property damage, we came out completely unharmed. Our losses are insignificant when compared to so many who had total personal property loss, suffered serious injury or loss of life...

It was Good Friday, and to most of you, spring was undoubtedly evident; however, when we looked outside, we saw fresh snow, the deepest snowfall that we have had this winter. Nevertheless, the days were getting noticeably longer and the temperatures were getting up into the thirties and so we had hope that spring was going to come

For some reason, Fridays seem to have grown as hectic as Mondays and so Knobby had said he would take me out for dinner Friday evening. When five o'clock came I was thankful the work day was over. I left my office about five-thirty and started walking the three blocks over to Knobby's office. As I was crossing Fourth Avenue going south, I felt as though I was fainting. I groped for something to hold on to, took a few more steps and grabbed a wood fence that surrounds the tourist information log cabin built on the city hall front lawn. It was there that I spent those five minutes (which seemed like

Editor's note: Knobby is her husband.

an eternity) in which the earth rolled, heaved, fell, and the buildings did likewise. Even though we witnessed this, it is still beyond us to realize the power of Nature and the destruction that was caused in such a few minutes. I really did not realize that it was an earthquake. I thought we had been bombed and that this was truly the end. This instant reaction came, I am sure, from the movie *On the Beach* which, you will remember, was the story of an atomic blast. In one scene, a mass of people stood in the street in panic and terror and in the next, the end had come and all the people were gone forever. So I cannot describe my thoughts as I hung on that fence and watched, as out of every store came all these people, men, women, and children, screaming, lying down in the streets, staggering for something to hold on to. Glass was banging to the ground, the streets were heaving and cracking, buildings swaying as though they were leaves blowing in the wind. Cars parked at the parking meters moved forward and backward at least four feet, and even though it sounds impossible they also moved sideways.

I was all alone hanging on to that fence! Now that I look back, I was actually in a relatively safe position. On the other side of the street are at least ten different shops with windows near the sidewalk. Some of the buildings had overhangs which crumpled. Just two blocks down from where I was an entire city block of businesses literally fell into the earth as it caved in. There were cars still parked at meters–twenty feet below pavement level.

After it stopped I got up and half running, half walking, I started for Knobby's office only to find he was not there. He had taken off at a dead run down to my office, only to be told that I had left before the quake. He ran the whole way back, a pretty far run for a little fatty like him, and found me pacing in front of his office. His office was a mess, files all over the place, furniture slid all over, neon light tubes smashed on the floor, but now our only concern was to get home and see what the conditions were there and to find our poor dog, Keeper, who was penned in the utility room.

Traffic was practically at a standstill. Some streets were impassable due to large faults; other whole streets had disappeared. It took forever, but I was so stunned I didn't even cry, that is 'till we finally got home. Each room was filled with a mass of broken china and glass. Seventy per cent of our lovely antiques were destroyed. Then I could not hold back the tears.

Our house is still on its foundation although badly shaken and will need some foundation work.

By a week later, utilities had been restored to most of the city and things began to settle down. Nerves were beginning to relax We took what few unbroken antique pieces we had left out from under the tables and set them back up to make us feel a little more stable–more like we really did live here.

Then Friday, just one week after the "big one," we had another severe quake. That one unnerved people who hadn't been (or hadn't admitted to being) unnerved before. Fortunately, it only lasted a few seconds.

After that second shake, we decided we would just put the antiques away for a while in boxes. It looks so bare now, but sure is easier to dust.

# Mittens, Boots and Diapers
## Hannah A. Frenier

We must have made quite a picture when going through the airport in Seattle in 1967 with our seven children. My husband says he looked back at one point and saw the children in order of eldest to youngest following him like a Pied Piper, in single file, each carrying items in each hand. I brought up the rear with the baby in my arms.

We were set for adventure, and it met us with below zero temperatures when the aircraft doors were opened in Fairbanks on February 2, 1967. We soon were in quarters at Fort Wainwright, had bought necessary boots and other cold weather gear, and settled into the pace of an Alaska winter. We never slowed down. It seemed the colder the temperature became, the warmer the hospitality flowed. Fairbanks was a town whose population never stopped because of the weather. Luaus at 50 degrees below zero were not uncommon. I gave one myself for a friend who was returning from a Hawaiian vacation. It did us all good to dress up in muumuus, with fur parkas on top, and gather in over-heated quarters to eat fresh pineapple, listen to Hawaiian music, and enjoy the warm company of friends.

Children's activities rarely slowed because of the weather. Our children walked to the nearby school unless the temperature dropped under 20 degrees below zero. At that temperature or below, the school buses transported them to and from classes.

Sometimes the winter weather was so cold the tires would freeze flat on the bottom. The sound of the thump, thump, thump of the lopsided tires often continued all the way to the commissary and home again. When the temperature was well below zero, many shoppers would leave car engines running while they were inside the stores. Temperatures that cold made one feel like a true adventurer. Of course we had all the modern conveniences and warm military quarters to call home. We didn't have to camp out or spend days on the trail like sourdoughs of old. However, just living in a land of dark and bitter cold was sometimes a trial. Five of our seven children were then younger than five years old. Most of my memories of Fairbanks are of mittens, boots, and diapers.

We had a dog team, which consisted of culls from the teams of local mushers. They were anxious to share their love of this truly northern sport with us. They invited us to their meetings, helped us learn about mushing dogs, and encouraged us to join their club, use their trails on Farmer's Loop Road, and even race in several events. We had seven adult huskies and eventually several litters of pups, which swelled our kennel to 21 dogs. Even on bitterly cold nights we would bundle up and carry food and water to the kennel that was located a mile or so from our quarters. Most nights my husband would go alone to feed and water and clean. However, sometimes we would put the younger children to bed and leave our oldest teen-age son in charge. Then we would harness Badger and Tanana, the two registered Siberian Huskies we kept at the house. We would put a five-gallon jug of hot water on the sled and I would snuggle against it with a blanket over me. My husband would drive the sled to the kennels where we would do the chores together. Then we would glide back home across the frozen landscape of icy crystals under clear skies or in light snowfall. There is nothing so peaceful as just the dark, the cold, and the sound of sled runners gliding on the snow.

The first summer we were in Fairbanks, family came to visit from Ohio. It was in August and we had a wonderful fishing trip to Valdez where we caught salmon galore. We were back in Ft. Wainwright to celebrate the baby's first birthday on August 14, 1967. The next day the Chena River, swelled with water from days of rain, overflowed its banks, and covered the post and surrounding city with more water than anyone could handle. We were in the midst of a full-fledged flood.

We had been on watch throughout the night. First we set things in the basement off the floor in the event we had water in that part of our quarters. Little did we realize the extent of the force of the water. The underground utilidors filled, and suddenly water came into the basement at an alarming rate. The downstairs toilet became "Old Faithful" with water clearing the seat in a geyser-like spout that turned our downstairs into an indoor pool in less than an hour. We plucked the four children whose bedrooms were in the basement from their floating beds and carried them through rising water to the stairs. We salvaged as many belongings as possible as quickly as possible, carrying whole dresser drawers to the stairs where a "fire brigade" line of children, and houseguests carried them to the main floor. We disconnected the electrical appliances, washer, and clothes dryer and ran to the other side of the duplex, because we were caretaking our neighbor's quarters while they were on vacation. What does one save for neighbors when time is so short and valuables are not in plain view? We grabbed guns and some albums of photographs before the water also filled their basement.

It was days before the water level receded. Actually it was over a week before the roads could accommodate regular cars and trucks. My husband went to work that week in an amphibious vehicle that picked him up early in the mornings and delivered him back home in the evenings. We were given a Civil Defense toilet, which is a cardboard cylinder with plastic bag inserts and a plastic seat. Two-and-a-half ton trucks delivered five-gallon cans of drinking water and emergency food supplies and picked up the bags from the CD toilet each day. Our guests had quite a vacation to tell about when they returned home after the runways were finally dry and airplanes could take off again. Even at the airport the excitement continued when a strong earthquake shook the terminal as we waited for their flight back to Ohio.

The children began school with no water or electricity. Fortunately the days were still long well into September, and light was not a problem. The military supplied generators and CD toilets and water trailers. Things went along smoothly considering the circumstances. Almost a month passed before electricity and water service were restored to the post. What an adventure!

We left Fairbanks two years later in the minus fifty degree February weather and returned to North Carolina. My husband had military orders to Vietnam. After he returned, we had a local man build us a "Back To Alaska Camper" and bought a white crew-cab Ford pickup truck to hold it. In June we sold our house, loaded everyone into the camper, hooked a utility trailer to the truck, and put our little green boat atop that. We set out to Anchorage and a tour of duty at Fort Richardson. We have lived here since then, and continue to enjoy the excitement of The Great Land.

# Black as Midnight
## Betty Smith Motes

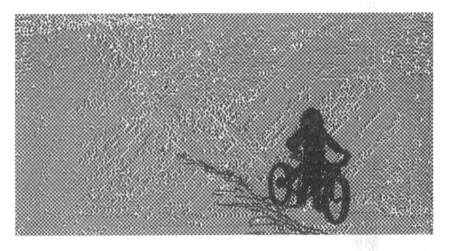

We had bought five acres off of Klatt Road in 1953. There had been a fire at the railroad in the blacksmith shop where my husband worked. While they rushed to rebuild it, they put together a temporary shelter. When the permanent shop was finished, we got the lumber from the temporary shelter to build our house. It was a shack about sixteen feet square. For the doors and windows we used surplus from old-time passenger cars–three windows and two doors. We added an arctic entry so that made two doors on the front of the house. We had two bedrooms on one end with a single bed for the boy and bunk beds for the girls. Then there was a closet and just enough space between the rooms for my husband and me to sleep on a fold down couch in the living room. They were sure small rooms.

That summer one of the kids came in and told me, "Mama, it's raining dirt outside."

"What are you talking about?" I asked.

"Well look," they went out and came back in and the back of their hands were covered with dust from something.

I rode my bicycle over to the neighbors on John's Road. They had a radio and told me that Mount Spurr had erupted.

I had a niece who had just come up from Montana. She was a Cheechako, and I knew she would be scared, so I rode the bicycle over there to let her know what was going on.

She was staying with a friend of my husband from the railroad, and he was home, so I decided to go home while I could get there. It was noon, but it was getting pretty dark. On the way down to the road to my place, I had to use the light from the neighbor's windows to tell me where I was, but when I turned into our road, there were no more lights. The only way I could find the way was to get in the ditch beside the road and follow it down to the house. It was like being in a blackout. It was as black as you've ever seen it at midnight, and here it was summer, when it is usually light all the time.

Flying Alaska

# Two Crashes, Same Spot
## Casimir C. Cechowski

It seemed simple enough to get in and out, but darned if this wasn't the second time I had survived a clobberin' in the same place. This was too much and I was getting tired of it. And I hadn't even been the one flying the planes.

It was the summer of 1952 and a very rainy one–sloppy and incessant. But the weather is never enough to stop a dyed-in-the- wool gold prospector. A well-known bush pilot (who shall remain nameless) and I were out to stake some claims so naturally we weren't about to file a flight plan and give away any secrets. Unfortunately, most gold claims are logistic nightmares in that they are never easily accessible, and this one ran true to form. It was upstream from Chitina on the opposite side of the Copper River. My partner owned the plane so he flew us both in and dropped me off at a sand bar. It was a used 60-hp Aeronca Chief, side-by-side, and it landed and took off easily from the sand bar. So far, so good. I then had the privilege of going through the brush to where the strike was located along the Kuskulana and clearing out a small air strip so the airplane could land with our grub and supplies. The plane was landed smartly and in good style, so the staking began.

The trouble started after a few days when we wanted to leave. The skies were overcast and it had been raining for days. You might say that there was heavy dew and marginal VFR (visual flight reconnaissance) conditions. In fact, you couldn't see the mountains. But we needed to get out and so we were setting out for Copper Center International (a small grassy airstrip). We were dressed for warmth and were carrying out lots of ore samples along with all the gear we had ferried in. Not being the pilot, I suggested politely that we would have to make two trips as the small plane was getting overloaded. Now no one likes to make two hairy takeoffs and landings unless it is absolutely essential, so my partner shut me up and gunned the engine. I think we would have made it except for the rain and the slop–a soft depression had formed in some unlikely spots after all the rain. When you're sitting next to the pilot and you're a pilot yourself, you can't help but second guess. I wish I hadn't been right this time. That darn plane just never gained enough altitude and we hit some soft spots and there we were–clobbered! Luckily, neither one of us was hurt, but no flight plan had been filed and no one knew exactly what our plans were. The plane was a mess so we salvaged what we could. We were a couple of mad roosters.

But the best was yet to come! We decided that they would come looking for us eventually. But since our food would never last, it was up to us to get ourselves out of there. Not far away was an old trapper's cabin, long abandoned, so we headed for that. We tore it apart and fashioned a freaky looking boat and set out to float down the Kuskulana to the Copper River.

We were singing and rowing and patting ourselves on the back until we realized two things: (1) The boat was not really that seaworthy and, although we both were bailing, we couldn't keep up with it. (2) With all that rain, the Kuskulana was high and kept getting faster and faster.

We entered a canyon, wilder than we both had imagined, and shot down the rapids like crazy as the boat kept sinking lower in the water. We knew we had to make a decision soon but the question was moot–as we rounded a curve in the canyon we crashed into a huge boulder–and that was the end of the "boat."

There went the last of our supplies though I managed to hang onto my rifle. My partner made it to shore but I was having trouble. Not wanting to waste all of our efforts, I had been wearing my heavy coat, its pockets loaded with rock samples in a coffee can. I got hung up on a sweeper in the river but finally got pulled out. Now I was really disgusted! We had used up supplies during the two days we wasted building the boat so we were worse off than before.

We emptied our pockets to take stock–some wet matches, a few grains of coffee, the trusty wet rifle and that darn coffee can full of rock samples. I think we both knew the situation was getting a little desperate even for a couple of macho men like us.

We were still lost and nobody knew where we were, so we started to walk through the brush toward the Copper River. This used up the better part of another three days as we couldn't get across a fast tributary and had to walk up the river to its headwaters, cross a glacier, and then walk back down.

Now we were really getting hungry. We finally spotted a mother duck and her ducklings. If you don't think we felt brutish chasing down those ducklings, capturing two, and stewing them up in my coffee can! Luckily the matches had dried out in the three days we'd been walking.

We finally reached the Copper River–mad, hungry, and thoroughly disgusted and disgusting. We hadn't spotted a sight of game, wouldn't you know? There, we spent two more days on the shore. We made signs out of rocks. HELP! We built fires, but no one noticed us. The brush is so thick and the trees so tall that no one could spot us with a dinky fire or two. By this time I was really mad and desperate so I selected an area between two streams, about a quarter mile apart, with a nice stand of timber between them. I gathered dead brush and started a forest fire. We had a fire that nobody could overlook. About the middle of the afternoon, a CAP plane out looking for some other party spotted the fire, spotted our messages, and spotted us. The best thing of all was that they dropped some C-rations. That day they were better than steak.

A tourist loaned his boat to a native with courage enough to brave the Copper River and pick us up. That tourist thought the rescue with his boat was the most exciting thing! He was thrilled!

About a month later I received a summons to appear in court for "campfire negligence." The prosecuting attorney was (later judge) Fitzgerald. They needed to make an example of somebody. Naturally I was incensed at this indignity and pleaded "not guilty."

When I told my story both the judge and the DA felt very badly, even the forestry man felt badly. No one had known the facts. The judge asked me if I would consider a $100 fine and a six-month suspended sentence. "No way, not guilty!" After some thought, the judge asked if I would consider a $10 fine. By this time, I felt sorry for the judge. He was embarrassed because he was stuck with the case. I had lit the matches even though it was in a good cause, so I became a criminal.

### Epilogue

I was bound and determined to get my rock samples so later I hired a bush pilot from Cordova Air Lines to fly into the same strip. I warned him. We landed okay. I retrieved my samples and got back into the Super Cub. I warned the pilot again and he turned around and snarled. "Who's flying this @%x#$ plane?

I just pulled up my bed roll, stuffed it in front of me, and hunkered down. We roared down the strip, hit the same soft spot, and over we went. This time, however, the pilot had filed a flight plan so, when we didn't get back in a couple of hours, the air line sent in another plane to get us.

I never did develop the claims!

# Up, Up and Away!
## Mikell L. Murphy

Back in the 1970s we could look up on almost any blue sky day and see brightly colored hot air balloons floating above Anchorage. How could anyone feel sad when they could watch such pretty shapes and colors bobbing playfully overhead with those majestic Chugach Mountains as their backdrop! Everyone agreed hot air balloons added a lot of pizzazz to our city's mood. Then the liability insurance rates were raised so high that the balloon owners were forced to fold their big toys into their oversized wicker passenger baskets and leave Alaska.

But before they went, I was lucky enough to ride in a hot air balloon. And what a ride it was! My then-husband arranged for us to take the "Champagne Special" one very cold day in January. We were scheduled to meet the balloon crew near the Bodenburg Butte, go up and float around the Butte for an hour drinking champagne and admiring the view.

When we arrived, the ground crew was already busy laying out the huge rainbow-colored bag in the field so that it could be inflated. Every balloon owner had a "ground crew" to help unpack and inflate the balloon. Then, once the balloon was aloft, the crew would chase along on the ground in a truck so they were handy when the flight ended and they could put the balloon away. It was a lot of work, but in return for their labor they got free balloon flights. This crew obviously thought it was a good trade-off because they weren't even grumbling about how cold they were as they struggled with the flapping balloon fabric in the sharp wind.

Hot air balloons get their hot air from a burner that ignites with a very loud roar and shoots flames up into the balloon cavity until it is full of enough hot air to be lighter than the air around it and *voila!* It floats up and off the ground. I didn't know that basic detail of ballooning so when the burner suddenly flared the first time I was so startled that I jumped away and landed on my back in a snow bank. By the time I was up on my feet again and brushed off, the balloon was upright and straining to take off in the wind. The owner had a worried look in his eye as he tossed up a handful of grass and watched it blow away.

"Too windy to fly today," he announced to the groans of his ground crew.

"Put her away and we'll try again tomorrow." Reluctantly the young men began to let the air out of their big ball and started refolding it.

"But what about our champagne deal?" we asked.

"Well, just because we can't fly doesn't mean we can't drink champagne, does it?" grinned the owner.

It didn't take long for us, the owner, and his crew to finish off two bottles of the bubbly, and somehow the day seemed warmer when we were done. The owner tossed another handful of grass up and when it landed nearby he declared, "Wind has fallen off, boys. Let's fly!"

I was thrilled to be getting my balloon ride after all and too buzzed on the champagne to worry about the wind, which definitely had not completely "fallen off." The ground crew was also happy and didn't complain about re-doing all their earlier work, unfolding the balloon and blowing it up again.

Along with the owner we scrambled into the basket below the huge balloon and the weights were tossed out. Up and up and up we went until we were floating high over the Butte and then still higher over the farms below. The owner was on his little radio trying to give our position to his crew in the truck somewhere below us. They were desperately trying to keep us in sight as we soared farther and faster than anyone had planned. The owner sounded worried, but I was having a grand time.

Balloon flying is so silent! You're actually in the wind so you can't feel it or hear it. You're just part of whatever is happening in the sky at that moment, and I loved the sensation. However, our pilot obviously was not enjoying the ride. He was trying very hard to stay calm and cool–to maintain the appearance of being in total control even though it was clear that no one was piloting this baby but the blowing wind.

"I'll just take her down to some quieter air," he said as he fiddled with something that let air out of the cavity and we sank down much closer to the ground. In fact we were bumping along whacking the treetops before he reconsidered and decided to hit the burner button and send some fire and hot air up into the balloon so that we could go higher again.

Our pilot was now busy on the radio trying to help his crew catch up with us and was muttering about how we should have been equipped with crash helmets. I was having a wonderful ride though and didn't worry about a thing until I looked down and saw that we were approaching the railroad bridge and highway at the end of Knik Arm.

No more Mr. Calm and Cool Balloon Owner. "We've got to get this thing down before we land the drink!" he exclaimed, "put the little one in the front!"

Now I'm not actually "little," but I was definitely smaller than the two tall men, so I got shoved to the front of the basket as we were rapidly falling toward the snow below us.

It was not a pretty landing with the wind as strong as it was that day, but as they say, "Any landing you walk away from is a good landing." Even after being dragged for what seemed like a long way with two big men on top of me and my face in the snow, I was still able to crawl out of the basket and walk away. We had come down into the flats between the highway and the railroad tracks, the last level landing space available before water and swamp. When I stood up I saw a long line of cars stopped along the road. People were standing there clapping and cheering for us. We had evidently made an impressive showing as we had abruptly smashed into the snow and bumped along until we stopped right in front of them.

It was a wonderful flight for me, even if it didn't go quite as smoothly as planned. I'll always be glad I got to float up in one of those big sky ornaments they call hot air balloons while we still had them here with us in Anchorage.

# Baby on the Wing
## Jean C. Persons, M.D.

Back in the early 1950s I was Medical Officer in charge of the thirty bed government hospital in Tanana under the Bureau of Indian Affairs, which had a number of similar hospitals scattered throughout Alaska.

The hospital took care of a tremendous territory, including all the villages below Fort Yukon down to and including Kaltag on the lower Yukon River, all the villages on the Koyukuk River and a few on the Tanana River, and, further north, Wiseman and Anaktuvuk, the latter one of the most nomadic of villages.

Early on when I first came to Tanana, I was able to hire Garfield Hansen from Fairbanks, as the main pilot for the Hospital. He put his trailer on a barge in Fairbanks and floated it down the river to Tanana, so he would have a place to live.

Each afternoon at three p.m. I would have radio call to all the villages that had a two way radio where someone, usually the trader, the teacher, or the missionary, would handle radio calls. Each village had a supply of medications provided by the government. In turn I had the same list posted next to my radio. When I had a medical problem I knew what supplies they had, and what supplies I needed to bring.

On one late winter day several hours after the regularly scheduled radio call, someone came to the hospital with a message from Father Baud in Nulato. One of his parishioners, who was in the late stage of pregnancy, had begun to bleed.

After receiving the message I hurried down the road to see if Hansen was available to fly me to Nulato, less than an hour's flight. In the meantime my head nurse was busy packing up the supplies I might need. All the supplies were stuffed into a pillow case to save room on the airplane. On this clear cool night we flew following the Yukon River.

We were met by Father Baud and several of the men when we landed on the short field in Nulato. They led us down the icy path to the village below, Hansen carrying the pillow case of supplies over his shoulder. Into the patient's cabin I went. Her bleeding had slowed down and the contractions had stopped. A brief examination revealed that the head was barely engaged. She was minimally dilated and almost no blood was present. She, her husband, and I had a conference. We could stay there for the delivery or go back to Tanana where we were better equipped should major problems develop. Because of the bleeding the risks were considerable. We decided to go to Tanana to the hospital.

To make more room Hansen removed the right front seat and the rear seat in the baggage area, my seat. Thus we got in, with me crouching over next to my patient who sat uncomfortably with her legs outstretched.

Off we flew. All was well until we were about twenty minutes out from Tanana. A touch on my shoulder. "Doctor, it's coming!"

Sure enough the baby's head was crowning, followed fairly quickly by the rest of the body. The delivery was awkward with me in contortions trying to ease the baby out within the tiny space available. However all was well except nowhere in the pillow case could I find the scissors. Ever helpful, Hansen pulled his penknife out of his pocket and handed it to me. Not exactly sterile, but I did wipe it off with alcohol before cutting the cord. I wrapped the baby girl in the blanket that Hansen had warmed in the front of the plane, and then in my parka, which I took off. By this time she was squalling away at the top of her lungs, always a good sign. I had to keep checking her to be sure she didn't slide out of the parka. Luckily the placenta came out with ease. It was at least thirty below zero by this time. My patient held the medications so I could fill the syringe to inject her to help the uterus contract. Hansen had been great, holding his flashlight for me so I could see, but he was so bashful he never looked back. I had to turn his hand so the light would fall on the right spot.

Inside the plane was a bit of a mess with all the amniotic fluid, but no one minded with the happy result of our trip.

Had the baby been a boy she would have been named Garfield after Hansen. Since it was a girl she was given a much prettier name. She was called Josephine Jean after me.

Somehow the story got picked up from the Fairbanks newspaper and I received over thirty pen knives from all over the country.

# God Is My Co-pilot
## Bill Churchill

After a trip to Ketchikan three of us got ready to board the plane to return to Wrangell, the pilot, Rev. Doug Moore, said that since I was the smallest I was to ride in the back seat. That was fine with me. The weather was not the best but we had flown in worse before. It was raining steadily with small gusts of wind coming across the water and white caps breaking. Rev. Moore always said to me, "God is my co-pilot."

It was 11:30 a.m. before we got airborne, heading out ahead of a storm. I was buckled in good and snug as we were bouncing around. Out the left side of the plane near the head of Helm Bay, I could see a nice little cabin. We were running into snow flurries and a lot of turbulence. Doug found one pass socked in, then the other, then tried the first again. There, we ran into a solid wall of snow, with no visibility. He kicked the plane into a steep turn, banking so we could get out of there. About half way through the turn the plane stalled out and we lost all air speed.

I was trying to get bearings when Doug yelled, "We are going in!" I looked forward and what I saw was not good. We were in a very steep dive, there was no pulling out. All I could see were big spruce trees, standing straight and tall as if on guard. I leaned over and crossed my arm and braced my head and arms on the back of the pilot's chair. I didn't figure I was going to live through this. I got knocked out when we hit the mountain. I don't know how long I was unconscious but when I came to I found that my left shoe was jammed under Mickey's seat and my nose was bleeding. I knew I had to escape that burning wreckage. Somehow I freed my foot, but my shoe remained jammed under the seat.

How I got out of the plane is still unclear. I do remember I got out on the left side, although I learned later there was no back door there. I made my way around the nose of the burning plane. It was difficult as the snow was several inches deep and very slippery. When I got around the right side I saw poor Mick and the condition he was in and I forgot all my pain. The poor guy was fighting for his life. The whole cockpit was on fire. He had taken a terrible blow to his front torso upon impact. Part of his lower pants had burned off. The fire had burned his hands and scorched his face and eyebrows. He was in shock. I reached down and unhooked his seat belt and pulled him from the burning cockpit as fast as I could. I dragged him away from the burning plane in case it blew up.

I tried to get back to help Doug, but he was already dead and the plane was really burning. I tried to make Mick more comfortable. I used my shirt sleeve for bandaging Mickey's left ankle and used the other sleeve for my left foot. I took off my belt and put a tourniquet on Mick's leg and made snowballs for him to suck, as he was very thirsty.

I crawled back to the plane and found that our sleeping bags and all our survival gear burned with the plane. I did manage to find some pieces of wood to start a fire. I knew it would be getting dark soon and cold on that January night. I took out my billfold first and dug out all the pictures and paper money and with those and what little wood I found, I built a fire. I was lucky to have a lighter with me. I left Mick in charge of the fire and went back to the plane to see what was left. One wing had been sheared off by a tree and was not burned. With a piece of Plexiglas as a knife, I hacked off some fabric pieces. I put the small pieces under Mick, and used the larger ones to cover him up. I unzipped my jacket and put my arms around Mick to try to save body heat.

Mick didn't make it through the night, and when he died I really felt alone. I sat back down on some small pieces of fabric, covered myself as best I could, put my back against an old stump and started thinking how lucky I was to be alive. The snow drops pooled on the glossy fabric over my legs and I began to notice a reflection of a light. I looked around in the darkness. Down the mountain toward the water there was a buoy of some sort blinking at intervals. There I was tired, wet, cold, hungry, lonely and freezing, and there was Helm Bay, where I had seen the cabin!

I put a plan together as I lay there. If I stayed with the wreckage I might never be found; the whole plane had burned and might not be spotted from the air. At the first break of light I would try to make it to the beach and the cabin.

At daybreak, I stretched my stiff muscles and made my way back to the wreck. There wasn't much I could salvage. I found a pair of water wings in a small plastic container which I cut open and, with one of the sleeves of my shirt, made a sort of boot for my left foot. I looked around the wreck one last time, bid my two friends, "Farewell" and started downhill.

The ground was slippery but in the cold morning air the visibility was good. I followed an old deer trail along a creek. Soon my makeshift boot came off, but I figured what the heck. I couldn't feel my foot anyway so I kept going. Heading toward the beach under a brightening sky I heard a small droning noise which I hoped was a search plane. That really made me feel good. They were out searching in the right area. The plane came and went.

The deer trail ran adjacent to the river, and then, coming around a hump, I saw another river, going in a different direction. Which to follow? I sat down to do some thinking and take a rest. I knew I had to make it to the beach before dark as I sure didn't want to spend another night on the mountain. I felt a panicky feeling in my stomach just thinking about the situation. Then I noticed a deep rumbling sound. I headed toward it and found that both rivers came together and dropped off into a falls. I could see sixty feet down over a logged off area not far from the beach.

As I came out on the beach, I found that I was almost at the head of Helm Bay. The first thing I did was to use my one and only good foot that had a shoe on it to make a big "SOS" on the beach, hoping it would be seen from the air. The cabin was a couple of miles away on the other side of the bay. I reached a fairly deep creek I had to cross. I made it, especially because I had no feeling in my left foot.

After what seemed like hours, I finally made it to the Sleeping Beauty Mine cabin on the beach. Was I happy! Inside was an old wood stove and dry matches in a glass jam jar, dry wood in the oven, a small can of lighter fluid and an old quart can of outboard motor fuel. There were two bunks with three mattresses, and an old purple dress hanging on the wall. Then I heard an airplane. I ran to the water's edge and waved my piece of airplane fabric. Coming into the bay was a big, beautiful Albatross from the Annette Island Coast Guard Air Detachment. The pilot came all the way into the bay, turned around and on his way out flew directly over me. I could look straight up and see the underside of that plane. When it headed out

I felt awful. Then I looked at things in a different light. I am alive! I'm down on the beach and I have a nice cabin to stay in with fresh water behind it. What more could I ask? I started a fire and wrapped that old dress around my left foot.

It wasn't long before I heard another plane entering the bay. This time it was the familiar sight of a Grumman Goose–Captain Jim Hickey with a State Trooper. He taxied in as close as he could get to the beach. I yelled to him, "Are you looking for that plane?"

He said, "Yes."

I said, "Well, it is up on the mountain and both the other guys got killed."

"How do you know that?" he asked.

"Well, I just came down from there."

I waded out to the plane and got in through the door in the back. Someone looked and me and said, "You poor man." I guess I was a sight to behold with my face all bloody, but I was so happy!

After getting airborne I started to get a little nervous. Captain Hickey tapped me on the shoulder and said, "It's all right. You will be okay now."

At the hospital the doctors checked me out and found nothing broken. I had some scratches on my hips where the seat belt cut into me. My left foot was frost bitten and the doctors took a lot of shale rock from the bottom of my foot. For months afterward I was still digging out small pieces of shale.

The people of Wrangell collected money to pay for my way home, my hospital bill, and then some. I will always be grateful.

# A Rustic Cocktail Party
## Elizabeth A. Tower

In the summer of 1965, I started working as Southcentral Regional Health Officer. My region included the Alaska Peninsula and the Aleutian Islands in addition to the rest of southcentral Alaska. That year, four communities in that area chose to initiate Headstart programs. The program stipulated that all participating preschool children should have physical, dental, and psychological evaluations. I volunteered to be the physician on the evaluating team.

Early in August I joined an administrator, a secretary, a dentist, and a psychologist on the Reeve Aleutian Airways flight to Cold Bay. At Cold Bay our team transferred to the Reeve Aleutian Grumman Goose that served the villages by landing in the water and taxiing up the beaches. Our first stop was King Cove where we stayed in a cannery and evaluated about twenty attractive capable four and five-year-olds. Three days later the Goose picked us up and transported us to Sand Point where we evaluated children of mixed Aleut and Scandinavian parentage. Next, we were flown to Chignik Lake on the Alaska Peninsula where every child was an Anderson, Carlson, or Skonberg.

We were weathered in for several days in Chignik. When the Goose finally arrived, the pilot informed us the visibility was so poor that we would not be able to land at Perryville so he would take us to Cold Bay to connect with the return flight to Anchorage. The Goose had to land at Sand Point to get more gas and the pilot agreed to take on several fishermen who had been weathered in at Sand Point. The fishing season was over and they were anxious to get home. The fueling at Sand Point had to be done with a hand pump and the pilot was anxious to get on to Cold Bay to make the Anchorage plane.

The weather got progressively worse after we left Cold Bay. With a ceiling of less than 500 feet, the pilot had to hug the coastline, making frequent banked turns out of the coves and bays. Finally he reached a position where he could intersect the low frequency radio range and ride it in to Cold Bay, so he climbed through the clouds. We broke out of the overcast at 7000 feet and were greeted by blue skies and a stunning view of Pavlov Volcano with its plume of smoke. As we tense passengers were finally relaxing, we were startled by a sudden complete silence–the roar of the engines had stopped. We could see the propellers drifting lazily and then we were falling through thousands of feet of overcast. Just as we were beginning to see the ground, the pilot pulled the flaps allowing the Goose to clear a low headland and pancake into the shallow water of Chinaman's Lagoon.

Everyone breathed a sigh of relief and applauded the pilot as he turned and faced his passengers. "I guess this is a good time to break out our emergency rations," he announced as he walked to the rear baggage compartment. Once he opened them, however, he realized that they consisted entirely of dehydrated food and we were in salt water. Our team saved the day because we had picked up a case of smoked salmon and some home brew at the last cannery. We all settled in for a rustic cocktail party while the pilot radioed our plight to Reeve Airways at Cold Bay. Soon a Reeve DC3 flew over and asked us if we had any wieners to roast. We assured him we were all safe, reasonably comfortable, and glad to be alive, but it was apparent that our rescue presented a problem.

After dark there was nothing to do but try to sleep. Sadly, a Grumman Goose is not equipped with a lavatory. Every time we had to urinate we had to climb out the door and get on top of the metal plane. Each time this happened someone would wake up and ask what was causing the noise.

Throughout the evening the pilot was in communication with several fishing boats. Eventually a boat got within about a mile of us and several fishermen waded to the Goose with enough boots for everyone on board. We all waded to the fishing boat and then spent about 18 hours on the boat in order to get to Cold Bay.

Cold Bay was crowded with fishermen and cannery workers trying to leave the Aleutians at the end of the fishing season. We were given priority for available seating, but it was two more days before we could get to Anchorage. The Goose had a broken strut, but could be flown back to Cold Bay as soon as it got some gas.

# Submarine C-123 in Nuyakuk Lake
## Hal Wolverton

The call came in the late afternoon during the latter part of November 1965. Mr. Herbert Johnson[1] of Eagle River Cold Storage was calling. His request was logical and the theory he presented was unique but valid. His research indicated that a significant market existed in the New York area for White Fish frozen in the round. White Fish were to be found in commercial quantities in the Tikchik Lakes, including Nuyakuk. Fishing beneath the ice for the White Fish during the winter months and freezing them on site for shipment to market would provide steady local employment. In addition this operation would enhance the Red Salmon fishery since White Fish feed heartily on Red Salmon roe in the Lake complex.

Johnson was calling the Alaska Air National Guard because we then operated the only large ski-equipped transport aircraft in Alaska, the C-123J. As Commander of the Alaska ANG, Johnson's request was referred to me. He was requesting at least two trips from Anchorage to the Tikchik Lakes to move a small cat, a pre-fab building, generator and other equipment to support the fishing operation. I advised him that we operated under a non-competition policy and that if any commercial enterprise could accomplish the airlift, we could not be involved. I indicated to Mr. Johnson that approval from the Air Force would assure all parties that we were in compliance with policy and regulations. Through the offices of then Senator Gruening, the Air Force approved two missions.

[1]Not his real name.

Since we at the ANG were unfamiliar with the ice conditions at the lakes, we contracted with a Dillingham fixed base operator to fly to Nuyakuk Lake to drill the ice and measure the thickness. The C-123J required a minimum of 23 inches of ice to support it at 60,000 pounds gross weight. After measuring the ice and plotting a drill-hole pattern, the operator was to mark out a runway of approximately 4,000 feet with spruce bows or other suitable markings.

The first mission, flown in early 1966 to deliver the small cat, was unable to reach the lake due to foul weather. The cat was off-loaded at Dillingham to be later trailed in to the lake. The second mission, flown in early February 1966, had aboard the pre-fab building, generator, support equipment and supplies.

After an uneventful flight from Anchorage we arrived at Nuyakuk Lake in mid-late afternoon. The spruce bow marked runway was easy to spot on the all white lake as we descended for a first look-see pass. Taking advice from Alaska "Bush Pilots" I intended to make a "skis down" pass down the runway to check for overflow (water beneath the snow) which if present, would dictate that we not land. There was none, so I maneuvered to land in the opposite direction. The landing and rollout were routine. As we approached the far end of the runway I executed a 90 degree turn to the right followed by a 270 turn in the opposite direction to have us end up on the end of the runway facing the opposite way. We could thus offload and be ready for takeoff without additional taxiing. A little past the mid-point of the 270 degree turn I felt the plane list some to the left and about the same time the Loadmaster shouted that we were shipping water in the left rear ramp area. I applied maximum power to both reciprocal engines and called for the copilot to bring up the Jet auxiliaries. This did little to move the stricken bird. The loadmaster and flight engineer were already moving forward as I called for evacuation and systems shutdown. We moved rapidly away from the slowly sinking plane and could do nothing but watch as the poor machine settled and came to rest on the horizontal stabilizer and under wing fuel drop tanks. Fortunately we had evacuated with enough winter gear to survive if necessary.

We were shortly approached by a homesteader who lived nearby with his wife and two children. He was familiar with the intended fishing operation and counted on employment when it became a reality. His wife had not planned on four additional people to feed that night but true to Alaskan hospitality dinner was superb. We were able to use their radio telephone to notify ANG Operations and our families of the situation.

The following day our previously hired fixed-base operator flew out from Dillingham with Mr. Johnson. He was to retrieve us and let Mr. Johnson view the mission progress. As the operator shook and scratched his head he *then* informed us that he had judged the maneuvering room

87

where he had actually drilled the ice depths as too restricted for our larger aircraft. He moved out into the lake another 3,000 to 4,000 feet to mark the runway but did not drill there or tell us what he had done. When the operator stopped scratching his head he spoke slowly, "I'd have bet a thousand dollars the ice was just as thick out here as in where I did the drilling." My droll copilot quickly replied "You know, yesterday we bet six hundred and fifty thousand dollars, and we lost." At this point Mr. Johnson, who likely assumed that some liability would come his way, turned chalky white and leaned heavily against the strut of the small plane.

Upon returning to Anchorage, the immediate concern and discussion was how to retrieve the plane. Since the Air Force had assigned the missions, they would assume responsibility and carry out the recovery operation. At that time most all Alaska Air Command projects were assigned code names which included the word "cool." This recovery operation was dubbed "Cool Rope." The "Rope" portion would eventually be translated as "Recovery of Plane Eventually." Two primary methods of getting the plane free of the ice were examined. The first was to let the sub-zero temperatures build two 20 foot diameter ice columns to the bed of the lake and then use these platforms to raise the plane with normal jack systems. The second suggestion was to blast a 40 foot wide channel to the shore permitting the plane to be winched on to solid ground for thawing out and repairing as necessary for flight. This second method was selected.

Unfortunately for the plane and for a rapid recovery, too little thought was exercised concerning the action of ice being blasted with high explosives. The shattered ice does not simply go away. It falls back in proximity to its original location. Larger charges of explosives and metal netting covering the blast location still did not accomplish the desired containment of the ice chunks. The plane's skin had been padded with mattresses, two inch boards and three-quarter inch plywood, but a huge ice chunk penetrated all this "protection" and damaged the horizontal stabilizer spar sufficiently to require its changing.

Eventually the blasting retrieval process was abandoned acknowledging that Mother Nature is, indeed, a tough opponent. Instead, inflatable Bridge Pontoon Bags were secured beneath the wings and horizontal stabilizer. They floated the plane and its icy cargo. Next, a log boom barrier was put in place around the plane to protect it from shifting ice as "break-up" approached. When the lake ice melted, the floating plane was towed to shore with an outboard motor and winched onto solid ground for enough repairs to permit the flight home.

One year and one day after the flight which left old 391 in the lake, I returned to Nuyakuk and flew the sorrowful bird back to Anchorage. Then after an additional year of extensive repair and refurbishing I was able to conduct the "test flight" to return the plane to service.

# An Alaska Flying Experience
## Martin Ondra

The year was 1957. The place was McGrath, Alaska, a quiet little village on the bank of the Kuskokwim River. I was an employee of the Federal Government doing work as a radio operator for what was then the Civil Aeronautics Administration (later, the Federal Aviation Administration). I had started working for the CAA only the year before. The station had family housing and I had a wife and two little children at the time.

I had a love of aviation since childhood. I grew up in Pennsylvania on a small farm about fifty miles north of Philadelphia. During the Second World War there were all manner of airplanes flying over our farm and I would watch them going by and try to identify them and wish so badly that I could be up there flying one of them. However, I was too young to join the Army Air Corps.

My time came in 1949 after I graduated from high school. I went to radio operator school for ten months to learn Morse code, the primary means of long range communications. I was assigned to a flight crew of six manning large cargo aircraft. We were home based in El Paso, Texas, but flew around most of the western hemisphere, including Alaska.

I had read so much about the territory in various hunting and fishing magazines. I could not wait to get to see it for myself! The Air Force gave me that opportunity and I liked what I saw, but the

Korean War was going on at that time, so I had to continue my Air Force commitment for the duration. My desire to move to Alaska was finally realized in 1956 when the CAA hired me as a radio operator (now known as Air Traffic Controllers).

So here I am, working at the CAA station in McGrath, talking to pilots, giving weather briefings, taking flight plans, etc. but I'm not getting up in the air myself! What do I do? Well, if I could get the use of an airplane and find an instructor to teach me to fly, that would be one option. Of course, there were no airplanes to rent in McGrath and Anchorage was too far away to commute for flying lessons.

Through conversations with other CAA employees I happened to hear of a Piper PA12 Super Cruiser (just a little larger than the original Piper Cub) for sale in Bethel. I learned that it was a good, forgiving, training airplane and in good shape. Before I bought it however, I would need to find an instructor in McGrath to teach me to fly it.

There were many pilots living in McGrath at that time, but I needed one that was a rated flight instructor and would be willing to take the time to teach me to fly. I found this man working for Alaska Airlines, flying their bush runs to the lower Yukon villages. His name was Gene Stolz. He was a former navy fighter pilot and had seen combat in Korea. A fine man and an excellent instructor! I was finally in the air on my own after Gene signed me off to fly solo. The skies around McGrath became my play ground!

The flying time toward the private pilot license requirements came quickly. It was very convenient to have my own airplane and have it parked almost in my front yard. I would fly almost every day, even through the winter, with the little Piper on skis.

Preparing for the private pilot's written exam was easy since I already knew most of the subject matter through my work as an air traffic controller. The flying experience took a little longer, but by the spring of 1958, I was ready to take the flight check to earn my private pilot's license. The ride went smoothly and I was now ready to really learn the fine art of flying my machine. Worthy of note here, is that I was working with a fine lady by the name of Dorothy Bryant. She had been a ferry pilot in the Army during the Second World War and was very knowledgeable about all aspects of flying. She taught me a lot about flying safely.

The wilds of Alaska were now open to me to explore, hunt, fish, sightseeing and more. Furthermore, I could take my family and/or friends along to share the pleasure of flight. The air over Alaska was good to me. I never had an airplane accident.

My 26 years of service with the FAA included working at Skwentna, McGrath, Sitka, Big Delta, Fairbanks, Deadhorse, and finally Merrill

Field in Anchorage. I retired in 1982. Between my work as an Air Traffic Controller and my hobby of flying airplanes, I was able to see almost all of Alaska, from Ketchikan to Deadhorse on the North Slope, from King Salmon to Northway, from Anchorage to Nome and most points in between.

The single engine airplanes (I owned nine different ones, mostly on floats) enabled me to partake of the bounty of Alaska to feed my family of six children with moose, sheep, caribou, salmon, grayling, trout, sheefish, and pike. It allowed me to be a part-time guide and enabled me to rescue a party of stranded hunters in the remote Brooks Range of northern Alaska.

The flying of 3000 hours in the air over a period of 38 years put a lot of aviation gas out of the exhaust pipe of my airplanes, but it was well worth it! My flying career finished up in 1995 when I sold my last little airplane. I still love to fly, but now I charter an air taxi when I want to go to my remote cabin. I am happy to let someone else manipulate the controls. What a ride it has been!

# Moose on High
## Martha Roderick

Our DC-3 had landed in Valdez and would continue on to Cordova. It was the summer of 1955, and I was a stewardess for Cordova Airlines.

As the Valdez passengers boarded everyone avoided the seat next to a man who had obviously had too much to drink.

I was getting ready to close the door when a man yelling, "Wait, wait," came running up. He was carrying a young moose calf! He said its mother was dead, and the calf needed to go to Cordova where people wanted to have a moose herd. Then he handed me the calf and left.

I managed to close the door and get seated for take-off holding the calf on my lap. I had to sit next to the drunk because my regular seat wouldn't accommodate me and my new passenger.

As the plane revved up for take-off, the calf started squirming and kicked the man beside me. He looked around then bellowed. "God dammit lady, it's bad enough to have had a night like I had last night without having a moose next to you on the plane…"

Then I gave him the good news. He would have to hold the moose while I checked on the new passengers.

I hurried, and in just a few minutes I was back, to find that he had fallen in love with the calf and wanted to hold it! He kept talking softly and singing to himself until we got to Cordova.

He carried the moose calf off the plane and had his picture taken with it before handing it over to the park service.

# A Thousand Mile Runway

### Evan Swensen

Many of my contractor customers were road builders, so I'd fly my old Stinson Voyager around the state and make sales calls wherever the customer was building a road. Many times there was not an airport or even a bush runway to land on. I had to find my own place to land when I arrived at many a construction site.

One day I flew from Anchorage to Fairbanks to call on Mort Shearhorn of Green Construction. After a routine visit, Mort announced that he had a new job near Old Man River at about Mile 1200 on the Alaska Highway. He needed to go there and check it out. He planned to drive there that afternoon and suggested that it would be good for my business if I went along with him.

I told Mort that my schedule wouldn't permit it, as I had to be back in Anchorage that evening, but would fly to the site, make the sales call, and fly back to Anchorage later in the day. He hadn't realized I had my own plane and had flown it to Fairbanks that morning.

"Well," he said, "you mean you're going to fly out there today and then back to Anchorage tonight? That would work for me if it will work out for your people out at Old Man River. If you're going out there today, why don't I just go with you and introduce you to the men at the camp. Then I'll drive one of the company pickups back to Fairbanks? We need to get an extra one off the job anyway."

It sounded like a win-win trip all the way around. The flight to Old

Man River was routine—if any flight in Alaska is ever routine, given the beauty and grandeur of the Greatland.

Before leaving Fairbanks, neither of us had considered a place to land when we arrived. I assumed there was an airstrip nearby, in as much as Mort had suggested we fly together, but Mort, a non-pilot, hadn't considered it at all. He assumed I knew. A few miles from the construction camp I asked Mort where the airport was. "I don't know. Don't you know?"

I told him I hadn't even thought about it. I just assumed there was a place to land near the camp. The job Green Construction was working on was improving a section of the Alaska Highway. I told Mort that, like many Alaska bush pilots, I landed on the road all the time in making sales calls. "Don't worry," I said. "We'll find some place close by to put down."

On arrival at the camp we discovered a short, straight stretch of highway right in front of the camp where we could land safely. Taking off would be another matter, as there wasn't enough room, but just around the corner the Alaska Highway went down a long hill where I could see any approaching traffic for three or four miles. The wind was perfect for a downhill-into-the-wind takeoff. We cleared highway traffic, landed, and taxied to a pullout where I parked the plane convenient to the camp, and where I could see any oncoming traffic when I was ready to takeoff.

The visit at the camp was brief and I was soon ready to depart for Anchorage. After checking oil, fuel, and outside of the airplane, I got in to takeoff. It only took a minute or two to warm up the engine and do an engine run-up. There wasn't any traffic on the highway, so I taxied around the corner to the straight, downhill part of the highway where the takeoff would be directly into a stiff breeze. It would be an easy, safe takeoff.

About the time I was ready to pour the coal to the engine, a motor home came into sight. It was big and coming my way pretty fast. I decided to wait until it passed. I turned off the engine, got out of the plane, and pushed it around with the tail off the road in the shallow ditch and just the engine hanging over the lane. The motor home had the entire other lane to go past.

It soon became obvious that the motor home driver saw the airplane, but it slowed, stopped; then crept slowly forward. Ashenfaced, the driver rolled down the window and asked, "Did you crash? Is everybody alright?"

"No, I'm just waiting for you to get by so I can get back on the road and take off."

"You mean you didn't crash? How come you're parked on the side of the road?

"I'm a salesman and I'm out here making a sales call."

The driver looked back where he had just been and then ahead. "Calling on who? Trees? Animals? What?"

I explained that there was a construction camp just around the corner. It wasn't really unoccupied wilderness like what he had just been passing through for the last couple of hours.

"Do you mind if we take a movie of you taking off?"

"Not at all. Just pull ahead enough so I can get back on the road."

When I got in the plane, started the engine, and was ready for take-off I decided I'd give the motor home driver a good show. The airplane was facing directly into about a 20 knot wind; and it was down hill. I taxied out on the highway, lined up with the center line, applied the brakes, and pushed the throttle wide open. The airplane hesitated just a moment and I released the brakes. Takeoff speed was realized in a short distance. At just the right moment I popped the flaps and the airplane jumped into the air. I kept the nose down for a few seconds and picked up airspeed. The movie makers on the highway would film looking down on the airplane.

Once I had good speed I turned back toward the Hollywood wannabees and came in low over their motor home. I could see them duck as I went overhead and out of sight. I didn't look back or turn around. I just kept flying low until I was well down the highway.

Some day I'd like to see the movie the motor home driver made—and to hear the story going along with it. It's been a few years now and I'll bet the tale is bigger than Grandpa's fish stories.

# Animal Encounters

# I Played Mother Goose
## Dolores Roguszka

The story of a family of lesser Canada geese began in the spring of 1969 at Campbell Lake, south of Anchorage, in an area that has long been a nesting place and migration stop for ducks and geese. At the first sign of waterfowl in the spring, Campbell Lake residents stock up on cracked corn, which is placed on the beaches for the wild birds. Mating birds take advantage of the free smorgasbord, and as soon as the young are hatched, introduce them also to the corn diet.

The spring of 1969 was no exception. Mallards, pintails, teal, canvasback, shovel bill, golden eye, grebes, Arctic loons, Arctic tern, Canada honkers and lesser Canada geese appeared at Campbell Lake in ever-increasing numbers. A flock of 15 trumpeter swans stopped in briefly. A number of ducks and one pair of lesser Canada geese stayed and built nests. A few weeks later, clutches of young ducklings and goslings joined the hens on the beaches to feed.

I was fascinated by the brood of lesser Canada's, five tiny yellow fluff balls. For several days they came to the beach with the hen. Hunting season was not open and the area was closed, but nonetheless, early one morning a shot rang out from the flats just west of Campbell Lake. The hen did not return to her goslings. The little birds, orphaned when they were far too young to care for themselves, drifted up and down the lake, cheeping for their mother.

They attempted to join a pair of domestic geese (also nesting), but the domestics would not tolerate the little ones, pecking at them until one of the goslings was seriously injured. The folks who were caring for the domestic geese captured the tiny birds to protect them.

And that's where I came into the picture. I offered to take them and keep them until they were old enough to fend for themselves, and until they were large enough so they wouldn't become a meal for the glaucous gulls and hawks in the area. Gene and Nancy Chavis, neighbors on the lake, brought down a pen and we made a shelter for "our" geese. Nancy was destined to join me as a "mother" for the orphaned flock.

We made a nest of dry grass in a box. A dishpan of water was put into the pen, with rocks placed inside the pan for stepping-stones for the goslings. Grain suitable for young birds was provided. Grass and weeds were put into the pen several times daily. The injured one recovered and grew.

The goslings soon adopted Nancy and me. One of us would sit inside the pen each day and wait for the tiny birds to crawl into our laps. We wore jackets so the goslings could climb into a warm, dark substitute for a mother's wings. They would settle down and sleep, with the tiniest of happy "cheep, cheep, cheeps."

It wasn't long before they demanded more and more attention. Each time we passed the pen, five little goslings, flapping tiny "thumbs" of wings, would jump up and down and "talk" to us, demanding attention. Their sign of affection, which continued as long as we had them, was a gentle nibbling of our fingers, hair, nose or clothing.

The intention had never been to keep them captive, and soon they were large enough to face the great outdoors. They had outgrown their dishpan pond and it was time to take them to the lake for swimming exercise. I called Nancy and asked her to come down and watch the first swim. We let the goslings out of the pen, walked to the lake, and there the goslings stopped. They pecked at the water, and then had a drink. But enter it, they would not do. Nancy and I looked at each other in amazement. What kind of waterfowl were we raising? The juveniles followed us up and down the beach. They cheeped, they ran; they flapped their still-tiny wings; they drank; they ate some grass, but they would not get into the water.

With a shrug and a shaking of my head, I said to Nancy, "I guess their mothers will have to show them how." So off came our shoes. We waded in while the goslings cocked their heads first to one side and then to the other. We splashed. We told the goslings what fun we were having. They watched. The water was cold and soon our feet were the same. But still we coaxed. And finally, one by one, they joined us. Soon they were swimming, bathing, splashing and cheeping. It was fun! And so, they learned to swim.

The "kids" continued to grow and thrive. It was amazing how fast they changed from downy fluffs to gangly, homely immatures. By this time they were free. They still slept in the pen, but the door was open and they could come and go at will. However, they did not leave the area.

While seated at my typewriter in the office, I could watch the young geese as they played, slept, swam, and fed. They could see me too, and whenever they wanted attention or company they came to the house and pecked on the window. I would go outdoors and talk to them for a while. Usually they weren't satisfied with a brief visit and a return to duties indoors produced a loud "Honk. Honk. Honk." Should their requests for a visit not be granted the geese would march around the house, up the hill and honk at the front door. Geese in a pen or on the beach or in the yard are fine. But geese at your front door! Each visit to the front door resulted in the necessity for hosing down the area to get rid of the abundant amounts of fertilizer they were sure to leave.

They were beginning at this stage to visit with the domestic geese, who had failed to produce young, and who had become more tolerant of the lessers. My geese would swim down the lake for a nice long visit, and when it was time for the evening feed, were not to be seen. I'd call them, and hear, off in the distance, an answering "Honk." So I'd get the boat, start the motor, and head down the lake to bring them home. As soon as they'd see the boat, and hear me call, they'd happily head for their "mother" and follow.

Nancy and I were beginning to be concerned at the amount of time they were spending with the domestics; afraid that when the wild geese came in the fall ours would not go with them. Our fears proved to be valid.

One evening I took the boat across the lake to look for blueberries. Naturally, the geese had to follow. When we reached the other shore the geese followed me up the bank and into the blueberry patch. They hadn't been taught about blueberries as food, so I handed them a few. It didn't take long until they decided they liked this new stuff, but instead of picking for themselves it was much easier to eat from my bucket! Consequently, I ended up with enough blueberries for only one pie, but the geese enjoyed them. I started the boat, five geese trailing along behind. They must have been tired by the time we reached the water, for they wanted to get into the boat and ride home.

By late summer they had attained their full growth. Wings were wide, characteristic markings of the Canada goose, *Branta canadensis leu-*

*copareia*, were in full evidence. They had been doing a lot of wing flapping but thus far had not started to fly. I decided it was time for them to learn if they were to join the wild ones in the fall.

And how does an earth-bound mortal teach five geese to fly? It's easy, if you don't mind the unbelieving, anxious stares of the neighbors. You start from the top of a hill, run downhill and flap your wings.

The geese run along behind, honking and flapping their wings. You run back to the top of the hill and try it again and again and again. Finally, if you're lucky (as I was), along about the seventh run a gust of wind comes along and lifts the geese into the air. They were aloft.

The problem then was how to get down. They flew around and around, squawking and honking, and finally made a landing that would get a student pilot grounded forever. This was the beginning. At first they flew for short periods, then more and more.

Nancy and I used our boats to give them more exercise. We would get into the boat and the geese would swim along behind. We'd speed up and so would the geese. We'd go faster until they couldn't swim fast enough to keep up and had to fly. Up and down the lake we'd race, wind full in our faces, while the "kids" squawked happy noises at us from the air.

Their friends, the domestics, did not take kindly to this new flying business and would continually call the lessers down. Our concern for our birds was mounting. We had hoped that when the first wild birds appeared they would join the wild ones on the annual migration.

I had to leave for an assignment in South Africa in September, so Gene and Nancy Chavis took over the feeding and watching of the geese. They reported later that the wild ones came, and though ours would fly with them from time to time, they did not go. About this time, Gene placed yellow bands on the legs of each of our geese. Apparently the five were regular visitors to other places in the An-chorage area, and one day only four of them returned to Campbell Lake. They had landed on the school grounds at Turnagain School where some avid "sportsman" shot one of them. The four left Camp-bell Lake again some time later and only three returned.

Winter came and the lake froze over. The three were still here, try-ing to land on the ice. They slipped; they fell. They squawked their indignation. After one flying sortie they landed at the far end of the lake, and Nancy walked them home over the slippery ice, the geese protesting the treacherous ice every step of the way. Gene built an-other pen and put the geese inside, where they were cared for dur-ing the winter.

In April I departed for the Arctic and while I was gone spring ar-rived and the lake began to thaw. As soon as open water appeared, the three geese were set free in the hope they'd join the wild geese during the spring migration. Two of them responded to the call of the wild and were gone. The last goose we named Esmerelda, and she stayed and stayed. She was far more interested in her own image in a mirror or plate glass window than she was in responding to a handsome gander who persistently wooed her. He must have been successful, however, for early in the summer of 1970, she followed him away from the lake for a day at a time, then three or four days, then a week, and finally she, too, was gone.

One evening in late August, Nancy and I were visiting at her home when we heard a familiar "honk" overhead. It was a greeting that Esmerelda gave each time she flew overhead. She didn't land this time. Was she bidding us farewell for the winter? We aren't sure.

We hoped that next year they would come back to Campbell Lake to breed. We also hoped they survived so they can rear their own young. We did the best we could, but playing Mother Goose to goslings is a job for a *real* Mother Goose!

'This story is a slightly revised version of a manuscript published in the December 1970 issue of *The Alaska Sportsman*.

# Memories of Annabelle
## Deborah Spencer

I grew up in Anchorage on O'Malley Road, not too far from the Diamond H Horse Ranch. The Diamond H was known for its horses, but they also had a reputation for accepting unusual and exotic animals from time to time. They had a seal named Oley, an ocelot, and an elephant named Annabelle.

Now I don't really know how Annabelle came to the Diamond H Horse Ranch. I think she was a result of a competition that was going on in Anchorage. Someone who didn't have a place to keep her won her, so, of course, the Diamond H Ranch took her.

One of the most remarkable things to me about Annabelle was that she was hairy. I didn't really know that elephants had hair. She was a baby elephant, not very big and she had a very sparse covering of long black shiny hair.

My story about Annabelle centers around one specific incident that happened when I was probably 10 or 11 years old. It was a summer day, with beautiful sunny weather. I was foot loose that day so I kind of meandered over to the Diamond H to watch the horses and to feed them grass and hang out.

When I walked down the driveway, I noticed that Annabelle was tethered out in the front part of the yard where it was kind of grassy. As I recall, the tether was a leather belt that went around her ankle and attached to a chain that had some kind of peg in the yard. It was not a very big chain and I didn't pay much attention to it.

Annabelle was playing with sticks. She was kind of tossing them around, dropping them on the grass, so I went over there and picked up one of the sticks. She grabbed it from me and kind of pulled on it, so I kind of pulled back. And so we played tug-of-war together for a few minutes.

She was small enough that she didn't really scare me. She had the most beautiful big brown eyes with long eyelashes, was very gentle with her trunk. She would wrap the tip of it around the stick and when I would pull back she would tug a little.

At some point it occurred to me that playing with the elephant wasn't such a great idea and that I might get into trouble so I decided to walk away and head home. I turned around and left. I was walking down the road when I turned around and saw that Annabelle was following me. She had crossed the road in fact and was now pretty close to the end of our driveway.

Somehow she had slipped her tether and I never did figure out how. Maybe it was broken or she just stepped out of it. She went all the way down the road, all the way across the road, not all the way to my house, but close.

I kind of panicked and I think I probably ran home. Mom was outside and looked at me, then at Annabelle, and I said, "Mom, she followed me home!"

"You can't keep her!" she said.

So that's my story about Annabelle. She later became quite the artist ...but that's another story.

# Reindeer Wrestling

## Jay E. Carlisle

One day late in the fall of 1986, a friend, Ron Brinker, called me and asked if I could help him the next day. He said he had a job he had to do and needed an extra hand. I told him, "Sure, as long we could do it early, because I have a 10 a.m. appointment."

Early the next day, before sunrise, Ron showed up with his truck, a cage in the back of the bed. He was doing a favor for a man who needed a female reindeer shipped to him. She had been left at the zoo earlier that year until after she had calved and recovered. The plan was for us to pick her up, put her in her cage, and ship her by Flying Tigers Airline to New York. If it were only going to be that easy!

We arrived at the zoo early. Were told by zoo personnel to, "Go on back and use the little catching pen off the large pen where all the reindeer were." Following those instructions, we entered the big enclosure and started along the sides looking for the opening to the smaller "catching pen." Ron went one way, and I the other.

A bull reindeer stood up and walked over toward Ron. He said afterward the reindeer was acting almost like it was expecting to be fed. I was following the fence on the other side of the pen, when I heard the sound of a fence being hit. I looked around and there was Ron on the ground, speared in the leg by the antler of the reindeer, and pinned against the fence with the reindeer continuing a full power charge.

I started running and as I got there I grabbed the antlers, did a football block, which rolled the reindeer and Ron up and over. Ron pulled the antler out of his leg, as I held the reindeer down, then ran and climbed up and over the fence. Blood was everywhere.

As soon as I could see he was free, I realized that I, too, was in a dilemma. I had to let go of the reindeer! Finally, I did so, and ran like crazy to the fence and jumped. I grabbed the top rung and hung there looking back at the bull reindeer, expecting to be his next target. Instead, he just got up, shook his head and ambled back to his harem.

Ron had to go to the hospital, in shock from the loss of blood. They operated on his leg to clean it of the debris to prevent infection from the ground and the antler.

We decided it was never a good idea to wrestle a reindeer before breakfast.

# McNeil River Bears
## June M. Thompson

It was during the 60s while I was working for the Alaska Department of Fish and Game that I learned about permits to go to the McNeil River Sanctuary to see the Grizzly/Brown bears fishing for salmon at the falls. Three of us ladies put our names in for a permit, not expecting to win, but I did!

After learning more about it, I decided I'd better get in shape to be able to do all the necessary walking, so I joined a spa for a couple of months before I was to leave. One biologist informed me of what gear we needed—warm clothes, raincoat, hip boots, a tent, sleeping bag, a container for water, cooking utensils, Coleman stove, dishes, silverware and food for four days. Luckily I had gone hunting and camping and had it all.

I drove to Homer where I was to take a float plane to McNeil River. It was so awesome to fly so close to St. Augustine, an active volcano.

We landed in the lagoon at McNeil River when the tide was in. Then it dawned on me that I should have worn the hip boots! Luckily, the biologist on site came to my rescue and carried me on his shoulders to dry land.

As many as ten people could have a permit, but there were only two of us, a young fellow who was a photographer and me. Usually there are two biologists stationed at McNeil River but this time only one was there, so I got to use the spare tent, which was roomy and comfortable and saved me from putting up my own!

Settling in, we had to hike over to a creek to fill our water containers. Our food had to be stored up a ladder in a cache. We cooked our meals in a "cook shack." There are no fences surrounding the fish and game camp but the bears seemed to know how close they could venture onto the camp site.

Fish and Game built a viewing platform at the river so people could watch the bears up above the falls. At first the bears would tear up the platform and each year it would have to be rebuilt. Finally, the bears got the message and left it alone. Below the platform was a photo cave where photographers could stand pretty close to the bears. One day while I was there, a bear did lunge at the photographer and he came flying up out of there in a flash.

The first day up to see the bears; we started out all decked in rain gear and hip boots. First we crossed the lagoon, which was muddy and I kept losing one boot in the mud. The biologist grabbed one arm and the photographer the other and pulled me along. We made it to the bear trail which was about a foot wide and a foot deep. We were to make noise in case of bears nearby. (I'm thinking "Would that scare a bear away?")

The next day we traipsed up to watch the bears again. What fun to watch them grabbing fish out of that rushing water from the falls! And the antics they pulled! They would stand in the water like they were taking a shower—brushing under their arms, etc. Others would pick fights—never a dull moment. The biologists had named several over the years—the Marx Brothers and Zubin who had a beautiful coat. One time a bear came up by the viewing platform only about fifteen feet away, but when the biologist cocked his gun the bear backed off.

I had been watching a mama bear and her three cubs as they were coming down the river toward us. She tried to entice them across the river, but one of them refused and just sat there crying. Believe me, they sound just like a child when they cry! I kept hoping they would come close to where I was, as I wanted a picture of the four of them. And believe it or not, that's just what they did! I got a picture of the four of them just below me and all looking up at me! It's not a very big picture, but I used it on my Christmas card that year.

We had four days there but one day it poured rain so we stayed in camp. I had heard that a tent leaked during rain if you poked the ceiling with your finger—of course I had to test the theory and leak it did!

At night we could hear animals passing by the tent. The privy was about fifteen feet away so it took all the nerve I had to go out there at night. The next morning, I would figure it was foxes because I saw them playing on the beach.

The last day, as we were returning to camp, the biologist said there was a Fish and Game boat we could use to cross the lagoon as the tide was in. Well, we found the boat but no paddles. The bears loved to tear them up too. So, he told me to get in the boat. Then he and the photographer pushed the boat across the lagoon and a little stream. The water was shallow but still hard pushing! I was so lucky!

All in all, it was such a memorable trip. I'll never forget it. And the bears didn't even scare me!

# My Pet Cub
## Donna Grant

I had a pet bear cub the summer I turned twelve. My dad worked for the Alaska Railroad and he and another fellow brought the cub home. It was orphaned when a hotel worker shot his mother at the Mt. McKinley Hotel garbage dump.

He was a darling cub, adorable as all young things are. I pampered him with Karo syrup, honey and condensed milk in a baby bottle. He was kept in a neighbor's secure yard and I took him for walks to the park overlooking the inlet (now the tank farm) where he romped around for hours.

The trouble would start when he'd scamper up a tree. Apparently he liked it up there because I often had to jerk his leash to get him down and that made him cranky. Somewhere I have a picture of me using fireweed to lure the bear cub onto a trike.

I guess I had him for a two or three months before he started to lose his warm little eyes and took on the beady eyed look of predator. It didn't help that neighborhood kids were pelting him with rocks. Eventually he had to leave and my dad told me that a zoo outside had taken him. Now I look back and wonder if he really did go to a zoo.

The prohibition against keeping wild animals is a wise one I think, but I have great memories of that little black cub.

# Fishing in Prince William Sound
## Donna Grant

One day in June my husband and I flew to Prince William Sound to do some fishing. George landed the plane, we got out and I, the non-fishing partner, followed my tireless fisherman through the tall grass by the river. I couldn't help noticing a lot of bear scat on the trail. It was not steaming, but some of it looked pretty fresh. I developed the ability to swivel my head much further than ever before, looking out for bear.

I soon lost interest in the fishing expedition. Tiring of the anxiety and boredom, I went back to the floatplane. From that elevated view I saw a brown bear in the woods behind where George was fishing (in what was the bear's spot no doubt.) I shouted to George, pointing and waving my arms and he, Mr. Cool, turned around, bellowed, "Whoof!" at the bear, which slunk back into the trees.

Needless to say I was wild with worry and not quiet about it. Finally, to shut me up I guess, George returned to the plane and we took off. As we banked we could see the bear close to the edge of the woods, waiting.

# An Unwelcome Visitor

## Camellia Buschman

It was a beautiful July day in 1995. After running errands I returned to the Anchorage Hillside home that my husband, Jack, and I had built many years ago. I found Jack in the garage, asked if he'd like a sandwich, and went up the outside back stairs to the second floor deck.

There I found the screen door open, which was usual as we had two cats that liked to wander in and out. Inside, a large floral decoration was scattered on the dining room floor. I had a few bad thoughts about those two rascal cats. After I picked up the mess, I stepped into the kitchen and almost fell flat!

The floor was covered in cooking oil. This couldn't be the work of the cats! Looking out into the hallway I saw oily tracks on the carpet. Not paying any real attention to the size of the tracks I stepped out of the kitchen and looked to my left down the hall. No more than ten feet away a black bear stood "smiling" at me!

I dashed down the main house staircase, out into the garage, and shouted to Jack that a bear was in the house. We called Fish and Game, who called back to make sure the call was not a prank. We then called a neighbor who was retired from Fish and Game. He rushed over with M80s (large firecrackers) and a shotgun. He and Jack decided against using the M80s to scare the bear, for fear of damage the interior of the house.

Meanwhile the bear was roaming through the house scaring the cats and eating gourmet chocolates, paper and all, which he found in two different bedroom stashes. He left bear claw holes in a couch and in the draperies where he must have tried to catch one of the cats.

The men decided to open the front sliding doors downstairs, and Jack went to the back of the house to the bedroom where the bear was prowling and began banging on the windows.

The bear made a swift retreat and dashed through the open slider. Our neighbor decided to fire his shotgun at the bear–but missed and hit the house with large buckshot.

Fish and Game finally arrived, but by that time the bear had gone up the hill, and climbed a tree, thus gaining access to someone else's second floor deck. He was peering in their windows, but when their dog began barking wildly, the bear returned to our house, where Fish and Game treed and finally were forced to destroy it.

To this very day, oily paw prints occasionally reappear on the carpet in the master bedroom as a reminder of our suburban bear adventure.

# A Lucky Guy
## Bruce A. Herrman

Way back when I worked as a commercial fisherman, I found myself extremely bored. You see, the Alaska Fish and Game had the
season on hold. Red salmon were everywhere. Not being able to
stand the tension, I decided to walk to the next village, Ekok, to visit
some friends. There was a brown bear in the area that was raiding
the set net sites so I decided to take the scenic route, which followed
the bluffs over the beach.

It was a beautiful day. There was not a cloud in the sky and just a
slight day breeze. The view of Bristol Bay and the surrounding tundra was breathtaking. There was a lot to see up on the bluff. Several
mallard ducks, ducks that I had never seen before, five cranes, and a
pair of swans that seemed to be oblivious to my presence all seemed
to demand my undivided attention. I even played with a porcupine.
What a lucky guy!

I was walking very slowly and not making much noise. After all,
I was very close to the wild birds and did not want to scare them
away. It was then that I had the most frightful experience of my 22
years—I came belly to belly with that brown bear!

I literally mean belly-to-belly! It seems that the bear was resting
next to the path that I was following. Well, the bear stood up and I
walked right into his belly. I looked up and the bear looked down.
The next few moments are a blur even now. I do know that I lost

all bodily functions. The bear started to run away. It was then that I got my legs back under me and stood up. I could not see but found my glasses a few feet away. They were broken and one lens was missing. There was a trickle of blood over my left eye. The bear was gone. The birds were all gone. But I was still there!

To this day, I do not know if the bear took a swipe at me before fleeing or if I lost the glasses as I fell to the ground. I do know that day I was indeed a very lucky guy.

# Traffic Jam

## Jean Cechowski

"It was a dark and stormy night," to quote Snoopy, but it was about 40 to 50 below zero out there, also. My friend, Pinky, and I were headed down the highway from Fairbanks to Anchorage in December of 1966. I had been at the University of Alaska in Fairbanks working with my advisor on my thesis. In those days there was very little offered on the graduate level in Anchorage, so you traveled to Fairbanks.

Once again I was going back to Anchorage with more questions than answers. The trips were beginning to be tiresome and not a little hazardous. The old Richardson Highway was just that–old–not well maintained–with little traffic on these cold, wintry days. Little did I know that the real hazard was going to come out of the dark, unexpected and unseen.

I had hitched a ride with a good friend who had run dogs and knew her way in the dark and cold. She had a fairly new van. Unfortunately it was not insulated. It was cold and the heater did little to warm the interior. Pinky was a slow and cautious driver so we were working our way carefully but surely on the approach to Delta Junction. There were large snow berms on both sides of the highway.

Buffalo were rather an innovation around Delta. I knew there were several herds wandering around, a curiosity rather than a threat to most people. I had passed through Delta Junction many times and stopped and looked around, but never encountered even a glimpse of a live beast. This time was different. First I heard a rat-a-tat rhythmic beat, not thunder–the beat was too even for thunder. Then the van started to sway side to side. There was no wind. Glancing out the side window, I saw brown, huge hairy beasts. We were surrounded on three sides by BUFFALO! Pinky was so shocked that she slowed and then we were surrounded on four sides. The drum beat was even louder now. The beasts were using the road as a pathway because the snow was too deep on either side. It was a herd of about forty. We were receiving some glancing blows that rocked the van, but they were passing us. Their heads were glazed with hoarfrost and they were a fearsome sight. Luckily they had no taste for foolish travelers. We were all just trying to survive the threatening cold and get somewhere. As the buffalo receded down the highway and disappeared in the dark, I gave a sigh of relief. Frankly, I will give buffalo the right-of-way any time.

Traveling in sub-zero weather is always a challenge. Buffalo have a right to survive but I do wish they would stay off of my highway. I've never seen a buffalo since this extraordinary encounter but I know they're out there somewhere!

# Go! Tex! Go!
## Roger Rabb

I was working on a road job up on the North Slope of Alaska. The job was far from home and family, and in a rather isolated location. We tried to keep ourselves amused, but sometimes things got pretty mundane and tedious. As part of the equipment we had a connex, a box that can be loaded on a trailer to pull behind a semi truck. It was sitting on the ground on the job sight. Inside the connex was a load of grass seed, which was to be used along the roadside to reseed the banks when the road job was near completion.

We also had a Texan working on the job, who never missed an opportunity to let us know what a great bull rider he was. He said he could ride any bull there was.

One day I walked out by the connex and there was a caribou inside eating on the grass seed. I quickly slammed the doors on the connex, keeping the suddenly frightened caribou inside in the dark. I then went in search of Tex.

"Hey Tex," I said, "did you say you could ride any bull there was?"

"You got that right," was the reply.

"Do you think you could ride a caribou?"

"Look, if you can catch him, I can ride him."

"I got something for you," and I led him over to the connex. Tex positioned himself on top of the box, and we got the doors ready.

When the caribou launched itself out the door, Tex jumped on his back. And then the fun started.

Of course a large crowd had gathered to watch the great bullrider in action. That caribou didn't waste any time at all putting his large rack of horns to work on Tex, and the next thing he knew he was on the ground. He soon sported a couple of black eyes and other assorted bruises.

We didn't hear much about his great bull-riding expertise after that, but we all had a good laugh at the expense of poor old Tex. And it seemed to me that caribou stepped a little higher, and held his head back a little further as he escaped across the tundra.

# Skier Beware

## Bruce Talbot

Cross country skiing in Alaska has always been something of challenge when trails need to be shared with various kinds of wildlife. Moose are a particular problem, since they understand that hard groomed trails are easier to travel than deep snow, and it is not uncommon to realize the necessity to back up, backtrack, and return the same way you came.

However, one chilly January night in 1989, I was going down a long hill. I was surprised and bewildered by a sharp strike to the back of my head. As I looked behind, I saw these rather large wings. I felt a tightening around my scalp and reached up and grabbed the legs of a very large, full-grown, great horned owl, which was attacking my gray pile ski hat. Did he think it was a rabbit?

While attempting to retrieve my hat, I also lost a glove. I escaped for a moment, but about forty feet down the trail I again felt the talons, this time imbedded in my back. Several other skiers, heard my calls for help, and assisted me in removing my jacket, vest, and T-shirt, which were all attached to the owl's talons. With the temperature at five below zero, I found myself stripped to the waist. Passing skiers were kind enough to loan me enough clothing to ski the two miles back to the Kincaid recreation center.

So, when skiing in Alaska, beware the great horned owl!

# My Bear Story

### Dolores D. Roguszka

With a lump in my throat I watched the small floatplane disappear over the treetops, then strained my ears to hear the last distant sound of the engine dwindle into nothingness. Cecil, my small black and white "cocker-springer type" dog, nudged my hand with his nose. For a moment I wanted to cry, "Come back, come back!" but realized that my voice would only echo across the lake and be heard perhaps by a solitary moose, the loons, a family of ducks, or a beaver building his dam across the outlet stream.

At that moment I wondered just what leave-taking of my senses had encouraged me to insist to husband and friends that I wanted to spend a week or ten days, absolutely alone, at our cabin near the foothills of mighty Mt. McKinley.

Back in the mid-60s I was a professional photographer and also doubled as secretary, bookkeeper and general Girl Friday for my husband, Gene, who had his own business as aviation consultant. We worked out of offices in our home near Alaska's largest city, Anchorage. For months I had been closely confined to home and office since Gene had spent a great deal of time traveling, and someone had to "mind the store."

I'm sure this confinement was the cause of my wanting to "get away from it all." The idea of a stay at our comfortable log cabin had seemed wonderful. I had envisioned peace and solitude. I would commune with nature. To prohibit complete idleness, I planned to brush log oil onto the logs, interior and exterior, of the cabin. "Ah," I had thought, "I'll be busy and happy, with only Cecil to share my 'vacation.'"

The pilot of the small plane, our friend, photographer and guide, Steve McCutcheon, had flown us in to the lake. He dumped my grub, supplies and gear on the beach, had a cup of tea with me, and then had taken off.

Gear was soon stored, log oil and brushes carried to a spot near the cabin, grub put away, some inside the cabin and those items that needed to be kept cool stashed on the porch.

While storing gear I checked to make sure the 30-06 Mauser was handy. Finding it in its usual place somehow comforted me. Gene had explained to me before I left home what I had to do to put a cartridge in the chamber, just in case I needed to use the rifle. The chamber was fully loaded. The five shots in the clip should be enough to protect me from whatever danger I might encounter. I pushed aside a vague, worrying thought. I didn't know the first thing about SHOOTING the 30-06, or reloading it.

That evening I felt that I had put in a good day's work, and after a meal, settled down to read for a few minutes before bedtime. The open fire in the Franklin fireplace crackled, snapped, and cast dancing shadows upon the wall and ceiling. Looking out the big picture window I could see Mt. McKinley bathed in a soft pink glow, seeming to settle down for a period of rest before performing the task of standing majestically overlooking cabin, my dog and me on the morrow.

The next morning dawned bright and clear, as only the crisp fall days in Alaska can. Cecil and I awakened in fine fettle, and began our day.

I started brushing oil on the exterior walls of the cabin while Cecil barked at every fish that jumped in the lake, every bird that flew near. Working my way around the cabin, my eye caught something unusual. I moved closer to get a better look. Strips of roofing material waved in the breeze, some strewn around the rooftop. I hauled over a box and climbed up. Not only was the roofing material torn loose, but also deep claw marks marred the thick tongue-and-groove lumber underneath. The strip of aluminum flashing along the edges was damaged. I had seen these marks before. Bear!

In past years I had never felt concerned about the beasts, but newspapers throughout Alaska this summer had reported many instances of black bears doing substantial property damage. Several men had been attacked. One man was killed.

Authorities suggested that wild berries, which the bears usually fed upon, were scarce. The beasts were looking for food. I recalled that I hadn't found the customary good supply of blueberries at the lake this year. Those thoughts flashed through my mind as I climbed down to the ground. I had a sick feeling in the pit of my stomach. I wished I had stayed at home.

I'd have to keep my eyes open. Thank goodness I had Cecil with me! The way he'd been barking at birds, jumping fish, and squirrels, I knew that a bear couldn't come around without my knowing about it. I'd stay close to the cabin, not go out after dark, and keep the 30-06 near. It *did* get difficult, holding a bucket of log oil in one hand and a brush in the other, all the while wearing the 30-06 draped over my shoulder. But I wasn't about to part with that gun.

Preparing breakfast a few mornings later I stepped out on to the porch to get the fresh peaches I had brought along. They weren't there! A plastic bag containing lettuce and tomatoes had been ripped apart. Sharp claws had raked the head of lettuce.

I had to sit down. I was shivering. I hadn't heard a thing! Apparently Cecil hadn't either. It was if a silent black ghost had paid us a visit, for there was no doubt in my mind that the bear had been here again.

I didn't accomplish much that day and when I heard the drone of a small plane's engine, I hardly dared hope that Steve was returning so soon. There he was though. The bright yellow and red aircraft dipped its wings as it flew over then landed and taxied to shore. I didn't think I'd ever be so happy to see anyone again—ever. That just proves how wrong one can be.

Steve listened to my story, inspected the roof, and then gave me a hand while I did a temporary patch job. We unloaded my supplies from the plane, and then taxied the half-mile or so to the McCutcheon cabin to unload supplies there. They, too, had had a visitor. Newspapers and magazines stored under one shelf on their porch were ripped to shreds. A gallon can of paint thinner had been punctured by sharp teeth, as had a coffee can.

We cleaned up most of the mess, and then Steve had to return to town. I'm not sure even now why I didn't go with him. Before he left, he suggested perhaps he should give me a few pointers on using the 30-06. I agreed. He set up a target for me, explained the mechanism of the gun, and I proceeded with target practice. I fired six shots and only missed the target once. Not bad for a beginner. Steve cautioned me, "Don't fire your last two shots, should you have to use the gun. Save them for the chance the beast you are hunting should turn and charge at you. At close range, two shots could make the difference between life and death for you." He was convinced after my short stint of practice that I could at least fire, reload, and handle the gun fairly well. I was secretly quite proud of myself.

This time when the plane disappeared from sight I didn't feel quite so desolate. Now I was armed. And knew how to use the weapon!

Back to work. Steve would return within a few days with fresh grub and more log oil. I didn't need much grub, only a few fresh vegetables and fruit. I told him specifically not to bring more canned goods or bread. I had plenty of canned goods and one whole loaf of bread, which should last me for the balance of my stay at the lake.

The logs of the cabin were gradually acquiring a gloss, and though I kept vigilance, the pride of my work banished thoughts of marauding bears.

Early the next morning I was barely cognizant of a peculiar sensation. The bed seemed to be moving! As consciousness returned, I discovered that Cecil had jumped onto the bed; trembling so hard the whole bed was shaking. He hadn't whimpered, barked or made any other sound. By this time I was wide-awake, and I too, heard the noise. SOMETHING was on the porch. I knew it must be the bear. All bravado disappeared. I hadn't guts enough to get out of bed. Cecil and I buried our heads beneath the pillows. After a while the noise diminished.

When I did crawl out, my knees felt as if they had turned to rubber. I hardly had strength enough to light the fire. Somehow I managed to get dressed and fixed coffee. After the coffee pot had perked and the coffee was consumed, I bravely pulled on a jacket, readied the rifle, and cautiously poked my head out the door. No bear. I checked to see what he had been into this time. He had overturned cans and bottles, pushed aside a stack of kindling wood; pawed around in the grub boxes, and carried off my only loaf of bread.

Cecil stayed hidden as I carefully moved outdoors to look around. The brush was so thick that the intruder could have been quite close. I'll admit that I didn't go far from the cabin door. Naturally my investigations didn't include poking around in the brush. Even armed I was still a coward.

All day I kept peering over my shoulder, as I brushed on log oil in a perfect frenzy of activity. Cecil was under foot constantly. The mutt never once during the day moved more than ten feet away from me. Every time I looked at him the hair on the back of MY neck stood up as I watched him stare into the wilderness. My dog paid no attention to his food, and soon he had me so "spooked" that I couldn't eat either. It's just as well, for I usually had a sandwich for my noon meal, but now, without bread, the sandwich would have been a thin one.

Every rustle of leaves convinced me that the bear was stealthily moving about, just out of sight. Every shadow took on the shape of a huge bear. I felt sure that the menace was hidden in the brush, watching me, and waiting for the right moment to pounce.

I used, slopped and spilled log oil until the last drop was gone. With no outlet for my nervous energy, I sat on the porch with rifle clutched tightly in both hands and watched.

As the afternoon wore on, tension increased. Soon dusk would be approaching, and the daily chores had to be done. They took more than twice as long that day, because I wouldn't, couldn't put the rifle down. Back and forth I trudged from the woodpile to the cabin, one armload of wood at a time. Wood box filled, I made two trips to the lake for water. Both times I stumbled over Cecil and spilled part of the water over the two of us.

On the third trip to the lake I discovered the remains of the stolen bread. Thirty feet from the cabin door the thief had consumed most of the loaf. Where was he now? Was he still watching me? I dropped the water bucket and quickly looked around. With Cecil close at my heels I reached the cabin, slammed the door, locked and secured it for the night. We were a long time going to sleep.

We did sleep however, and early in the morning Cecil nudged me with his cold, wet nose. This time I was awake in an instant. Again the sound of thumping, banging and rattling on the porch! As I jumped out of bed, Cecil jumped in and burrowed under the covers. I grabbed the rifle and started for the door, pausing to glance out the window. And there he was! Standing on his hind legs, looking in the window!

While I stared, momentarily unable to move, the bear dropped to all fours and moved away from the cabin. I quickly had a cartridge in the rifle chamber. Slowly I opened the door and peeked out. He was still moving away from me. I stepped outside, raised the gun to my shoulder, aimed and fired. I hit him. With a roar of anger he whirled to face me. From inside the cabin I could hear Cecil's muffled howls of fright. I wanted to howl too. I steadied myself to fire the final shot, aimed and pulled the trigger. The gun jammed.

The beast had begun crawling away. Apparently the shot had broken his spine, but even so he was pulling himself along toward the protective cover of the brush. I couldn't let him get away. Wounded, he was more of a menace.

I flew into the cabin and frantically pried the shells out of the gun. With shaking fingers I reloaded. It seemed hours before I was ready to fire another shot. By now the bear was out of sight. I could see a clump of brush move slightly, and heard the sound of his tongue as he attempted to stop the flow of blood.

After a while the brush ceased moving. I thought perhaps the shot had been a mortal one, although I didn't dare approach near enough to find out. I suddenly felt cold, and realized that I was dressed only in my birthday suit and a 30-06.

Returning to the cabin I pulled on my clothing; built a fire; made coffee and viewed, from the window, the spot where I had last seen my quarry. I continued to watch while I warmed myself and swallowed a cup of coffee. Not a movement.

I decided I'd sit right there and wait for Steve to arrive. This was the day to return home, and TODAY I'd really be happy to see him! But no, I couldn't take a chance on his coming in to tie the plane down at the very spot the wounded animal was hidden. Steve couldn't know of the danger. I had no choice but to find that bear.

Cecil stood on the porch as I took the rifle and circled toward the beach. Step after wary step finally got me to water's edge. I peered at that formidable spot. No bear. My eyes searched the brush, further and further down the shoreline. There, some two hundred feet away, he sat, hindquarters in the water, nose in the air, head swinging to and fro. I felt dismay. The first shot at him had been at a distance of maybe fifty feet, target practice at eighty feet, and now, here was that bear sitting at what looked to be a half-mile away!

Gun loaded, I raised it to my shoulder once more, aimed and fired! Too short. The beast turned his head and looked at me. I fired again. Still too short. At this, he roared and lunged in my direction. Tears of frustration blinding me, I raised the gun once more, aimed at the blurred image, and pulled the trigger.

I heard the thump of the bullet as it hit. He raised his head and bawled. The sound sent a tremor through me. He sounded as if he were crying, "Ma-a-a, m-a-a-a" and the thought that his mama could possibly come tearing down the hillside toward the beach unnerved me. A more heart-rending sound I have never heard. I had to shut it off. As I raised the rifle I heard Steve's words, "Don't ever fire your last two shots...." I only had two shots left. Mama could be on her way. I flew back to the cabin, reloaded, and with that dreadful cry ringing in my ears, raced back to the beach. I was close to hysteria.

I fired one more shot. It was done.

Abruptly, I sat on the rocky beach. As tears flowed freely, Cecil crawled out from beneath the cabin. He came to comfort me with a gentle brush of his tongue on my cheek. I made a vow. I'd never be a hunter, but from this day on, I'd become a better marksman. In the event it was ever necessary again, neither beast nor I would suffer, as this one and I had surely done.

This story is a slightly revised edition of a manuscript published in the January 1965 issue of *The Alaska Sportsman*.

# Me, My Cat, and Mr. Bear
## Bruce A. Herrman

September 2006, it will be eighteen years since these events took place. The scars are almost completely healed, but the memory will never fade...

At the time I was living in a small remote fishing village accessible only by boat or plane. It was early autumn. Some buddies invited me to tag along on a caribou hunting trip. Well, I loved to hunt and had not hunted caribou for several years. Without question, I accepted. A few hours later I advised my wife of the upcoming event. Her first questions were: "Where are you going?" "How long will you be gone?"

These thoughts had never occurred to me. "I'll find out tomorrow," was my reply.

The place was named, No Name Bay, somewhere near Foggy Cape. We were going to be gone about ten days. This seemed to make all of our wives happy. Whether this was because we apparently did not know where we were going or because of the length of our stay, I never quite figured out

The hunt, itself, went very well. All six of us got a caribou. We were, however, stuck in "No Name Bay" for two and a half weeks due to bad weather. As it became apparent that we were going to be stuck for a while, we started to catch and put up silver salmon. Just imagine, six fishermen, more than a week free time, and a bay full of returning silvers. What a holiday!

Eventually, we made it home and proceeded to take care of our meat. I hung my caribou in a game bag inside a shed, which was designed for curing meat.

There was a slight breeze and not a cloud in the sky. It was time to butcher my caribou. "Not in the house!" was my wife's only comment. She has a weak stomach and left for the day. I did know better than to work in our little one room cabin so set up in the side yard.

Everything was going along well. Then without warning or provocation, my cat climbed up my back and perched himself on top of my head. He made sure to use every claw he owned several times as he climbed and proceeded to hang on, again using all of his claws. Believe it or not, this really hurts! With my own blood dripping in my eyes, I grabbed the cat and tried to throw him away from me–I tried because he now had his claws firmly embedded into my arm. At this point I was extremely angry with him and managed to throw him some distance away. I cleaned up my wounds and continued on with my task, intending to deal with the cat later.

To my surprise, he did it again! My cat had obviously gone mad and had a death wish. I now had twice as many claw marks, scratches and puncture wounds as before. This time I used both hands and grabbed the cat, spun around, and with both hands over my head grasping it… I froze.

There was a black bear sitting there about three feet away just looking at us. What was this bear thinking? He was looking at a six foot-one, 240 pound man holding a mad tabby over his head. My blood was running down and off my arms and down over my face, and all I could do was stand there frozen. Someone had to make a move.

Still holding the cat, I back pedaled very slowly up the path that leads to the cabin door. As I entered the cabin I realized that the cat still had me. I shook him loose, and used my CB radio to call the local constable to ask him to scare the bear away, because my cabin was only a few hundred yards from the local school.

As I looked out my window, the bear was taking a large piece of my caribou. Then he started away, up the hill behind my cabin.

For the first time, I realized this was a rather small bear. He looked to be smaller than me and might have been recently abandoned by his mother. His first kill? Also he could not have been very smart; he left behind 240 pounds of human and an entire hind quarter of caribou meat. All he took was the ribs. I bet he didn't want anything to do with that cat!

As for the cat? Well, he lived for several more years and never scratched me again. We made a silent pact that day. He could live if he promised to never attack me again.

# Bear Tag

## Adam Minnicks

I was back in the Eagle River Valley with Jack Wagner digging power cable line ditches. When I finished work that evening I went back up to Jack's house, which had a stairway on either side leading to the front door. As I rounded the corner a black bear met me, and at that moment he seemed like the biggest bear I had ever seen. Sounding braver than I felt I told him, "I'll see you later." Then my automatic reflexes took over and I changed directions and went around to the other side of the house and up the stairs. Just as I reached the front door from this direction, I met the black bear, who had gone the other way around and up the stairs. He did not seem quite as frightened as I felt at that moment.

I had a pick axe in my hand, and I told the bear, "I don't want to bury this thing in your head." I was shaking so hard I wasn't sure I could even land the necessary blow. Fortunately Jack came out about that time and scared the bear away. At least he was armed with a shotgun, but fortunately for all of us we created enough commotion that the frightened little black bear took off into the woods, and I could safely enter the house.

# A Close Encounter
## Dale Minnicks

I was up at Petersville moose hunting with my friend Don Snoville. We had ridden the 4-wheelers up the road and as close as we could get to a slough. From there, we walked about 45 minutes through the woods to where we thought we might be able to see if there were any moose.

We stepped out into the slough where we could see a big spruce tree. I glanced to my left. There was a Mama bear and two little ones. She stood up, snapped her jaws, dropped down and here she come. Don and I both leveled our rifles on her, but held off hoping she would stop. She came a little ways, stopped and popped them teeth again. She was now within about thirty yards. We stood real still; we knew bears had poor eyesight and looked for movement. She dropped down and started to walk back toward the cubs.

As soon as she turned to leave we took a step back, but she heard us, and turned around to face the danger. She charged again and we were just on the verge of pulling the trigger, when she stopped, stood up, and snapped her jaws. She was slobbering, so close we could almost feel the saliva.

Meanwhile, her cubs were getting farther away. Finally, she dropped back down and started after them. We just stood real still and waited for her to get on across to them.

Finally, after what seemed an eternity, she was far enough away we thought we could move, and move we did, It had taken forty five minute to get in, but it only took fifteen minutes to get back.

Back at the cabin, we had a good stiff drink. Don wanted to clean his trousers, which was a good excuse for staying. We hung around there the rest of the afternoon to get down from the high of the adrenalin rush.

# Willow Creek
## Elaine Held

June 2004. At Willow Creek the kings were running heavy. Every-where you heard, 'Fish on!' I had caught my limit so was relegated to camera duty, which was way too tame. I wanted to feel that power-ful hit one more time. Oh well.

I decided to cross Willow Creek to photograph the boot to boot excitement from the other side. After crossing I walked along a small bluff on my left which was cleared of trees. The trees started thirty yards to my right. Two Alaska fishermen walked in front of me. I knew they were Alaskans by their swagger that said, "I am tougher and meaner than any Texan."

Within a heartbeat the two men froze and I knew enough to copy them. I looked to my right into the trees and saw nothing. The hair on my neck stood up as I sensed real danger. Slowly I looked to my left into the creek. In the water ten yards away stood Mama moose and her small baby. Mama's neck hair was stiff and she stood as if she were a statue. Suddenly she booted the little one with her snout and he ran across in front of us to the trees. That left two frightened men, one terrified woman and an enraged moose. The possibility of being stomped was very real. There was no movement from any of the four of us. We stood that way so long my legs began to tremble.

The men whispered back to me, "Don't look her in the eyes!"

"Don't look her in the eyes?" I couldn't control myself enough to do anything my brain told me to do. I had reached the point where I was going to have to move or go down when, without warning, mama exploded out of the water charging us. My fearless companions ran over me as I tried to get my legs to work. Just as suddenly as she had charged, she stopped six feet from me, whirled, and sauntered off into the trees.

I collapsed into the grass working up the courage to make my escape.

# Urban Moose Tales
## Ruby Ketola

Following the death of my father, my mother spent winters in Anchorage with me for a decade. After all, Anchorage winters were milder than those of northern Minnesota. As she does not drive, she was housebound in Minnesota, whereas with me she could attend most cultural events and keep an active social life with all my friends. We also used long weekends to travel to warm destinations such as Hawaii and Phoenix. My working did leave her at my home in east Anchorage during the days. Normally, I would call her at my morning break when she was just awakening, join her for lunch, and call her again at my afternoon break. She never wanted to "bother" me at my job, so I was understandably surprised when Mom called me one bright afternoon.

She was in such a state that she didn't even apologize for disturbing my work before blurting out, "There's a moose in the back yard and it's looking right at me through the kitchen window, so I'm sitting on the couch in the front room so it can't see me. What if it wants to come in? What should I do? Call the police or animal control? I'm afraid to go over and shut the blinds." She was so obviously frightened that I tried hard not to laugh when I told her that this was a normal occurrence in Anchorage and the police wouldn't come out just because the moose was eating the greenery under the window. While still on the phone with me, she got up and looked out the windows again and reported to me: "Now it's in the carport and looking right at the front door. What do I do?"

Unable to control myself, I replied, "Mom, the moose is just there for a photo-op. Open the door and take a picture." She didn't think it was funny then, but now she still enjoys telling everyone in Minnesota about the moose who regularly came to check on her while I was at work.

# II.

People who live in Alaska know that you have to keep busy during the winter months so that you don't get "cabin fever." One way of doing this is to volunteer. So, one year I volunteered to be the welcome/sendoff chairperson when Eagle River was the host for the Arctic Winter Games. Though the games were in March, work for such a large project began a year in advance. In the fall prior to the games, the representatives from other countries came to Anchorage to check out the various sites for events and housing. We had arranged a school bus to take people to the parks, schools, and other locations. One of the first stops was Kincaid Park. We stopped at the "Municipality of Anchorage, Kincaid Park" sign. On one side of the sign stood a large moose and a yearling, and on the other side of the sign was an older calf. Making the most of an opportunity, I immediately stood up and said, "And, here, of course, is one of the families of my welcome committee to greet you. Feel free to take pictures." The three moose calmly stood there until everyone who had wished to take pictures had done so. Events like that made the Arctic Winter Games a resounding success.

# Life in the Bush

# Blue Eyes, Permafrost, and Karma

Patricia Garrett

Horrified, I watched the oozing muck that smelled like rotten meat spread from around and under the melting permafrost. I began to question my own sanity. Could it be that I was a conservationist, or did I need hormones? I turned my back to the four miles of destruction of tundra and borealis forest land that once was the walking trail I loved and returned to the cook-cabin to bake and eat brownies.

Growing up in a rich mining district, I found the lifestyle of camp cook for three men at a placer gold mine above the Arctic Circle to be ideal. But now the scenic trail was gone for good and in its stead ran a gully of mud. My second summer on Prospect Creek was not at all what I expected.

It is important to say that two things greatly influenced my move to Alaska in 1963. One was the movie *North to Alaska* starring John Wayne and the other was the sound track to the same movie sung by Johnny Horton. It came as no surprise that I jumped at a chance to go mining in 1978. At 33, I was financially independent after working on the pipeline, single, and up for adventure.

The miner was good looking and smooth talking. He had me believing I was the best thing since sliced bread that first year I cooked for him. His eyes were Paul Newman blue, and he praised the ease in which I caught on to the chores. The woodstove soon began to offer the scent of cinnamon rolls, moose roasts, and fresh perked coffee. I especially enjoyed operating the Maytag wringer washer on the creek bank. After becoming a fair shot with the bear gun that hung by the pantry door, I eagerly accepted his offer to return for the mining season of 1979. In February, the miner surprised me with a phone call and an invitation to join him in Hawaii. Not even the smoking ash of an erupting volcano on Kona Island clouded my enthusiasm for a second summer.

Convinced that I was in love, had found my prince, and had a home at the mine, I sold my home in Anchorage and put my belongings in storage. To his specifications, I purchased a big blue generator/welder to the tune of $18,000, ordered a large red water pump on runners–a steal at $10,000, and bought a $2.50 bright yellow cotton valance for the cook-cabin's one window. Giddy, I planned menus for five, ordered replacement parts, belts, hoses and tracks for his two dozers; purchased diesel fuel for the mining equipment and ordered propane for the backup kitchen stove. I splurged for lanterns for the cabins and bunkhouses. Soon my $100,000 had swindled to $50,000.

It was too good to be true. I would become a permanent resident on the picturesque west bank of Prospect Creek. The camp sat on a wide part of the valley, surrounded by rolling hills of quaking aspen, birch, and spruce trees. Willow, caribou moss, and bearberry proved delicate groundcover in the Arctic. Patches of blue berries, high bush and low bush cranberry all promised jam and lively pancakes.

Prospect Creek, where I was determined to live, is famous for holding the North American record cold of minus 80 degrees in the early 1970s. I begged to go to camp early, and stay there alone until the creek thawed for mining. He gave in, and we cat-trained up the solid creek in late March. Still deeply frozen with winter, waiting in the shadow of the north ridge, the camp resisted human contact.

The dry snow creaked beneath my heavily booted feet. My gloves quickly froze to a crescent shape while holding the old hammer. My jaw ached from the shrill screech of nails ripping from the frozen plywood panels that I had nailed over the door and window of the cook cabin last fall. These panels that had kept bears, wolverines, or human vandals out, needed to be removed quickly or we would die of exposure. Beneath my layers of down, wool, and silk I felt my body temperature dropping. Ecstatically, I used the wood stove and propane back up stove to thaw out the cook cabin where I would stay alone after he returned to Fairbanks. Tired, we crawled into our double sleeping bag on the bench close to the stoves. We made love before falling to sleep, and I had no way of knowing then that it would be for the last time. The next morning I assured him I would survive and I watched him slowly cat train back down the frozen creek toward to Dalton Highway.

I used those six weeks to clean the bunkhouse and inventory the tool shed. I had the lengthening days of sunlight, my seven-year-old calico cat, Momma Kitty, and a young camp dog with gigantic feet, that I called Lady, to keep me company. Late March is famous for surprise storms, and despite blizzard conditions I proved to myself that I could make it alone on the creek. When the ice finally went out, I ecstatically radioed the miner. "Come up and let's start mining!"

He arrived within a couple days, driving in a large orange backhoe on tracks and with a crew of 15 men. The loud garish hoe rumbled into camp across my beloved walking trail, crushing berry bushes and diamond willow, with no regard to the aesthetics of the camp I loved. Surprised, I questioned him. "Who the hell are all these men and why are they all here? Why do we need this huge hoe?"

"The men are here to build a road into camp. We need the hoe to build the road you will need," he stated.

"Yes, but I like the walk into camp. I enjoy looking at the ground cover." I tried to reason.

"I ain't running no summer camp," he responded and dismissed me with a cocked eyebrow. His electric blue eyes sparked in the sun.

"I hope to hell I have enough food to feed everyone." I stomped off to the cook-cabin to consider this surprising change of events.
So much for being in love and living in La La Land - those days were over. Within a week I had commandeered a 16x16 foot skid shack, hooked it behind a small John Deere dozer, and pulled it out of camp. I faced it toward an undeveloped part of the creek around a bend, hoping the constant sound of the equipment couldn't be heard.

The miner was obsessed with his road building. Permafrost lay under a shallow overburden of soil and vegetation. Day after day, as the gyrating hoe pounded the ground, the bucket slammed against permafrost, while dark oozing gashes of mud appeared. The drone of the equipment echoed off the hills and my peaceful dream in the valley ended. I avoided the yellow-valance window of the cook-cabin that perfectly framed the on coming destruction. As the melting permafrost spread, my dissatisfaction with road building grew. Again and again I berated him in front of the crew, telling him it was a lame idea to build such a monster road, and that it was time to start mining to recoup my investment and pay operating expenses.

"I know what I am doing," he told me. "If you didn't have shit for brains, you would have thought this through yourself. Living here year around requires better access."

"If you didn't have delusions of grandeur and weren't enamored with that big hoe we'd be mining," I shot back.

In July on a supply run to Fairbanks I frantically sought out a lawyer. His office was above the Mecca Bar on 2nd Street. As Willie and Waylon wailed about Luchenbach Texas, I lamented my own tale of woe. The lawyer couldn't believe that I had been so stupid as to invest the biggest part of $100,000 into a gold mine with nothing in writing. I admitted that it seemed stupid now, but last winter it had seemed like a reasonable plan. I asked for suggestions on how to get out of the mess.

"You go up to him in private. Tell him you will put liens on his claims if he doesn't give you something in writing. Do not leave that creek early or he will say he doesn't have to repay you, because you didn't uphold your bargain."

I practiced that pitch on the 300-mile drive and four-mile walk into camp. I saw the miner off to the side of the permafrost mess scratching his butt, and I marched straight up to him.

"I saw a lawyer in Fairbanks. I want you to put in writing that you will pay me back all my money, or I will put liens on the claims." I was pleased that I made direct eye contact and sounded so sure. However, my knees soon buckled and my stomach knotted as he returned my stare and calmly stated, "You will not get off this creek alive."

The next morning I found, Momma Kitty, my magnificent mouser shot dead, and nailed by her calico tail to my skid shack when I returned after breakfast. That sealed it. Determined to last him out, I would not leave early. War was declared! Stuck in the middle, the crew tried to avoid us both. The days slowly dragged, as the road project continued to be a stinking muddy mess with no end in sight.

August came, a hint of fall was in the air, and the leaves took on a yellow hue. The sun rose later, but I had difficulty sleeping and still woke up early. I enjoyed my brief time alone in a quiet camp. By the time the crew stumbled into the cook-cabin I would have the canned bacon rinsed and frying, bread rising for the next day's lunches, and plenty of fresh coffee perking.

"Mornin'," the guys mumbled as they picked up coffee or warm water to wash up. They brushed their teeth outside and spit on the ground, leaving toothpaste droppings like pigeon poop on the trail to the outhouse.

"Don't forget to lime," I told them time after time. With seventeen people using one outhouse, the lime was vital to keep down the stench. Our outhouse was an old three-sided packing crate that offered the morning sun. Cinderella blue skies with pink tendrils of clouds spun like cotton candy across the valley. Sitting there, gazing at the undeveloped creek and the hillsides that formed the valley I saw bear, moose, caribou, fox, wolves and a bazillion migrating birds and different waterfowl.

By late August the morning fog shrouded the valley. I could see my breath hang in the air when I whistled for Lady the young camp dog. Wolves were in the area and she leaned against her chain and howled to be free. The miner claimed she was a wolf hybrid and cussed her for not breeding with his grumpy old German shepherd. The entire crew threatened to shoot Lady if she didn't stop howling at night. I suggested we set her free and I even offered to take her to my shack at nights, but the miner said she was a camp dog and needed to stay on the chain in camp. He said if she went to the pack, they would kill her, that she was too domesticated to survive. One morning she was just gone. There was no evidence of her breaking her chain. Since the entire crew complained about her, I never knew if they turned her loose or shot her.

I was out of money. I had advanced wages all summer and bank-rolled the operation with all the money I had. The day's light grew shorter. We were all tired and tempers flared easily, but we all caught our second wind when the miner announced we would start mining. The orange hoe that tore up the trail attacked the creek and its banks with equal vigor. The miner told me to run the hydraulic giant that hosed the material through the sluice. I rushed to prepare meals, and then suited up in bunny boots and rubber gear to stand just inches from the gapped toothed bucket of the hoe I had cussed all summer. Each bucketful that dropped into the sluice, I hoped would be the glory hole and I prayed that large nuggets were filling the hot box below me. At the same time I cried to see my beloved valley chewed up at such a rapid rate. The miner had the crew empty the riffles into white five gallon plastic buckets and haul them to his cabin each day. At night he panned the material and kept the results to himself. Time was running out and I desperately wanted to pay expenses.

As the weather turned colder the constant drizzle chilled us to the bone. Musky wool socks and wet muddy gloves dried behind the wood cook stove. The cook-cabin stayed crowded with the un-washed crew as they played cards by lantern light. I baked sweets and tried to keep morale up, but my own heart was heavy. This time last year I was wildly in love and thought I would live forever on Prospect Creek. This year I was homeless, broke, and feeling mighty worried about the debt we had incurred during the mining season. This wasn't the way it went in that John Wayne movie of my inno-cent youth. My mood was as soggy as the weather.

We continued to mine until the metal sluice box iced over and the water became slushy. The trail into camp was still a gully of muddy runoff and I wondered how we would get out. The miner isolated himself in his cabin and wore a gun. He was the only one that knew the results of our short mining run. I assigned the crew duties to clean up camp, winterize the equipment and buildings, and to prepare for our trip home. I urged them to trust me for their summer wages. I worried someone might get killed. The miner seemed paranoid and edgy.

Then one frigid morning, toward the end of September, two of the guys came in and announced they thought the cold weather had set up the trail enough that we could cat-train out. That day the miner snowshoed the trail, gave it his blessing, and came back to announce we would leave camp the following day.

That night the miner pulled me from my mummy sleeping bag to help him lash down the heavy tarps over the loaded sleds. He had hidden the gold for the smelter on the sleds. He kept his gun visible and tied to his thigh. I felt stuck in a bad John Wayne movie, and I prayed the trail would be hard enough that we wouldn't tip over, lose the gold or be killed.

The temperature had dropped and it hovered around zero. I remember feeling the itch of my frozen nose hairs as I nailed plywood back over the cook-cabin's door and yellow-valanced window. I wondered what the future held for us all as we pulled out of camp - the Dalton Highway. Tucked in snug on the back sled, lulled by the slowing rocking rhythm, I watched the valley fold up and disappear from my sight. I watched for tracks made by a big-footed camp dog.

Three years later, a sleepy judge commented that since I didn't get anything in writing, it was just the miner's word against my word that any money had changed hands. Somehow a miner, who served in Viet Nam, sounded more credible than I did in that hot Fairbanks courtroom. "Your Honor, you know how those redheads are, always raising hell and causing trouble. Why, there isn't a woman in the world that wouldn't want a goldmine."

Later I heard that he scammed a couple more folks to finance his operation. When the gold played out on Prospect Creek, he sold his claims to an unsuspecting newcomer and took his accumulation of funds to Southeast Asia. His plan was to buy Thai beer, import it to the USA, and make a killing. Instead, he got robbed of every cent, beaten badly, and left for dead in the jungle. He is alive, crippled, and driving cab in Seattle, where he lives close to the VA hospital. You might see him sometime. He has blue eyes, like Paul Newman.

# Nome Days
## Russ Arnett

I arrived in Nome in January 1952 to become United States Commissioner. In Territorial Alaska this position had at least ten judicial and administrative functions. The compensation was entirely by fees. In Nome at the time you could earn about $4000 a year if you did all your own secretarial work which included considerable typing. Some Commissioners earned only $500 a year. Few had legal training. Even so, you had the power to send someone to jail for a year or in a sanity proceeding, after a verdict, to Morningside Sanitarium at Portland for an indefinite period. In the old courthouse in Eagle is a letter from Judge Wickersham from about 1910 to the U.S. Justice Department requesting that something had to be done about the sad condition of the Commissioners. Forty years later, nothing had changed.

One of the duties of the Commissioners was to instruct accused persons of their legal rights. I told them that they had a right to legal counsel but then added that the nearest attorneys in private practice were in Fairbanks and there were no public funds to pay them. There were no public defenders at that time.

I presided in a preliminary hearing for a soldier accused of raping an attractive Eskimo girl who may have been only sixteen. Witnesses testified that the defendant entered the barracks and threw the girls panties on the table. The victim had T.B. and was spitting up blood. I inquired what could be done regarding this condition and was told nothing could be done, although about this time new drugs effective against T.B. were coming into common use. In the early 1950s the Seward Sanitarium was treating Native T.B. patients.

One of the Commissioner's jobs was Coroner. I investigated an air crash where there were three immediate deaths. One of my duties was to examine their frozen bodies in the morgue. I interviewed one of my friends in the hospital who was the fourth victim. He said they just flew into whiteout conditions and crashed. He died the next day. On another occasion, a liberty boat from a freighter was swamped in the surf. Some of the crew drowned and some survived. We interviewed the survivors at an inquest. The description of the wet seamen coming out of the surf was very graphic. Another time a young Eskimo man died while swimming in the Arctic Ocean on a lark. Once we flew to Saint Lawrence island for a sanity hearing. The Eskimo wife of a white government employee, while in an emotional state, had cut off most of her hair. The six members of the jury were leaders of the community and appeared in their furs. They were quite intelligent and deliberated in their Native language. They arrived at what I considered the proper verdict which was that she was in a very emotional state but was not insane.

I shared a cabin with Don Perkins who later was a very popular mayor of Nome. He made a mean chili and insisted it contain cayenne. We often had fried ptarmigan. Ptarmigan, when stripped of their plumage, have large breasts and small legs, not unlike some women of the time. When we had a real banquet Don would insist that we include smoked oysters.

I developed a high regard for the Eskimo people. In court proceedings they were much more honest than the average white defendant or witness would be. I found the oldest Eskimos, some with little or no formal education, to be quite intelligent.

In summer there did not seem to be a particular bedtime for Eskimo kids. They were usually smiling and I liked them a lot. I walked often and sometimes with my hands behind my back. I would look back and see a string of Eskimo kids following me with their hands behind their back and big smiles on their faces.

Like many Alaska towns of the time, Nome had a church crowd and a bar crowd. Usually, I identified with the church crowd. Nevertheless, I agreed to perform a wedding of a bartender to a waitress. It was at the home of the owner of the Board of Trade bar. The guests were prepared to start consuming spirituous liquor before the wedding ceremony. I stopped that. After the ceremony the reception was at the Board of Trade. The main drink was French 75s which was made of gin and champagne and served in a large punch bowl.

Someone took a picture of me holding the bowl up and drinking directly from it. About that time I have a cloudy memory of one of the wives telling me that she liked me better than her husband. I have a clear memory of falling in a snow bank on the way back to my cabin. Oddly, nobody told me I should behave better.

When I arrived in Nome, the Marshal told me that, because of my public position, I should not go out with any of the Eskimo girls. There were about five marriageable white girls. Don Perkins became engaged to one of them that summer. I had pretty well worn out my welcome with the others. (In the past, the Nome School Board had given considerable weight to personal appearance in hiring new teachers as they were regarded as prospective wives as well as educators.) We bachelors learned that a new welfare worker was soon to arrive and that she was single and attractive. It might be too strong to describe us as like chained beasts, but we were very anxious to meet her. I managed only one date with her before she became engaged to one of my friends. Finally, seeing no other course open to me, and aware that the Marshal might disapprove, I asked one of the Eskimo girls to go out with me. She turned me down.

So, I migrated to Seward. There I worked as a janitor and longshoreman, and fell crazy in love with one of the housemothers at Jesse Lee Children's Home. We have been married over fifty years, and I cannot imagine having three children I would like any better than ours.

# Teacher at Adak
## Dorothy L. Arnold

The summer of 1952 my sister, Rachel, and I drove from Montana to Massachusetts in her Nash and camped out the entire way. On the way home one said to the other, "Where shall we go next summer?"

The other promptly replied, "Alaska."

Who knew it would change our lives.

In May of 1953, with two older teachers who had decided to join us, we set off in my new 1953 Plymouth. At Calgary we noticed we were riding low, so at Edmonton we had air bags put on the car to reinforce the springs.

From Edmonton north it was either dust or mud with rough, and very rough, road. There were steep hills with very winding turns and narrow bridges over which only one car at a time could pass. In the narrow places, if we saw a big truck coming from either direction, we pulled over and stopped because the dust kicked up by the trucks caused visibility to go to zero. Most of the time we chugged northward at 25-35 miles an hour and were passed by cars going 50, only to pass them later, while they changed a tire. We met many travelers that complained about flat tires, yet we only had one.

We camped wherever we could find a spot until we reached the Yukon which had campgrounds. When we arrived at Liard Hot Springs, we hiked to the Lower Pool expecting to go for a swim and get cleaned up. However, the water was so hot we decided to hike up to the upper springs. There my sister ran ahead shouting, "The last one in is a baby." She did not quite make the water when she found herself mired almost to her hips in the soft gooey mud. She would not allow us to help, and was finally able to get herself out. All of us went around to the point where we saw a diving board. Although the mosquitoes were thick we stripped and got into the water. As we did so, we laughed because each of our backs turned black with mosquitoes and the only solution was to stay underwater while trying to tread water and take a bath. We got dressed in a big hurry to avoid being eaten alive.

Despite the mosquitoes we felt good at having been able to get clean from head to toe. As we drove north on the ever dusty road my sister looked at me and said, "I thought you washed your hair and face."

I replied, "I did."

She said, "It doesn't look like it; your face is gray and so is your hair."

Then I looked at her and laughed as I said, "So is yours."

At Whitehorse we took the paddle wheeler on an overnight trip to Carcross. What a beautiful journey! Next came Haines, Juneau, Sitka and then Skagway where we took the train to Lake Bennett and back. Each small rail car had its own wood heater. From the windows of the train we could see the trail used by the early gold seekers. From there we drove to Fairbanks and then to Anchorage.

In Juneau we had learned from the State Education Department that teachers were needed in several places. In Anchorage, Rachel and I tried to get a teaching job in the same school but that was not to be. She took a position in Kenai, while I decided on Adak.

In late August I left the car with Rachel and flew home to gather the items we needed for the coming school year. I shipped Rachel's things to her, flew to Seattle and took a military plane back to Alaska, via Elmendorf to Adak where I was met and taken to my quarters.

The teacher's quarters were in Quonset huts with two teachers sharing a half of each Quonset. We ate nearby with the officers at the BOQ. My roommate, Pat, and I became wonderful friends, even though she loved to sit and read or do other things indoors while I wanted to be out the door at every opportunity.

The wind on Adak governed our lives. The rule was that if the wind was forecast to be 25 miles an hour with gusts to 35 it was safe to hike, but not if the forecast was 35 with gusts higher. If caught in a strong wind and you were facing it, you were to lean into it, leaning even further as it gusted. Of course there was always a danger of falling on your face if the gust suddenly stopped.

Because of the wind, buses were run for teachers and students. When the wind was high, the older children had to hang onto the younger ones and escort them safely to their doors. Many a time it was two high school students with a young child. The older students hung onto either side of the child while the wind lifted the child parallel to the ground. Sometimes rain accompanied the wind and then, without the proper clothing, a person would get soaked through in seconds. At times the wind was so strong that someone inside the BOQ had to push the door open for us to enter. Ninety mile an hour winds are strong!

Before the snow came a group of us checked the weather and set off for the summit of Mt. Moffet. At the top we signed our names to the notebook in a coffee can. We did not tarry as we could see a storm moving our way. We managed to return to the Base just as the storm hit.

Hiking could be adventuresome. The weather could change unexpectedly, and "Willy and Waw" would come to play along with torrential rain. Walking after dark was dangerous because there were deep holes filled with grass all over the terrain.

Besides hiking, there was roller skating, and in the winter, skiing, especially on Mt. Moffet, where heavy fog was a problem.

There was no ski patrol on Adak so the science teacher and I went to the officer in charge of recreation and explained why we felt there should be one. Thus a patrol was begun. The first thing we tried to do was to get a safety gate put on the tow, as we had seen small children lifted off their feet and then fall to the ground at the upper end of the tow. We made a rule that there should be no loose scarves and asked that all watch to make sure that this rule was followed. Since there was always fog, we made the rule that when it was extremely foggy, skiers must ski together in at least groups of two. If partners could not see each other they were to talk together so that they knew where their partner was. Many times, skiers would miss the tow as they descended and use sound to find their way through the fog.

The next year I taught at Ft. Richardson, then decided to finish my degree requirements. I drove the Alcan alone, sleeping under the stars using the tent as a cover.

*A williwaw is a sudden sharp gust or a small whirlwind common to the North.*

# Helping the Girl Scouts

## Marjory S. Bailey

Here I was headed for Alaska in August 1947, when I had really planned to meet a friend and visit the Grand Canyon. I was on the National Staff of the Girl Scouts, assigned to Oregon and Idaho to assist in training, promotion, and support for the Councils.

After a bad day of visiting camps in hot, tick country, I received a call from the Regional Director asking me how I would like to go to Alaska. "Well," I said, "sure, I'd like to go to Alaska, but not now." She said I should think it over it's a wonderful opportunity, and she'd call me in the morning. I don't think I had much choice; the person assigned had become ill and I suspect I was at the bottom of the list. I was told I would be on this assignment for three months.

Trying to get winter clothes was a big challenge. I still laugh when I think of the white oxfords that I was able to buy, but they kept my feet dry during all the rains and mud.

My first stop was Juneau. I can remember the beautiful mountains that reach straight out of the ocean, some snow covered in the distance. Then there was the wake from the boats that plied the waterways. It was all very unreal to me. I had lived with mountains, but not like these.

One event stands out about my visit to Juneau. A group of ladies took me to visit their camp. We drove out north of town and stopped at a trailhead, where we were each handed a bucket with rocks in it. Finally, one lady explained that this was bear protection. Mentally I'm thinking, "Why would you put a girls' camp in this location?" Off we went, swinging our buckets of rocks, and nary a bear did we see. This method has worked for me all these years.

My next trip took me to Fairbanks, past the Malaspina Glacier, a river of ice larger than the State of Connecticut. It was awe inspiring with the Mt. St. Elias Range in the background and the glacier coming right to the ocean.

Upon arriving in Fairbanks, a lot of other passengers and I had hotel reservations. The man ahead of me got a room and then it was my turn, but I was told to go around the corner and the hostess would take care of me. The hostess had a deep purple dress. At her waist was a huge buckle and fresh tulips blooming! Quite a sight! I later read a *Reader's Digest* article on the most interesting person the writer had ever met. It was about my hostess, Eva McGowan. She was an interesting person to say the least. There were rumors that she had been a mail order bride from Ireland.

After much telephoning I was handed an address and told, "This is where you'll stay." In the taxi, we passed some cute little houses, not much larger than a tool shed that looked alike and I was curious. The driver explained that this was "the line." Police headquarters was close by and prostitution was quite legal in the territory.

The taxi drove up to a rather large home with a lovely large living room, a formal dining room and the kitchen. There was only one bathroom, which was connected to my small room. There was barely room for a cot and chair. I had to keep my clothes in my suitcase. In checking with the other passengers the next day, I found I had great accommodations; some were sleeping on couches in the living room or cots put up for a night. I had paid a weeks rent when I moved in and after hearing their stories, I decided to pay for the rest of the stay. Probably the smartest move I ever made.

About a week later I came back to the house to find all the living room and dining room furniture had been removed; temporary partitions put up, with a cot placed in each space, about ten cots in all. I found the owner placing a curtain to cordon off my room's entrance to the bathroom. When I studied the situation I realized that the entrance to the bathroom was to be through my room. That evening I announced that I didn't go to bed until midnight and didn't get up until 8 a.m. and the bathroom would be off-limits during those hours. Early the next morning I had someone pounding on my door and what he called me was not pretty!

My work went well and one of the highlights was visiting with Leonard Seppala, the dog musher who ran the longest and most difficult stretch of the Serum Run to Nome. This was a bit of history unfolding for me. I was fascinated with his stories and later, when the Girl Scouts in Anchorage said I could name their camp, I chose to honor his lead dog, Togo. The camp is now called Togowoods.

After three weeks in Fairbanks my next stop was Anchorage, so I boarded a plane for the short trip, or so I thought. Shortly after take-off we lost an engine and returned to Fairbanks for repairs. There was a long wait, and since we were on the military base there were no snack bars. At last we boarded the plane again, but the flight had only begun when the co-pilot announced we had lost our communications so we were returning to Fairbanks. This apparently entailed going down through the clouds to look for landmarks and then back up through the clouds. We finally made it back to Fairbanks. Many passengers opted out, but I had no choice as I had no place to stay in Fairbanks. It was now after 2 p.m. and still no food. After another delay, we boarded again for another try, this time with no problems, at least until we got to Anchorage, where our destination was to be Elmendorf. The runway was closed, so we landed at Merrill Field. It was great to finally land but how I got off the plane is a mystery to me as there were no steps. I may have jumped off I was so happy to finally get to solid ground. One thing I learned from the trip was to always have some food with me when flying in Alaska!

Anchorage had but one paved street, Fourth Avenue. This was fall and so the dirt streets would freeze at night and then thaw during the day. My white walking shoes announced that here was a newcomer, or a fool.

A trip to the post office often took at least half an hour and sometimes longer. There was no mail delivery and few mailboxes, most of the population stood in line at the general delivery window. You visited with everyone and maybe took care of some business. No one was a stranger very long. There didn't seem to be a big rush since life was at a much slower pace.

Hunting season was a big event for families dependent on game for their winter meat supply. If you needed your plumber or carpenter you might just have to wait until he got back from a hunting trip.

While eating lunch one day, I heard a gentleman from "Outside" as we called the states, who demanded a glass of water. The waitress said she'd get it for him, but was sure he wouldn't want it. Sure enough, when it came it looked muddy; during break-up that was not unusual. Everyone else took it in stride, no big deal.

Another man always ate dinner at the restaurant the same time each day. Seemed he was in jail next door. He didn't like the food served so he bought his own. As there was only one road–and it went north, it was unlikely that he could get very far if he decided to run away.

With no road to Seward, you took the train or flew. On one occasion when I was returning from Seward, I found a moose draped over an oil barrel in the shack which served as the terminal. It was raining and a low ceiling; the pilot looked up at the sky, shook his head, and said he wouldn't be going for a while. He advised me to just go back to the hotel and he would send for me if it cleared.

About mid-afternoon someone came for me. There were a few other passengers going, too. We boarded the plane which had no seats, just a long bench on the side of the plane. I don't remember having any seat belts. The pilot had started down the runway when a car came chasing the plane. Seems some lady wanted to send a birthday cake to Anchorage. The pilot opened up the hatch and handed me the cake. He said he could depend on me to get it there. It was a bit of a challenge to hang onto the cake, as the flight was quite turbulent.

When I returned to Seattle, I, like everyone from the Territories of Alaska and Hawaii in those days, had to go through Immigration to get into the United States. That law wasn't changed until the pressure to approve statehood began in earnest.

# When a Man's Alive He's My Friend

## Jack D. Johnson

Two guys were hunting off of thirteen mile hill on the Denali High-way. They hiked down and shot a caribou about a mile off the road, then rolled it up to dress it, with one guy sitting on the front quarters leaning up against the body to hold it up while the other worked. When the hunter looked up, he saw his buddy had fallen down over the caribou and onto the ground, with a little trickle of blood running out his mouth. Scared, he shook his friend and kept talking to him while he sat him up against a tundra hump. He finally figured out the man was dead.

The hunter just dropped everything and ran to the road to find Dad and me. He knew we were using the weasel to haul meat out to the highway for hunters. Of course it had to start snowing so by the time he found us we couldn't follow his tracks back, and although we looked, we never found the body that night.

The next morning we got up, and talked to the guy, who had calmed down a little. He told us what the area looked like where we should be able to find the dead man. It took us about two and a half hours of driving around to find him. He had fallen down, was lying almost flat, and was frozen. As stiff as he was, we couldn't get him in the weasel, so we laid his coat on the rim, his neck on one side and his feet on the other, and he just kind of rode there rocking back and forth all the way back to the road.

We went back to the lodge where we had a two bedroom house trailer that wasn't heated and put him in there. We called the highway patrol and they were going to come up, but they hadn't come. We didn't know anything other than what the guy told us, and then he went back to try to contact the family. About three or four days later this guy was still laying out there in the trailer, and we hadn't heard from anybody.

These two guys came down from Fairbanks to do some fishing. They were sitting at the bar, having a few drinks and some laughs.

It got so late, these two wanted a room for the night. Dad said, "Well, all we have is a trailer down there. There's a dead guy in there, but he won't bother you any." Of course, they laughed and went out to look at the trailer.

When they came back in, one guy was just shaking his head and the other guy says, "M-M-M-Mr. Johnson, there's sure enough a dead man out there. When a man's alive he's my friend, but when a man's dead I'm finished with him."

Dad gave him a drink, and decided to have some more fun with him. He had these little male and female fishing lures he showed people and a little weighted eyeball. When the one man wasn't looking he would drop it in his drink. When the unlucky guy went to take a drink, he would just look away and set the glass down on the counter. Then Dad would fish the eyeball out, and wait. Finally, the man would take a drink. Then Dad would drop the eyeball again. This went on until Dad got caught. As if the poor man hadn't had enough of a shock!

# Sawmilling at Bird Creek
## Doris Rye Rhodes

We had run sawmills on the Oregon coast and the small gypo operations had lost out on the available timber, so we decided to relocate to Alaska. We came up the Alcan in 1955 in a caravan of four vehicles to start a sawmill at Bird Creek twenty-four miles south of Anchorage on the Turnagain Arm of Cook Inlet. The sawmill and machinery came in pieces on a barge and arrived before we got here. Alaska wasn't even a state yet.

The planer was located between the log Bird Creek Lodge (later called Jolly Vi's) and what later became the Bird House Bar. Our sawmill was one mile up Bird Creek where we developed a road on an old trail.

It was living a lot like homesteading, but the highway to Seward had been paved a year earlier, so there was access to Anchorage. We didn't have any electricity for the first year, except when the mill was running. There was no school, bus, or post office. Mail was received in Anchorage by general delivery in the old Fourth Avenue Post Office. It was picked up whenever anyone came to town.

On weekends we took a station wagon with garden rakes and wash tubs and drove to Portage Glacier. There we raked in the glacier ice, carried it up the bank in wash tubs and brought it home to Bird Creek. Buried in the sawdust pile, it kept until it was needed to cool food.

There was an outhouse and I recall being marooned in it one time when a black bear came galloping by.

My folks, who had settled in a trailer house nearby, had two Siamese cats,

Ming and Toy. Old Ming took great pleasure in sneaking up on magpies as they fed on extra pancakes Mom threw out. Ming would creep up on two or more birds, pounce, and watch them scatter. This went on for several days. Then, Mom looked out one morning and a whole flock of magpies had isolated Ming under a lumber pile. Never again did he go outside and harass the birds.

One of our employees at the mill was Bob Burseil who lived in Girdwood. He was later instrumental in starting up Alyeska Ski Resort and in getting a small one-room grade school started at Girdwood. Bob was an excellent artist and he drew pictures of our mill for use on Christmas cards.

We placed an ad in the Anchorage Times to trade lumber for a moose/caribou hunt and arrived at an agreement with Al Lee at Glennallen which lasted for years. He would send us a letter saying what dimension lumber he would need next spring for a hangar, etc. We would call each fall and go up to Glenallen on a three day hunt to get moose or caribou for our winter meat. By then we had electricity and a freezer.

Once the army came charging in, all around our mill site deep in the valley up Bird Creek. They made such a mess of the road that we could not get lumber down it to the planer and they came close to putting us out of business. They slashed and laid out a small city all around the mill. Streets were even surveyed. Dad and my husband went to the base in Anchorage to see what could be done. The army did put a little gravel on the road but for several weeks we hoped they would buy us out. It turned out they were preparing for an offensive missile site, but Washington D. C. deemed later that we would not get offensive missile sites in Alaska at that time.

There is no trace of the sawmill or planer any more. But three structures still stand that my parents built and owned, and I have fond memories of jams, jellies, catsups, and syrup made from local berries, a copper boiler full of clams from 20-mile Creek to clean, grind and can, eating loads of hooligan, and eating salmon out of Bird Creek that my husband caught at 4 a.m. before going to work at the sawmill.

# Rural Life in the Daysof the Husky Dogs

## Rosanna Troseth (Sis Laraux)

I was born and raised in Western Alaska in the remote village of Akiak, on the Kuskokwim River. It is located 90 miles east of the Bering Sea and 400 miles from Anchorage. My father, Arthur Laraux, was a gold miner who came to Dawson from Quebec as a teenager during the Gold Rush in 1898. From Dawson he moved on to the Iditarod Stampede in central Alaska and then down the Kuskokwim River to Akiak. There he met my Eskimo mother Lena Venes, married, and made Akiak their home. I was the third oldest of seven siblings.

Papa built a carpenter shop and also a blacksmith's shop for building sleds, boats and furniture. He made dog harnesses to fit the dogs and became an expert at building sleds of all types, many of which he sold. Basket sleds with sides were built in two sizes, the larger for village traveling and hauling heavy loads and the smaller sleds for hunting or water hauling. Water was hauled from the river for all home purposes. Toward spring large cubes of ice were chopped and hauled into our ice-house where it was packed in sawdust for summer drinking water. Another type, called a bob-sled, had two sections and was used for hauling logs from a wood camp, where spruce and cottonwood trees were cut at Papa's small sawmill. Wood was used for heat in our furnace and kitchen stove and was sold for home heating and to the sternwheelers which then were powered by wood furnaces. These boats traveled up and down the Kuskokwim River hauling freight and passengers during the summer months.

My father had from twelve to fourteen work dogs of different breeds—Malamutes, Siberian and even hound, mainly for their longer legs. Some had wolf strain for a heavier, stronger work dog. Dog houses were built for each dog. We would gather straw before the frost to spread in the houses for warmth throughout the winter. Dogs were named according to their personalities in many cases. There was Mr. Bear, Jack, Blacky, Susie, Dubbie, Queenie, Ring, Pinkie, Trouble and Jimmy. We treasured our dog team. Our brothers and Papa made sure the dogs were watered and fed properly every day. They were an important part of our family and were treated accordingly.

Jimmy was the lead dog and Trouble was trained for that position, too. When they were hitched up to the sled for a day's work, they would be excited to start off, barking and yanking on their harnesses. We never said, "Mush" like in the movies. The dogs were so anxious to get started we had to hold the sled brake steadily and, when ready, would say, "All right" and off they'd go, full speed ahead. We'd have to brake going down the banks or small hills to keep us in control. To turn the team right, we'd call out "Gee" and to turn left, it was "Haw." Usually when one team met another on the trail, you had to steer or take your team off the beaten path to prevent a dog fight. Jimmy, our lead dog was so wise, he'd automatically lead our whole team off the trail and back without any orders from Papa. He was an excellent leader.

In a government venture in the early 1900s, Laplanders from Norway were sent over with their herds of reindeer to different locations in Alaska. One Laplander family group settled in Akiak and grazed their reindeer approximately 75 miles east of the village, toward the Alaska Range where the tundra had ample feed for the animals. Reindeer became our staple meat supply, supplemented by wild game.

The men of the village would hitch up their dog teams and make a trip to the reindeer herds at slaughter time. They would come home with a sled load of reindeer carcasses, at $10 a carcass. Since there was no refrigeration yet, the meat was hung out in our woodsheds or caches which soon resembled a slaughter house. In winter, keeping meat was no problem, but when spring or warm weather arrived everyone got busy, preserving. The meat was cut up, canned, jarred, salted down in barrels or dried, just as the fresh fish was preserved.

In summer months, the dogs were moved to the river banks or beaches where the breeze off the water would help keep the mosquitoes away. We had skiffs, Johnson or Evinrude outboard motors and nets for fishing. In early days, there was no a limit on the fish catch except that imposed by the need to quickly take care of the day's catch. A wooden cutting table was placed close to the waters edge for cleaning and cutting up the fish and galvanized metal tubs were used to wash it. A fish rack was built for hanging the fish to dry. The scraps were cooked in a metal container for dog food. Salmon of all types were preserved. The king salmon were the first to arrive in spring, weighing anywhere from 40-50 pounds. Our mother, Lena, took charge of them. With the use of her Eskimo knife (called an ulu) the large fish were scaled, split, and filleted. Salmon strips were cut about one-inch wide, and whole slabs from the belly were flake cut for dried smoked fish. The split fish were then washed, soaked in brine a short time, tied two together with twines and hung on the fish racks to dry. From there they were moved to our smoke house to be preserved. A fire was kept constantly burning with certain wood smoke, from trees cut down in our nearby woods. Smoked salmon is very delicious if preserved properly and was one of our staple foods during the winter. We were able to keep the smoked fish hanging on the tallest rafters for future use. We also salted down salmon bellies in wooden kegs, with brine. When needed we took some out and soaked them in cold, clear water for about three days. Then the fish was ready to cook or pickle.

The Eskimo knife was homemade then–the handle was formed of wood, bone from antlers or ivory from whale tusks. The steel was usually cut from old saws. Ulus are widely used to this day for just about any cutting chores, such as fish, meat, vegetables or pizza.

The chum salmon, nicknamed dog salmon, were preserved for dog food. They were filleted and hung up to dry connected by the tail. The back bones were tied together and preserved also. Usually we older children had the honor of splitting the dog fish.

Supplies in bulk were ordered and shipped north from Seattle, by steamships. There were two shipments, early spring after the river ice break-up and in late fall before freeze-up. The steamships were only able to come up the Kuskokwim River as far as Bethel. Stern-wheelers and private scows or barges met the ships and stayed busy all summer hauling freight up and down the river. Local stores carried general merchandise of every description but it was much more reasonable to order in bulk. Items such as food in case lots, dog food by the sack, gunny sacks of potatoes and flour, wooden barrels of real butter to name just a few.

Akiak had a small trading post where the store keeper carried home necessities, groceries for over the counter purchase, dry goods and kerosene and gasoline in five gallon tin containers. Gas was used for outboard motors, gas mantel lights and the saw mill, kerosene for lamps. The fuel was normally sold in wooden case lots of two each. Empty, the tin containers served many useful purposes. They were cut in half and edges were bent properly and made into dog dishes for water or food. They also made up into interesting garden planters. The sturdy wooden crates were very useful and were improvised to serve as temporary cupboards, furniture or step-stools. It wasn't surprising when visiting someone's home to pull up a wooden gas case for a seat.

Our mother was the main hunter in the family, teaching my brothers her many skills. She would hitch up a few dogs to a small sled, dress in her parka, and wolf mukluks, take down her 22 rifle or 20 gauge shotgun from the gun rack, and off she'd go for a day of hunting. I can't recall her ever coming home empty handed. Her catch included rabbits, ptarmigan, spruce hen, willow grouse, and early spring or fall ducks and geese. In summer or fall, sometimes she would walk, with her packsack over her shoulder. She'd come home loaded down, with our father hurrying out to help her carry the game.

Sunday was our day of rest and pleasure. We would hitch up the dogs and go out for a family ride, sometimes to the reindeer camps. The Laplanders would give us children a swift ride on their small sleds drawn by a reindeer. Often we visited our friends in other villages. Whenever we went to Bethel, usually for a doctor's appointment or for supplies, we'd stay long enough to take in a movie or dance and come back home during the night. It was great fun being all bundled up in the dogsled, the moon shining brightly and hearing the steel sled runners practically sing going over the snow trail portages.

In the large shop was a 50 gallon drum wood stove for heat and for cooking dog food. One year an epidemic of distemper hit Alaska. Many good dogs were lost. It was a sad time for all. Since there were no veterinarians, the men would try different remedies. A cleansing of the stomach systems was necessary. One method was a concoction mixed with a spoonful of kerosene, which seemed to help. The sickest dogs were moved into the shop for warmth and were forced fluids until well. We lost a few good dogs ourselves. Other times a dog would come down with rabies, usually from fox bites, and all infected dogs would have to be destroyed. Sometimes our dog team would encounter a porcupine on the trail. Papa and our brothers would have the task of pulling out the quills one by one with a pair of pliers. It was very painful for our dogs to bear. Whenever the snow was crusty or icy our dogs would get cuts on the pads of their feet. Our father would make them snow moccasins out of white canvas, with ties.

In the summer of 1939, men from Admiral Byrd's expedition force to the Antarctic arrived in our area. They were told to select the best and strongest sled dogs for their government sponsored journey. Fortunately none of our sled dogs were chosen; however dogs from Grandpa Joe Vene's and others were selected and never seen again. It wasn't a happy order for the owners to comply with.

The U. S. mail was delivered around isolated Alaska by designated dog mushers with good strong dog teams. They traveled up and down the Kuskokwim and Yukon Rivers and points in between. Normally, the trading post owners were selected as post-masters. During the summer months, the mail was transported by boat up the river as far as McGrath and down again. Our large volume of mail was catalog orders from the Sears, Roebuck catalog, the "Alaska Bible."

Once airplanes started delivering the postal mail, it was much more regular. Air delivery began in approximately 1934. The first pilot to deliver mail down the Kuskokwim River was Harold Gillam, originating in Fairbanks with his Pilgrim. That type of plane was loud and so noisy that you could hear it for miles, but it held a large load and was very reliable. Deliveries were so dependable we could "set our clocks' by them. That ended the hauling of mail by dog mushers in Alaska.

Gone are the days of hard working husky dogs that were such a necessity. Airplanes, boats and snow-machines have taken over. Dogs of today are bred for racing in the popular races held throughout Alaska in winter.

Not forgotten are the cold nights, lying in bed, ready for sleep, when we'd hear the "Malamute Chorus" begin. One dog would start a lonely howl, then another and soon all the village dogs were chiming in. It lasted for only a few minutes and then quieted down. It made us feel as though they were bidding us all goodnight and happy dreams.

# Culture Shock!

## Jean Paal

Before 1976, when the State of Alaska settled the Molly Hootch case, and agreed to provide equal education to all of its citizens, boarding schools were the only educational option beyond eighth grade offered to Native youth in villages. These schools, located hundreds of miles away from home, were operated by the Bureau of Indian Affairs (BIA). Spring and Fall transportation for the students was provided by the BIA. Trips home at holidays had to be funded by families, who rarely could afford such luxury. At that time, the only telephones in most villages were in the store and the school. The shock and homesickness of the youngsters and the sadness of the families can hardly be imagined.

Transportation of these rural students was a logistical problem for the BIA and the airlines, extremely difficult to plan and amorphous in actual progress. At the time, I worked as a reservation agent for PNA[1] and became, somehow, the chief organizer, "cook and bottle washer," for the 'School Kid Movement," as we called it.

The main boarding high school was Mt. Edgecombe in Sitka, with others in Oregon (Chemawa,), and Oklahoma (Chilocco.) There was also a Junior College in Haskell Kansas, an Art School in New Mexico and a grade school in Wrangell, where children as young as six, from villages too small to even have grade schools, were sometimes sent. The children came from villages all over the state by small (four to six seats) planes to connecting feeder points like Bethel or Nome. There they changed to larger planes, usually DC-3s with about twenty seats, and brought to Anchorage or Fairbanks, where still larger (then big, hundred seat) planes took them most of the rest of the way. If they were going to Wrangell or Sitka, they had to change to smaller planes again at Juneau. Except in the rural areas (the "Bush") these were not charter flights. The children had to be fitted in along with the regular passenger traffic. The program started months in advance, with an often-rancorous meeting among the many airlines involved and the BIA.[2] (A dispensation from anti-trust law had been obtained.) Using the list of accepted students, we worked out the airline shares on each flight leg. Then, I would take the preliminary mess and work out an integrated plan which included a route for children from each village that would get them to the school on time, with as few layovers as possible, while not overly crowding any individual scheduled flight. Once the plan was approved by all concerned, blocks of seats were reserved and blocks of hotel rooms arranged.

Of course, it never worked as planned! If a bush pilot couldn't get into one village, or the kids weren't ready, he would try another (not necessarily with the same number of children.) If an airline operating from a feeder point had too many passengers, they would put on an extra section (later in the day, of course.) Children misconnected, flights were cancelled, or delayed, or full. Through it all, I had to reroute on the fly in a manner that kept the distribution among the airlines as fair as possible.

Competitors were usually understanding, but not always, and my own boss was as likely to get on my case as representatives from any of the other airlines. Fortunately, what fur flew soon grew back, because most of us were primarily concerned for the comfort of the children.

Teachers from the BIA schools were sent to the main connecting points to act as chaperones. In Anchorage, I worked with them, keeping them advised on arrivals and departures as best I could. There were daily surprises, however. Perhaps it was sixteen kids from Kwethluk walking off a plane on a Monday, five days ahead of schedule, or perhaps not a single child on the plane from Nome that was supposed to have twenty. Therefore, every flight had to be met. Of course, each child had to be chaperoned until take-off and counted on board. All involved, chaperones, local BIA officials, and I, worked long hours, every day during the ten days at the height of this bi-annual migration.

When it slowed down, the teachers went back to their schools, and I went back to my regular job, notifying the local BIA office when

I knew of stragglers, so they could handle it. Once in a while, they would ask me to meet a child if I was on duty anyway.

One such time, I was working the swing-shift, due to get off at 9 p.m., when Bob, of the BIA, asked me to meet an unexpected child on a Reeve flight that was due in at 9:30 p.m.. She had just been accepted to Mt. Edgecombe, and had a reservation on our 7 a.m. flight to Juneau the next morning. He had called the Westward (now the Hilton) for lodging for the night. All I had to do was put her on the limo[3] to the hotel and she could take the limo back to the airport in the morning. He had just found out she was coming and was tied up (at a party, as I could hear).

"Sure. Glad to."

Of course the flight was an hour and a half late. When she arrived, she seemed to cling to me. I usually rode the limo home, so I offered to go all the way to the hotel with her. I could walk home from there. She was perhaps thirteen and said very little. At the hotel, I led her to the desk to check in. She turned pale, so I handled the check-in and led her to the elevator. It was there that it finally dawned in my thick head that she had never been out of the village, and what that might mean. I asked if she was hungry, and, though she said "no," we scrounged a sandwich from the closing restaurant. Then, I showed her how to work the elevator, took her to the room, showed her how to unlock and lock the door. Her continued shaking told me there was more she needed to know. I led her to the bathroom and turned on the tap, explaining about cold and hot. I had her flush the toilet several times. I didn't bother with the shower; I was sure she would be afraid to use it. Then I turned her bed down, persuaded her to lie on it. She shyly took off her shoes and lay down fully dressed. I showed her how to turn the light off and on.

I could not stay with her, for family reasons, but the deer-like fright in her eyes made me promise to come to her room and take her back to the airport in the morning. I explained the telephone, and left a call for her for 5:00 the next day.

When I arrived at 5:15, she was dressed and sitting on the edge of the neatly made bed. Not a thing, not even a towel, was out of place. I gently led her out, down the elevator, and rode with her to the airport, where I waited until she was safely on the airplane. Then, I teletyped the Juneau office to meet and transfer her, and went home.

By the time the "Molly Hootch" settlement was reached, the airline business had changed and so had my title. I had not handled the *School Kid Movement* for several years, but I assure you, there were very few Alaskans happier than I was when I heard the news that the State was mandated to provide a high school education in each village that had an elementary school and at least one high school aged student

Today I have only a few reminders of that exciting time–a photo of me leading a flock of little Wrangell kids across the ramp, an ivory bracelet made for me by a gifted Mt. Edgecombe student (Myrtle Snow), and the frequent articles in the papers that mention "my" students, now providing important services to our state as leaders in business, politics, and many other fields.

[1]Pacific Northern Airlines, formerly Woodley Airlines, one of Alaska's pioneer (meaning pre-W.W.II) airlines. It was bought by Western Airlines in 1967.

[2]For old timers, here is a list of the major carriers involved: PNA, Alaska, Reeve (the Aleutians) Northern Consolidated (primarily in the Southwest) Wien (primarily in the Northwest and North) and Ellis and Alaska Coastal ( Southeast.) Pan-Am and Alaska flew between Fairbanks and Seattle, Northwest and PNA between Anchorage and Seattle.

[3]For many years, a private company provided transportation between the airport and town. Since it had started out using actual limousines, that's what it was called, "the limo."

# Poliomyelitis Recalled
## Arne Beltz

When I was young my mother, like most parents, was terrified of poliomyelitis. This was conveyed to me and I recall crossing the street in order not to pass a home where there was a case of this disease.

In my time as a public health nurse in Alaska there were two polio epidemics. The first was in 1951. Fortunately I was in Southeast Alaska, which was not infected. There were over 90 cases in Seward and many in Anchorage and Fairbanks. Friends have told me of the many iron lungs in use at Providence hospital. For years after the epidemic orthopedic clinics were filled with victims.

In 1954, polio struck again. I was in Fairbanks working in the Fairbanks health center. The town exploded in fear. Parents called in panic asking what to do to protect their children.

Assistance came to Fairbanks through the Red Cross and military. A supply of serum immune globulin left over from the Korean War was given to the health department. The medical orders given by the health officer were to set up a clinic to administer the serum to school children. The dosage was to be zero point one cc per pound weight of the child. We were to inject it into the gluteus muscle (the buttocks). This entailed weighing each child and adjusting the dosage.

At our disposal were five cc syringes and twenty gauge needles (which are very long–fearsome to a child.) The syringes were numbered. The inner cartridge had to be matched to the outer envelope of the syringe; if not done right the syringe might either leak or not fit. Immune globulin is like egg white; thick and easy to gel. This meant that after use the syringe and needles had to be thoroughly washed, especially before sterilizing, or any remaining serum would harden and block both needles and syringes. Also needles developed burrs and had to be sharpened or discarded. We had a very limited supply of needles and syringes, and a small electric sterilizer. All this was a recipe for disaster.

The clinic was held in the Presbyterian Church. Children were delivered in class groups. They were weighed and dosages established. Then they were called in the clinic room one by one and asked to lie down on their abdomen and pull down their pants. The serum was drawn up and injected.

It sounds simple but things happened. With supplies low sometimes children had to wait until a supply of syringes was sterilized. This added to the awful anticipation already upon them.

Often the syringe and needle functioned well when filled and then plugged up when inserted into the child, entailing getting a new syringe and re-injecting. You can imagine the agony of both giver and receiver when this happened. In addition, there were medical orders that a child weighing a hundred pounds would receive ten ccs of the serum with five going to each side of the buttocks.

In the midst of these problems was the heart rending screams causing terrible apprehension to those who heard it and the constant hopeful, but doubtful question, "Is this going to hurt?" It was chaos, sweat, pain, fear, and noise. We could have done it better, but it was such a rush. It was a day to remember. The good thing was that none of the children developed polio.

A few years later when SALK Polio vaccine came into use it was a pleasure for us to hold clinics. We would have worked many hours overtime with great joy. Even better was the later vaccine which was given by mouth.

# Howling Through the Night
Bud Rice

On a beautiful sunny Saturday morning in April 2000 my wife, Lulie Williams, and I traveled to the upper Tokositna River with six of our dogs: LilleHammer, Casper, Hudson Stuck, Horace Smoke, Doc Lombard, and Payson. Lulie ran her four dogs with a loaded Bernie Willis' dog sled, and I had Casper and Doc pull a loaded pulk with me skijoring behind it. The pulk had a hand brake for going down steep hills. We traveled about 17 miles from our cabin, which is about 10 miles north of Trapper Creek, Alaska. Trapper Creek is about 114 miles north of Anchorage on the Parks Highway. Across frozen swamps, lakes, and over snowmobile trails we went to the Tokositna River. We enjoyed spectacular views of the Alaska Range with 20,320-foot Denali looming as the centerpiece of this magnificent land.

About three miles up the Tokositna beyond Bunco Lake we stopped for a lunch break in the bright snowy expanse. While sitting there a brown form slithered across the snow across the river from us. At first I thought it was an otter, but quickly I realized it was a beaver with its flat, rubbery tail. As soon as I alerted Lulie, the dogs riveted their attention on the large rodent, appearing hungry for it. The beaver, feeling a bit exposed, retraced its steps to a hole in the snow and returned to the river.

We continued along on this gorgeous day looking for a nice campsite. The 7,000-foot Tokosha Mountains eclipsed our views of Denali, but their jagged forms left nothing to be desired. We found a nice camp among live and dead spruce trees on the floodplain. We followed a snowmobile trail to the base of a large spruce where we found the remains of a campfire and an empty bottle of booze. (We packed the plastic bottle to haul it out.) It was early in the afternoon, but sunny and reasonably warm. We set up camp and tethered the dogs to a stakeout cable line. We pitched the tent near the dogs, and took short walks with the dogs in the brushy woods to let them relieve themselves. LilleHammer pointed four willow ptarmigan, but we returned her to the stakeout line after she broke point to chase the birds. We decided to make a short foray on our snowshoes to explore the immediate environs and take photographs. We found fresh beaver tracks, including parallel scratchings in the crusty snow where they dragged brush. We found a slide where beaver had slipped back into the river, but it was frozen over now. We saw a few other old tracks but could not identify them all.

Back in camp we fed the dogs and ourselves and gathered wood for a fire in the cold morning. We lamented the noisy snowmobile group swirling about an open area about one mile farther up river. By 5 p.m. they had rumbled down the river corridor, presumably back to their cabins and RVs. Now it was quiet, and we reveled in the wild beauty. As the earth rotated us away from the sun and a pink glow lit up rocky spires to the west, we heard the mournful wail of a wolf. Shortly a few others joined. As darkness settled more howling ensued, and we really felt we had arrived at a wonderful and wild place.

The howling continued as night came. Our dogs howled back, and the wolf howling got louder and closer. I tried to count the number of individual wolf voices, but after counting 10 or so with all the echoes, it became impossible to identify all the voices. In a short while our dogs barked and acted nervously, and we emerged from our tent to peer around with our headlamps. Lulie spotted the glowing eyes of a wolf not far away, but I could not see it without my glasses on. I grew concerned for our relatively small, short-haired dogs. We've heard of dogs being attacked and killed by wolves in the Anchorage Bowl and in villages like McGrath. We decided to build a fire between the tent and the dog line to keep the wolves at bay. As soon as we returned to our sleeping bags in the tent the howling resumed and got louder and closer. We got up three times before I realized I needed to stay up all night to tend the fire. It was uncanny, but within a few seconds of returning to the tent the howling would resume. We felt watched. I remembered the words of an Alaska Native to Richard Nelson in one of his books, "Remember the animals always know way more than you do in the woods."

The howling grew so intense, that the hills reverberated, as did the space between my ribs. I never felt personally in danger, but I was concerned for the dogs. We needed them to get home, and they are our family members as well as valuable racing dogs. We clapped hands loudly when the wolves sounded near, and I shouted at times to let them know a surly human was present. Some of the wolves barked and others wailed in a tremolo as if celebrating a grand rendezvous.

I broke dead branches off dead spruce trees, nearly denuding one old snag. I used Lulie's little folding Sven saw to cut down another 10-inch diameter dead spruce. Periodically I cut this tree into manageable lengths to drag to the fire site. The fire melted down into a five-foot pit in the snow, never reaching bare ground. I built the fire sideways making a trench rather than melting my way to China. The howling continued all night.

Though concerned for the safety of our dogs, it was interesting to stay up all night. The northern lights glowed with a pale green arch above the northern horizon and bright stars twinkled across the clear skies. The howling was eerily beautiful too, but ominous. I've heard wolves howling in Denali National Park, Eagle River, and other locations around Alaska, and I've seen wild wolves on numerous occasions. It was always something to celebrate, but this time felt different. I felt we were unwanted; this area is the wolves' domain. And, it appeared to be hungry country with few signs of moose and no caribou in this snow-smothered landscape. The night sky seemed darkest between 3 a.m. and 4 a.m., when I was most sleepy, but the wolves seemed as lively as ever then. I watched the light of the sun appear to the east around 5 a.m. as the earth spinned in space to face the warming sun. Morning finally broke, and I thought I would be able to sleep, but the howling persisted.

I roused Lulie and convinced her we needed to go to leave the wolves to their place. She thought we could relax then, but I was not so sure we could completely drop our guard. We watered and fed the dogs, and ourselves, then we hitched up and sped down the river. The dogs seemed anxious to go. (I secretly wished I had been in a pulk race at that moment!) I noticed near our starting point some fresh moose tracks in the snowmobile tracks. Now I wonder if we inadvertently camped near a fresh carcass. Did the wolves drop a yearling moose in the crusty snow? It's entirely possible, and this would explain their persistence and agitation with our dogs in the area.

I'll never know the full reason for the howling through the night. But one thing I do know. I'll never forget that night and the howling. I can hear the sounds this evening, echoing in the recesses of my mind.

Traveling the Alcan

# On My Own at Fifteen
## Charles Dickey

In 1946, when I was fifteen years old, my brother Dave, came home from the military after having served in the Army Air Corp during the war. He had been to Alaska prior to WWII and upon returning announced that he was going back to Alaska. I was not doing well in school, had no interest in school, and was probably spending as much time at the pool hall as I was in classes. I was able to convince my parents that the thing for them to do was to let me go to Alaska with my brother.

Much to my surprise they agreed to it. My brother bought an old 1932 Chevy truck from a farmer in the eastern Montana area. We bought some surplus building material and loaded the truck with that, what personal effects we had between us, and drove from Glendive, Montana to Seattle. Upon arriving, we found that there was a shipping strike going on there. The longshoremen were out. We had to wait in Seattle for a few weeks before we could get passage.

On his way home from Korea, Dave had stopped over in Seattle and made reservations for himself on the Alaska Steamship Company, but none had been made for me. So when the strike ended, his passage came up fairly soon and about the middle of April he left Seattle. He left me there. I was living in a fifty-cent a night hotel room on Jackson Street on Seattle's skid row. I lived there by myself for two months until about the end of June when I was able to get passage north.

My passage was steerage class. My bunk was right alongside the drive shaft that drove the propellers of the ship. I could lie in my bunk and this huge shaft was turning practically above my head. By this time it was late June and into the fishing season. At each of the fish ports, canneries and fish traps there was freight to unload. They were short of stevedores or longshoremen to unload at small ports so they came into steerage and asked if there were any passengers who would like to work to help unload the ship. I worked at practically every stop they made from the time they got into Alaska until we got to Seward.

I had some money when I got on the ship, maybe a hundred dollars. My passage was all paid, including my fare to Anchorage from Seward on the railroad, plus I made $50–$60 cash, at $1.25 an hour working along the way. Right after we stopped at Valdez and started to steam around to Seward, I had gone to bed when the purser came down and said he needed my social security number to record my deductions. I dug out my billfold which was in my pants under my mattress, and gave him the number. Instead of putting my billfold back in my pants and under the mattress, I just laid it on the mattress. Some time before we got to Seward, somebody came along and emptied my billfold for me.

I arrived at Seward about the first of July absolutely broke. I had just a little bit of change in my pocket, probably less than a dollar. We got into Seward about eight in the evening. The cabin class passengers were allowed to stay on the boat overnight until the boat-train left for Anchorage and Fairbanks in the morning, but they kicked the steerage passengers off as soon as we got into Seward; so I spent my first night in Alaska sleeping on a baggage cart on the Alaska Railroad depot platform.

I got off the train in Anchorage and walked up C Street to Fourth Avenue and down Fourth Avenue to the Federal Building and went in there looking for the employment office. I was told the CAA (Civil Aeronautics Administration) was making up a crew to go out to Northway for the remainder of the summer. The CAA office was down the hall. There I talked to the engineer who was going to be running the job. I convinced him that I was a couple of years older than I was and was hired as a construction laborer. They sent me down a couple of blocks to Doc O'Malley's office and I got my physical that afternoon. The next morning I caught a bus on the O'Hara bus lines that ran between Anchorage and Whitehorse.

It was a two day trip. We stayed the first night at the old Santa Claus lodge at Gakona and the next day we were dropped off at Northway. We graded and planted grass on the shoulders and aprons of the runways to control erosion. In the two months I worked there, I learned how to run a D8 cat, a motor grader, and a dump truck. It was quite a learning experience. At the end of the season we went back into Anchorage and about the day I got there I got a job on Fort Richardson, which was where Elmendorf is now, working as a bull cook in a construction camp kitchen. I worked seven 12-hour shifts from 6 p.m. to 6 a.m. scrubbing the kitchen and dining room floors, scrubbing pots and pans, peeling potatoes—everything the cook needed done to clean up from the dinner, prepare a midnight meal for the men who worked all night and helping with breakfast.

About 3 one morning I picked up a copy of the *Anchorage Times* and saw in a want-ad where a guy was advertising for someone to drive a truck from Anchorage to Williston, North Dakota. That made me a little homesick. I had been away from home for six months, and I was only fifteen. I thought this is my chance to go home for the winter.

When I got off work I went downtown and was camped on the man's doorstep when he came out of his house in the morning. I was the first person to see him about the job, and was hired. The man had three trucks that he had been doing some hauling with during the war and he wanted to go home to Williston.

I had not seen much of my brother Dave, so I hunted him up and told him I got a chance to go home for the winter, driving a truck out. Dave decided well, maybe he would go with me. My new boss was happy to have him, so we packed our stuff and on the 20th of October I started my first trip on the Alaska Highway.

The highway was not officially opened to civilian traffic at this time. In fact it didn't officially open to civilian traffic until about the spring of 1948. We started down the highway midmorning. We saw our last pavement about C Street. At that time there were only about nine blocks of pavement in Alaska, and that was on Fourth Avenue in Anchorage.

That first day we got as far as Sheep Mountain Lodge. During the course of the night it snowed about a foot, a wet heavy snow. The driving conditions were really bad. There were no tracks to follow. The only way you could find the road was to steer about halfway between the trees on both sides. It was still snowing and the windshield wipers and defrosters on the truck weren't very effective, so I drove most of that morning in first and second gear with my head out the window trying to keep the truck on the road. In the truck with me were Dave and another man who had contracted with the boss to haul about a thousand pounds of personal effects out onto the Alaska Highway. He was going to look for a likely spot to start construction on a lodge for all the tourist traffic that was going to be coming along the Alaska Highway in future years. As we went down the road my brother and this man, D. Jasper Heath, got friendly and Dave got excited about this project so they decided they would go in partnership. On the 21st of October, in about a foot of snow they found their spot. It was at mile 1238½ on the Alaska Highway about halfway between Northway and the Canadian border.

It was a beautiful spot up on the side of the valley looking out over the Chisana River Valley toward the Wrangell Range of mountains. That evening they unloaded their half-ton of gear which included a tent, a couple of cots, some groceries, and an axe, a saw, and a few other tools. They were going to build a cabin and spend the winter. That's where I left them the next morning as I drove on down the road.

It was an interesting trip. I was driving one truck, and my employer was driving one, and towing one. All of the trucks were just pieces of junk. We carried spare tires, spare parts, and gasoline for the trip. We had barrels and barrels of gas on the trucks. We had probably a couple of dozen spare tires, none of which were in decent shape. During the war, new tires had been impossible to get. We blew or punctured tire after tire on rocks. We went down the road making about 100 to 150 miles a day.

We'd get up early in the morning and from about 6 a.m. to 10 a.m., repair the tires that had gone flat from the day before, breaking them down with hand irons, patching and booting them, mounting them on rims, all by hand, pumping them up with hand pumps, and loading them back on the truck. We'd go down the road and every twenty miles or so we'd have another flat. We abandoned a lot of tires along the way.

The guy was supposed to be paying me $5 a day and my expenses, but I had never been able to get any money out of him. I wound up paying most of my meals and my rooms along the way, that is, when we actually stayed in rooms. Lots of times we just slept in the seat of the truck wherever it was that we stopped. We'd sleep until it got so cold we couldn't stand it any more, then drive down the road to warm the trucks up a little bit, and then stop and sleep some more. He also kept giving me a bad time, I thought. I wasn't at all happy with my employment.

We broke an axle on my truck and it took us a day and a half working alongside the road in the snow and the ice trying to repair it. Finally, we gave up. The truck I was driving was a 1941 Chevy. We took the axle from that 1938 GMC that he was towing (backwards) and mated it up underneath the truck I was driving. We got it to work, but it had different sized tires and we didn't have many spares that size. We had to start mounting the 8.25 tires on the 7.50 rims, which was more difficult, and harder work. And that put the tires so close together on the rims that we couldn't get on a set of single chains any more, but they were also too close to the spring shackles so we couldn't get on dual chains. From that point on, I was not able to chain up at all. The truck the boss was driving was four-wheel-drive, and chains, and often he would have to take the truck he was towing to the top of the hill, leave it there and come back and tow me up.

Another thing that was constantly going wrong, the gas that we were carrying was contaminated with rust and water, so we were always having plugged filters and plugged fuel lines. The truck I was driving had a 90 degree reducing elbow from the saddle gas tanks. The water and rust would get down in that reducing elbow and it would plug up with rust and then freeze. Two or three times a day I had to get under the truck, take the fuel line off, screw this elbow out of the bottom of the tank, lay there on my back with my thumb over the hole in the bottom of the tank, while I tried to get the ice and rust out of the elbow. I would blow on it and bang it on rocks to get it cleared. Then I would have to screw it up into the bottom of the tank and as I did this, the gas would spew out in a circle soaking my arms with raw gas clear up to the shoulders. It was cold, down around zero. My arms were just blistered from this cold raw gas.

So that's how we progressed down the highway. It took us 18 days to get from Anchorage to Edmonton. The day we arrived, as we drove through town, my gas line clogged for the fourth time. I was following and at first he didn't notice I was not with him. He got back to me just about the time I got the gas lines cleared and I was dripping gas off my elbows, and my arms were raw. He said something that didn't quite go well with my Irish temper. I told him what he could do with his truck, and I pulled my suitcase out of the back of the truck and started hitchhiking.

I was able to hitchhike the remaining 800 miles from Edmonton to Glendive, Montana in only two days. I arrived on the 10th of November, four days before my sixteenth birthday and was really glad to be home.

The next spring after spending one of the coldest winters ever recorded in North America, Dave came home to take care of some business (That winter the temperature at Snag, 60 miles east of their cabin, set a North American low-temperature record of 83.6 degrees below zero.) He wanted to buy a truck for much-needed transportation at their cabin, and drive it back over the highway. My dad had an old 1917 Model White Touring Bus that he'd bought surplus from Yellowstone Park. They had sold them off during the war when there weren't any tourists. My brother bought this old bus from my dad and we cut the three rows of seats behind the driver's seat off and put a box on it and that was to be our vehicle for our drive to Alaska.

It had been a beautiful old bus, with a canvas top, bows to support the canvas, and curtains you could pull down in case there was a change in the weather. It had wood-spoke wheels, big brass carbide gas head lamps, and no electrical system. It had a vacuum tank instead of a fuel pump to bring gas from the tank up to the carburetor. It was really an antique. This was in the spring of 1947 and it was 30 years old. We loaded it up and headed back over the Alaska Highway.

It was March, during spring break up, and it was another interesting trip. We made pretty good time from Glendive up to Edmonton, but on north we started having our problems. When they originally built the highway all the equipment, materials, and men had been shipped by rail to Dawson Creek where the actual highway began and the road between Edmonton and Dawson Creek was very primitive. It wasn't even graveled. It was just a dirt road across the prairie. Now it is less than 300 miles, and you can drive it in four or five hours. At that time it was nearly 500 miles. The road went north out of Edmonton, crossed over above the Lesser Slave Lake and came down into Grand Prairie from the north.

At the same time we were going up, there was another shipping strike on the coast, and the army was sending a big convoy up there to re-supply their bases in Alaska. The road was so bad and so muddy that if we'd ever let that truck convoy get ahead of us, we probably would not have been able to continue. When they got done churning up that road it looked like a plowed field. Big chunks of gumbo mud would roll up on the wheels of the 6 x 6 and break off and leave clods of mud as big as 50 gallon drums laying in the road.

Another fellow by the name of Del Winkler came with us. He was driving a brand new 1946 Ford car. (He got one of the first new cars that came into Montana after the war. He had his name on a waiting list for four years.) Our truck had high wheels, 8.25 x 28 inch tires, and we were able to put chains on the rear wheels, so we were able to churn through the mud on those roads, and do it better than a lot of the weapons carriers and 4x4 jeeps and ambulances. But the Ford wasn't having that kind of luck, so we towed him. The mud would pack up under the car and into the fender wells, 'till the tires just quit turning, and we were sliding the car along like you would tow an old stone boat or a sled. We dragged that car for most of the 500 miles from Edmonton to Dawson Creek.

Near Grand Prairie, we had to cross the Little Smokey River. We had been pressing hard because we wanted to get there before the ice went out. If we didn't, we would be delayed for two or three weeks until the ice cleared and they were able to get the ferry launched. We came down to the bank of the river about 11 p.m. one night. As we came down to the bank of the river we could see the water running and the slush running on top of it. There was a guy manning the cabin where the ferry was still pulled up to the bank.

We asked him, "When did the ice go out?"

He said, "There was a truck went over about four hours ago and he didn't have any problem. There is about 18 inches of running water, but the ice is solid under there."

We started out across that 450 foot wide river in the middle of the night, our lights shining out across the slow moving water and slush, towing this poor car behind us.

The truck's plywood cab up over the front seat had only one door, about 18 inches square. On the left hand side the spare tire was mounted on the fender and the cab we built came down to the sill. Hearing that slushing ice against the side of the vehicle and knowing that, if the ice broke, we only had an 18 inch hole to get out through, was the scariest experience of my life.

Another time, the brakes went out completely. My brother was kind of handy. He cut the tops out of a pair of engineer's boots and riveted the leather strips into the brake linings and that was what we had for brakes.

When we got to where Dave and Jasper were building their cabin, we left him and the truck. Del Winkler and I headed on into Anchorage in his Ford. The roads were still breaking up. The Tok Cutoff (the original road that followed moose and game trails across the country) was the narrowest, windingest road you ever saw. It started out along the edge of a valley, and where it was cut into the hill, the water would seep out, and freeze up, forming a glacier across the road. The highway department had cut a trench every two or three hundred feet to drain the water and keep it from building higher. These trenches were V-shaped, a couple of feet wide and 18 inches deep. The only way to cross them was to hit them hard enough so that you could bounce across. The front end would bounce in and out; then the back would bounce in and out. Then you'd go on down the road another few hundred feet until you came to the next one.

That only lasted for a few miles and then the road came down off the side of the hill and started out across the Chistochina River Valley. We looked out across this valley and it was running with water and all glaciered up. Del had a spotlight on his car, and we shined it out across the valley nearly a quarter of mile across. We could see an opening in the trees on the other side and we decided the road must go from here to there and we just headed across. As Del drove, I was looking down wondering where the side of the road was. I kept seeing the butts of piling sticking up maybe an inch or two out of the water on my side, but didn't really know what I was seeing. We made it across fine, and went into Santa Claus Lodge and stopped to spend the night. The lodge keeper fixed us some dinner, and we got to talking about our experiences coming across the Cutoff that day.

He asked, "What did you think when you crossed the Chistochina River bridge back here?"

We said, "What bridge?"

He said, "Where you crossed the river, there is narrow planked bridge about a thousand feet of bridge on piling." Here we were crossing this bridge and didn't even know we were on one. There were no guard rails, or anything. That explained the piling I had been seeing. That was our last hairy experience on our trip into Anchorage.

Sometime after we arrived in Anchorage, Del sold his car to a taxi-cab company. I don't think they knew what they were buying. It was just a two door, but there were no new cars to be had, and they were glad to get even a two door. I often wondered how long it held up. It had taken more abuse in that trip over the highway than any car I had ever seen.

Whenever I hear someone tell about how tough their trip was over the Alaska Highway, I have to laugh. They don't know what a bad trip over the ALCAN is all about.

# Dreaded Canadian Border

## Elaine Held

The only time my husband and I have crossed the Canadian border without incident was the year after 9/11.

The first year we crossed we were too innocent to recognize that there was a problem even though the border personnel were wearing bullet proof vests. We found out only later that the United States and British Columbia had almost come to blows over salmon. It was the year some Canadian fishermen took an American ferry and held its passengers hostage, an international offense.

We excitedly pulled up to the little booth. I noticed an instant change in the demeanor of the person who approached us as soon as she saw our California license. Instead of the usual questions she asked, "Do you have any weapons?" When she seemed satisfied that we indeed did not have an Uzi with us, she asked us to pull over to a large open area. Should we be worried?

Two scowling men approached. "Get out of the motor home. Take any valuables with you. Stand to the side."

I looked at Bill. I thought to myself, "I think I am going to lose my apples." Then the seriousness of the situation hit me as I remembered I had a needle with a strange looking substance in it in the refrigerator. Sweating, I couldn't look at Bill. I was going to spend the rest of my life in a Canadian jail! One of the men was trying to lift our ice chest out of the shower and was having a difficult time. Not thinking, Bill stepped on the bottom step to go in to help.

The man whirled on him shouting, "Do not come in here. I told you that!" Oh boy, we are dead. Suddenly they were finished and told us to get in and leave. We didn't argue. After we were a good way from the border we began to shake. I told Bill about the needle. That was when we pulled over to recover.

The next year we were old hands at this so we didn't worry about the crossing. Again they pulled us over. The man asked Bill for our poultry. It was so off base I sat there thinking, "Poultry, what is that?"

"I want your eggs, chicken, or any poultry."

"Huh??" We only had three dozen eggs so we gave them to him. We were traveling with another couple who had a dog. We got out to go back to help them, since this was their first crossing. Sure enough, the man was asking them for their poultry. Sharon, being the nice person she is, did not think to hide anything. She told him she had a frozen chicken and turkey so he took that and her eggs. For some reason she volunteered that she had dried dog food with chicken in it. He asked to see it and then took that too, all three bags of it. Poor Truffles had nothing to eat all the way across Canada.

At the US side of the border, we found the Americans were confiscating all beef because of the mad cow thing. We gave them a bad time about eating well, the border guards from both sides getting together for meals—one side fixing breakfast and the other dinner.

# Slippery Slope on the Alcan
### Sherry Eckrich

"Are you trying to kill me?" I screamed into the dark. I untangled myself and made my way back up to the road by kicking little hand and foot holds in the ice-crusted snow. My left hip was bruised and I wasn't feeling very kindly toward Jan, but I had survived the van's impact remarkably intact.

How I got there is our favorite tale when people ask us about our trip to Alaska. It never varies much in the telling, except the temperature has crept downward a bit over the years.

On November 2, 1982, six of us—my husband Paul and I, our friends Jan and Bill, their son Bryan (twelve), our son Tekle (eleven) —set out to move to Anchorage from St. Louis, Missouri. The menagerie also included two dogs.

We drove two vehicles—the Dodge van and a retired Sears delivery truck we affectionately christened Bouncing Blue Bertha. Bertha towed my small Toyota. Both were stuffed full of possessions. I just needed to bring some of St. Louis with me, the way a toddler carries her worn blanket as a transitional object.

We had planned to stay at lodges along the Alcan but hadn't made reservations, because we couldn't predict our schedule. "We'll get there when we get there," was our motto.

Midway through the eighteen-day trip, we decided to stop for the night at Liard Hot Springs in British Columbia. The thought of soaking in hot mineral water enticed us after a rough day of driving. When we arrived, the inn was full. A holiday weekend in Canada, and the nearby hot springs drew partying Canadians. Not suspecting we would have trouble finding lodging in winter, we hadn't made contingency plans.

Darkness had fallen and we were road-weary. We had plenty of blankets and sleeping bags, but we hadn't come prepared to camp. Our vehicles weren't the warmest. Even with the heater in the van running full tilt all day as we traveled, water from an overturned thermos jug had glaciated into a mound of ice on the floor behind the front seat.

The next roadhouse wasn't too far—thirty-eight miles, a little over an hour at our average road pace. The truck was exceptionally slow going up hills. Sometimes, on a long uphill slope, I would watch the needle on the speedometer move slowly to the left and chant, "I think I can, I think I can...."

Paul and Bill led the way in Bertha, still towing the Toyota. Jan drove the van. Stationed next to her, I handled the CB and rode herd on the restless boys.

Although it was dark outside, our headlights on the snowy landscape, revealed we were traveling on a raised roadway, just wide enough for two vehicles to pass carefully. On either side, the shoulders sloped down six feet to a smooth snowfield.

Suddenly a distress call came from the truck. "Stay back! We're jack-knifed, slowly sliding back down and the Toyota is hanging over the ditch! It's slicker than whale shit up here!" Bill screamed. "We're going to have to chain up. Paul is getting out to check the Toyota." Paul stepped out of the truck and found the only way he could progress safely was on all fours. Our first attempt to chain up would have to be in the dark.

The van had studded tires, and Jan stopped it on a relatively flat stretch. We had just descended a long slope and were a few hundred yards behind the truck, too far back to see how serious things might be.

"I'll go see if I can help them," I said, opening the door.

"I'll stay here with the kids." She turned on the emergency flashers.

I got out, and as I turned to cross in front of the van, Jan suddenly started it up again after she heard a trucker yell on his CB, "Get the hell out of the way! I'm rolling downhill and I can't stop!" She knocked me over. On the icy road I slid ten feet, landing in a heap in the ditch on the right. Unaware she had hit me, Jan continued to pull ahead.

Back on the road, I couldn't stay upright on the black ice. I crept across crab-wise to where emergency flares marked the truck's position.

With the Toyota sloping tail down into the ditch and threatening to pull Bertha down with it, Bill sat in the truck, body straightened, legs extended, both feet pushing on the brake pedal as hard as he could. The truck was in gear and the emergency brake was on, but still Bertha slid slowly backwards. Paul wrestled with the recalcitrant tire chains.

Another large truck whizzed by, barely missing Bertha's nose. It took a long time, but Paul finally hooked chains around the tires. A third truck approached; it slowed down and stopped. "Need help?" the driver called out. He got out and walked with a kind of gliding gait that made it look as though he had been on this stuff before. He looked at the chains setting loosely around the tires. He didn't snicker, even as he undid everything Paul had done and deftly hooked the chains three or four links tighter. We thanked him and he went on his way.

"Ease 'er forward, Bill," Paul said.

Bill tried to get Bertha moving with the Toyota hanging over the edge of the roadbed. Each time he started to take his foot off the brakes, the truck inched closer to the edge.

"I guess I'll have to unhitch the Toyota," Paul said. Once freed, the Toyota slipped silently backward into the ditch.

The temperature was near zero. I wore moon boots, mittens, and a down parka. The boots kept my feet warm in the van but not for long outdoors. Appendages began numbing, and I knew I wanted to be just about anywhere besides out on the road, trying to tame cantankerous vehicles.

Bill eased the truck forward a bit, and Paul tried unsuccessfully to drive the Toyota up the slope to the road. Paul is six feet plus some, and the car was packed so full he could barely squash himself into it. He steered with his head tilted sideways, right ear against his shoulder so that he could see out the windshield.

"Sherry, can you take some flares on up the hill? You'll have to flag down trucks coming that way so they slow up before they start coming down." Luckily, no one had come from that direction yet.

Grabbing our last three flares, I trudged up the hill in the ditch three-quarters of a mile or so and clambered back to the roadbed. I was far enough from the top of the hill that I couldn't see what was happening with Bertha and the Toyota, but a truck driver could brake some before he started downhill.

In an earlier, more poetic mood, I had likened a frozen Canadian landscape to the enigmatic emptiness of a lunar surface. That was when I was watching it roll by through the window of a faintly heated vehicle. Now my concerns were more pragmatic. In the frigid dark, my nose was beginning to harden. I had no idea what kinds of predators were lurking nearby, and I worried about whether I could ignite the flares correctly and quickly. I couldn't afford to practice with only three left.

From the distance, I heard the sound of a truck approaching from ahead. I fumbled out of my mittens to break the cap off the flare. How soon should I light it? Sound seems to carry a long way in the clear Northern cold, and I couldn't really tell where the truck was. The road curved just beyond where I stood. By the time I saw the headlights it might be too late to get the flare lit, especially if I screwed up. I took a stab at the timing and scratched the flare into life, burning a few holes in my coat and my numb hands. The red sparks were comforting in a way...if only they didn't attract the attention of the bear I was sure I heard snuffling in the brush behind me.

My prayers must have been answered. That truck and two more saw the flares, slowed, and passed safely. Before long, I heard the unmistakable strain of Bouncing Blue Bertha's engine chugging up the hill and saw her headlight beams wobbling in the dark. Behind her, Paul drove the Toyota, and Jan followed in the van. Paul had driven a quarter mile in the ditch until he reached a spot where the slope onto the road declined and frozen vegetation provided extra traction. While they were traveling in tandem along the road and the ditch, Bryan had grabbed the CB and began singing, "Oh, you take the high road and I'll take the low road..." They all joined in. The caravan stopped to pick me up, and we took off down the high road once more.

It took us six hours to cover that thirty-eight miles. Six hours of adrenaline and grit. Well past midnight, we reached a lodge near the confluence of the Coal and Liard Rivers. We knocked on the door and asked the proprietor, "Please, can we have a room? We don't care how big it is, we'll fit in."

The middle-aged woman peered at us as though we were road dirt. "My rooms are all taken."

"Please, could we just put our sleeping bags on the floor of your garage? We won't disturb anything."

"No." She slammed the door.

"We're going to have to conserve body heat," I said. "We'll have to sleep as close together as we can."

In the back of the van Bill had built a plywood platform with two foam pads, just wide enough for Jan and Bill to sleep comfortably. The four adults sardined ourselves head to foot on the platform. One of the boys slept on the bench seat and the other on the floor in front of it. The dogs curled in tiny nests on the bucket seats, noses buried under their tails.

To say we actually slept that night would be a distortion. The cranky little voices of the boys could be heard complaining periodically through the night. Any movement by one of us in the back affected everyone else in the sandwich. We all stayed cold.

Through the night, fighting back tears, I wondered why we had gotten ourselves into this whole mess. Would we survive? Would we ever make it to Alaska?

We thawed out and survived, however. On November 20th, we arrived in Anchorage. Five days later we celebrated our first Thanksgiving here, realizing just how much we had to be grateful for.

# A Trip to Remember

## Jean Matyas

My husband was transferred to Alaska from San Antonio, Texas in 1960. He drove up here alone in February, flew back the end of May and drove our family of five up here in seven days in a '55 Chevy wagon.

We carried a Coleman stove and a big cooler. The tailgate was my kitchen. The highway had not been paved or straightened, it was miles and miles of gravel and unbelievable dust, and there were signs at every curve informing us of how many deaths had occurred at that particular spot.

Now, fast forward to 1966. We were being transferred to Virginia. We had added two children to our family, a boy, two, and another boy, two months. Thinking he was doing us a huge favor, my husband bought us a fifteen foot Aloha camper trailer. This time we had another station wagon, a small Buick. The day arrived and everything was ready, food and clothing packing in the trailer for the seven of us, not to mention lawn chairs, toys, golf clubs, etc.

We got an early start and got as far as Eagle River before our engine overheated. Fortunately, we had friends living in Eagle River who put us up while the two men worked feverishly during the night installing a new thermostat and doing whatever else they thought might alleviate the problem. Off we went the next day. This time, we barely made it to Palmer. We limped into a garage, thinking we might need a new radiator only to be told it wasn't the radiator. The engine was not powerful enough to pull the load back to Eagle River. We left the kids with our friends and went back to Anchorage and bought a bigger station wagon, leaving the Buick with our friends to sell.

Our third departure was anticlimactic. I'm sure our friends were hoping they had seen the last of us. We were barely past Sutton when we had a blowout on the trailer. My husband put on the spare and we drove until everyone was worn out. Upon stopping for the night we opened the door to the trailer to discover the inside boiling with dust and the cabinets shaken completely loose from the wall. Somehow, we managed to clear enough of the dust to fix a bite to eat and cram our seven bodies into what sleeping space we had.

We had nine flats on that trip and along the way, our baby, Greg, developed a raging case of Thrush and our two year old, Mike, had infected mosquito bites and his usual sunny disposition was anything but.

We did finally make it to Virginia but never used that trailer again. My husband sold it to an eager buyer and we said, "Good riddance!"

Looking back, we can laugh at our frustrations and trials along the way. We were transferred back to Alaska in 1970, but that's another story.

# We're Celebrities
## Dr. Darryl L. Gremban

My first trip to Alaska was in 1970. I had just gotten out of the service and we were moving to Eagle River, Wisconsin, where I was building a dental office. While it was under construction I said, "Let's go to Alaska."

Mom and Dad said, "Yeah, we'd like to go to Alaska, too." So they bought a new motor home, and come September six of us headed for Alaska–my wife, our two kids, Mom, Dad and I.

I can remember driving the Alcan Highway, 1228 miles of gravel road and dust like you wouldn't believe. We taped every single crack and crevice in that motor home but dust still filtered in. Then we found that if we ran the generator and turned the air conditioner on, it would build a little air pressure inside and push the air and most of the dust out. Motor homes in 1970 weren't really built for that kind of road and something was always rattling and we were always tightening. I remember that when we got to Whitehorse, they had, like, three whole miles of black topped road, and it was so smooth we said, "Okay, let's just drive around for a while." Nothing was rattling and we thought that was pretty neat.

We took it easy. We'd just drive along until we found a stream and stop and fish. If the fishing was good, we'd stay a day or two, but if it wasn't we'd move on and try the next stream.

One evening when I was down at a river fishing, a guy came up alongside, and says, "Are you catching anything?"

I said, "No not here, but …"

And he said, "Which way are you going?"

"We are going up."

"I am, too. I haven't caught a fish yet."

"Really? We've had fish every night for supper."

"Where have you been fishing?"

"Every creek that we come across that looks good and we're in the mood, we stop and fish that creek."

He says, "Man, I stop at these lakes and take my boat off, put the motor on and fish the lake. I don't know where to go, and don't catch any fish and have to come back and then I have to take my motor off and put my boat back up on top, it's killing me."

I said, "We just jump out the door, grab our poles, and start fishing."

One day, I can't remember what river we camped on, my dad and I took off fishing. We got into a hole and we were catching fish and it got really dark. We had thought we could probably cut across country and get back to the motor home quickly, but in the dark, I said, "We could wander around in there forever, let's just follow the stream back even if it takes longer."

By the time we got back to the motor home, the girls were a little scared and pretty 'ticked off.' But, we enjoyed the trip simply because we did those things.

We stopped at Liard Hot Springs. We walked back up a path, and sure enough, there was a hot springs. We put on our swim suits. There was a little pool, just right for the little kids. Fortunately, before we could put them in, someone warned us off. That pool was where the hot water came down, and it was way too hot, so we all got into the big pool. After traveling as far as we did in the motor home, without all the great facilities like we have now, we were really glad to have a nice hot bath.

In 1979 we made a second trip up the highway, driving the same motor home, and doing the same kind of traveling. Just before we got to Liard Hot Springs there was a road block. They told us they were taking a survey about the Hot Springs. Apparently they were thinking of damming up the river to make a lake, which would have flooded the pools of hot water. "What would you think about that?"

"Well, we wouldn't like that at all. We stopped at Liard in 1970 and here we are, looking forward to stopping again."

She thanked us and gave us a few tokens and coupons, and a British Columbia magazine. Back on the road, with Dad driving, I was leafing through this magazine, when I suddenly saw a picture and said, "Geez Ma, here is a woman who looks just like you. It is you! It is us in the hot springs!" Somebody had taken our picture when we were there in 1970 and here we were in the new book. We still have the book, and we show it to friends once in a while. Here we are, we're celebrities; we have our picture in the book.

# The Alcan-1946
## Lewis J. McDonald

My father always wanted to go to Alaska to homestead.

My mother said, "We need to get a new truck." In 1946 you had to be on a waiting list to get a new vehicle.

One night Dad came from working a late shift at the local sawmill and told my mother, "There is a new Studebaker truck for sale, and nobody wants it." The next day, we owned it.

Dad and his older brothers built a bed on it. We loaded the furniture, piano, and washing machine on first. The mattresses were on top for sleeping. We children sat on the kitchen cabinets on a mattress.

We all left Burney, California on August 8, 1946 in a half-ton Studebaker truck pulling a trailer with a John Deere tractor on it.

The first night it rained on us, the tarp leaked, and all the bedding got wet. At Creston, British Columbia the trailer broke an axle. Dad left the trailer with the tractor at the train station to ship to Alaska via Seattle.

From mother's log book I learned that we had lunch in Edmonton and spent $5.40 for eight people. Twenty gallons of gas was $2.40.

Canada required you to carry extra tires and gas. At Dawson Creek we had to get a permit (#38) to drive the Alcan Highway. One day the road was so rough that Dad only drove 20 mph all day, in third gear. The road was dusty in places and muddy in others. There were three days we didn't see anybody. We camped out in gravel pits, much as RVers do today.

Dad was told he needed a two speed axle to climb up Steamboat Mountain. He made it with one gear to spare. Somewhere near Teslin, Yukon Territory we reached a bridge that was too narrow for dual tires. Mother said, "We can't cross there."

Dad said, "I can't back up that hill." So, we crossed the bridge.

All our possessions didn't get to Alaska with us. Mother left four chairs by the roadside in Canada and we also had to jettison a bicycle, but my brother was able to sell it for $100, Canadian.

The McDonald family crossed the Alaska border on August 28, 1946 and two days later we arrived in Sutton and stayed at the Alpine Inn. The family joke was that we would have turned back except all of our clothes were dirty, and the washing machine was in the front of the truck.

My parents bought a colony farm on Hyer Road by Wasilla Creek, because it was cheaper than homesteading. The first winter was cold, 50 degrees below for a long time. That was tough on people from California.

I have made twenty trips over the Alcan Highway since then, but that was the most memorable. The pioneer spirit of my father made it possible for us to live all these years in Alaska.

True Alaska Adventures

# Danger on Twenty-Mile
## Don Lietzau

It was a beautiful, mid-October day when my wife Cindy, our German Shepard, Lady and I slid the twenty-foot freighter canoe into the gray, turbulent, icy water of the Twenty Mile River, south of Anchorage. We planned for a weekend of goat hunting at the upper headwaters of the river where it falls from the Chugach Mountain Range.

Cindy was in the front seat, Lady and a mound of gear at mid-ship and I was in the back managing the fifteen-horse Evenrude motor. With a quick pull of the starter rope the motor sputtered to life. A thin cloud of gray-blue smoke kicked into the air as I shifted the motor into gear and checked to be sure the engine's water pump was moving water through it. We slid quickly toward the middle of the river.

The Twenty Mile River is swift except at the lower end, where it broadens out and dumps into the saltwater of the Turnagain Arm. There the current slows and is quite manageable. I rolled the throttle and we surged forward, swinging northeast up river. I had some experience in this particular river so my confidence was high. Pushing along at maybe fifteen miles per hour we were soon far upriver. As we gained elevation the river got narrower and swifter. Angry whirlpools and long hanging sweepers lined the banks. We were pushing forward, bucking the swift current and coming to a sharp left-hand bend in the river, when suddenly a huge floating cottonwood loomed from around the corner. This massive 100 foot tree, with a root ball at least twenty feet across, was headed toward us on a collision course. The giant twisting mass of limbs and roots was being hurled down the river at an impressive speed. The log lurched over a huge boulder, teetered briefly and then moved forward, swiftly closing the distance between us. With sweepers on the left bank and the tree bearing down on us on the right, I slid the canoe to a stop. Holding just enough thrust to maintain our position in the current, I quickly assessed the situation. I kicked just a bit of power to the prop and the big canoe moved as far to the left side of the river as possible. My hope was to let the tree wash past us. This seemed like a good plan, but then all plans need a backup, right? The tree, vaulting down the river like a runaway train, slammed into a small island, just upstream to our right side and stopped. Then, with water spray flying, it spun on its root ball and lodged across the stream in front of us. It hit the canoe on the bow as it came to a stop hanging at a right angle to the force of the current. Bobbing slowly up and down like a giant dragon sizing up its prey, it loomed over us. Scared? Yep.......but what next?

The water was not deep, maybe three feet, so Cindy jumped out of the canoe and tried to force it to the left and around the top end of the tree. No good, she was just not strong enough to manage that while fighting the cold, swift current. I held the throttle about half open while keeping the canoe steady, but Cindy couldn't crawl back with her boots full of icy water and the current threatening to hand her to the saltwater gods down stream. Realizing it was now my turn, I bailed out of the boat and made my way, hand over hand along the left side of the canoe to the front. I grabbed Cindy by the back side and launched her head first into the bow of the boat. Grabbing the tip of the canoe, with one hand on the bow and the other against that rocking tree trunk, I slowly made my way toward the island only thirty feet away. I was almost to safety when, on the next step, I was over my head.

Icy water swirled over me; I was so cold I could hardly catch my breath. I lost my hand on the log, but held fast to the top of the aluminum bow of the canoe and jerked myself toward the surface, fighting the current. My boots, now full of water, were trying to drag me deep to a watery grave. Fighting hard, I broke the surface just as Cindy grabbed my arm with a death grip like none other. (Guess she must have forgotten to pay my life insurance that month.) Anyway, with my head above water it became apparent we were far from over the ordeal. The canoe was spinning in a savage, counter-clockwise trip down the rapids and heading straight for the inside curve of a sweeper-filled, boiling rage of water. I frantically tried to touch bottom while fighting the current. Cindy was also fighting my efforts to touch bottom, trying to get me back into the boat. Realizing we only had one chance, I screamed at her to duck as we smashed through a birch sweeper. Then I convinced her to let me go and move to the back of the boat and give us some outboard power. Convinced that I was okay and not going to loose my grip, she swapped ends and on hands and knees, crawled over the mound of gear and dog, just in time to have the motor quit. Never, ever, does a plan go smoothly. Now we were at the total mercy of the mighty river. A quick glance over my shoulder showed the cottonwood tree was still holding on top of the island. We hurled down river, everything in a blur, but seemingly in slow motion.

I kept reaching with my foot, hoping to touch bottom. Then I felt it, a small bump on the gravel bottom with my right foot. Then a solid hit, then both feet touched. I realized in a flash that the bottom was coming up fast and suddenly I was dragging in three feet of water trying to bulldog that hurtling mass of aluminum and gear. I thrust my feet out in front of me and held tight on to the bow. Jamming my feet down into the rocks, I tried to stop the downstream momentum. Big rocks, the size of footballs were shoved aside. Looking down stream, I saw the inside-sweeping river bend with it's under-cut bank, looming closer with every second. I screamed at Cindy to jump into the river and help me. In a flash she hit the water and locked on the brakes. The canoe came to a slow stop, bobbing in the current. We dragged it to the shore on the bottom end of the same island that held the cottonwood tree that started this whole mess.

As soon as we made dry land I was in self rescue mode. Freezing and soaked to the skin, Cindy cried, "I want to go home." She stood there dripping wet, shivering and barely able to move. Yelling at her to strip off her wet clothes, I did the same. Now I tell you that an October breeze, when one is soaked with ice water, is not a pleasant experience. Cindy was busy getting naked as I was trying with numb, stiff fingers, to unhook the gas can from the motor. They throbbed with pain as I undid the hose and jerked the gas can out of the boat. Under my stern instructions, my lovely, pale-blue, teeth-chattering wife dragged the dry-gear bag and our dry, warm cloths from the bottom of the water logged boat. Hobbling in bare feet to a nearby snag, I dumped a liberal amount of gas on a pile of driftwood and then lit the pile with the flicker of a match. Whoof, and the gas-soaked wood roared to life with fiery heat.

Within minutes we were dry, in warm clothes and sitting in the warm glow of the fire. Only then did we have a chance to realize what had just happened. Scared, you bet. It was a few hours before we got up the nerve to get back to the canoe and head home.

You know, I don't believe I have been up Twenty Mile since. Every time I pass that river I get a cold chill, knowing all too well that death was very close that October day.

# Afloat?

## Maxine Rader

When Bill and I married in 1951, it was still expected that a good wife would follow her husband to the ends of the earth, and, to my mother's way of thinking, that's what I did in 1956. We moved to Alaska after Bill finished his internship. We came with the idea of staying a year or two, just to have a little adventure, before setting up practice in Kansas.

In '57 Bill floated the idea of homesteading at Pt. Mackenzie, his notion being that he would work in town, while the children and I fulfilled the living-on-the-land requirement. With two children under the age of three and another on the way, I was unenthusiastic. Bill had to assuage his lust for adventure by hunting and fishing and taking flying lessons, until we headed to Cincinnati for his psych residency.

We returned to Alaska with five children and another on the way. Bill began casting about for something exciting to do as a family. Dr. Perry Mead decided to sell his 16 foot cabin cruiser, the *Galea*, which he had built himself using sealastic, normally used on artificial limbs, instead of fiberglass. Bill's admiration for Perry's innovative approach inclined him in favor of the boat.

When we first saw the *Galea* it was sitting high and dry in a dimly lit warehouse in Seward. It had a broad beam—good for stability—nice lines, and beautiful Philippine mahogany interior woodwork, but how could we really tell whether or not it was seaworthy? Couldn't just take it for a trial run the way you would a car. We bought it on faith and trailered it to Anchorage.

Bill had done some tinkering with old cars and balky tractors, but he couldn't even get the *Galea's* engine to turn over. It sat in our back yard for a discouragingly long time while Bill tried first one trick and then another. It wasn't until he called in an expert mechanic, Harry Patton, that there was any real progress. Harry gave the engine a vicious kick and swore at it, maybe in more professional and mechanical terms than Bill had been using, and the engine roared to life. Harry pronounced it seaworthy. I won't say it never gave us trouble after that, but its attitude was decidedly more cooperative.

The boat made it possible for us to explore the tidal pools and beaches of Resurrection Bay and Prince William Sound. We had close encounters with humpback whales and listened to them scraping the barnacles off their backs on the bottom of a rusty barge. We had the thrill of catching king crab and halibut, salmon and Irish lords and of experiencing the special beauty of Alaska scenery in a way that is impossible from land, but then we did have some scary moments. I'm not prone to seasickness but I remember some nausea, probably from sheet terror, the time the engine quit as we were passing near jagged cliffs in an on shore wind.

The *Galea* had one troubling idiosyncrasy, which was that, when the motor reached certain rpm it set up a vibration that activated a phantom leak. We would have to man the handheld bilge pump and pails until we reached a higher rpm and the water stopped gushing in. My parents, Kansas farmers whose marine experience was in a row boat on the stock pond, found this particularly unsettling on their first and only trip to Alaska. We took them to Thumb's Cove, where we showed them an especially beautiful tidal pool. When we started halibut fishing, a rope got snagged around the propeller and pulled the shaft loose. Of course, the engine quit and we had to find some other way to get the boat to the beach. I still remember the sight of Bill rowing on the leeward side with the boat's oar, while Dad manned a broom on the port side.

We tied the boat to a big stump. The little children, Mom and I went ashore and the men considered the problem. There was no way to get the prop back in, except for someone to dive into the icy water and shove it in. Bill tried to convince Cam, our oldest boy, that he could do it. Probably thought it was undignified for the captain to be stripped down to his underwear to perform such a lowly chore, but that's what happened in the end. I imagine the job was more excruciating, because there was a boatload of interested, hooting women tied up nearby. Once the prop was reseated, before anything else could go wrong, we headed for dry dock to inspect the repair job. No one seemed anxious to go out again after that. Mom, an inveterate fisherman, seemed content trying to catch flounder off the end of the dock.

The next season we moved the boat to Whittier. We had some memorable and enjoyable adventures, but once when Bill forgot his captain's hat, everything seemed to go wrong. It wasn't just the hat that was still in Anchorage. Bill had forgotten the boat key, too. Not one to give up easily, he tried hot-wiring and got the engine running. It was a beautiful sunny day, maybe a little rough, but everyone was having a good time, until daughter, Carrie, missed a handhold while coming around from the bow and fell overboard. I saw her go and yelled at Bill to turn around. I've never been sure whether the sound of the engine drowned my voice or he (who was supposed to have given up smoking and was obliged to pay the kids a buck if they caught him smoking) didn't want to be discovered puffing away, but I had to pound on his back to get a response. Carrie was beginning to disappear in the wave troughs. I was frantic, but Bill –once alerted—responded with cool dispatch, turned the boat around and brought her close enough for Cam to snag Carrie neatly with the boat hook. Her life jacket had held her well up, so well that though the seawater was streaming from the ends of her pigtails, her little cat's-eye glasses were still firmly in place on the bridge of her nose.

We motored on until the smoke began to rise from the control panel—the hotwire job coming undone. By that time we were in a quiet cove. Bill suggested that we occupy ourselves catching crab while he made repairs. He got the engine going before we caught a crab and we headed for Pigot Bay, where we had the Forest Service cabin for the weekend. We anchored the boat on the longest line and went ashore. It was a beautiful spot, but we lacked readily available drinking water. One of us had to drag a ten-gallon milk can around the cliffs to a little waterfall some distance away. It was heavy to start with and heavier full. We didn't know either, that Pigot Bay completely disappeared at low tide. The next morning, when we woke up the boat was lying on its side. We feared for its prop but could do no more than wait for the tide to come in and see if it was still working. We had breakfast and waited. I sent Cam for water. He decided to take a shortcut over a log between two shale cliffs. When he tried to cross back over with the full can, the log gave way and he fell onto upturned shale as sharp as knives and gouged a chunk of meat out of the inside of his thigh. Fortunately, it didn't cut an artery and his doctor dad was able to bandage him up and get him into the boat. We loaded up and headed for Whittier, where we had to wait several hours—until 4 p.m. for the train to return to the highway. Bill and Cam spent hours in ER while the doctors picked shale out of the wound. Even with a skin graft, it was months before the hole finally granulated in. Taken altogether, the experiences of that day were too much for me. I never wanted to set foot on the *Galea* again. We sold her and I, for one, considered us lucky to be alive. I'm not superstitious but I would never get on a boat with a hatless captain after that day.

# Climbing the Golden Stairs at 70
## Betty Arnett

Boulders! Huge rocks challenging our every step! It is hard, hard going as we keep climbing steadily, gaining an elevation of 3500 feet. We were into our third day of hiking the Chilkoot Trail beginning at Skagway, Alaska on June 21, 2000, and ending at Lake Bennett in Canada on June 26. We saw a few rusty relics here and there that had been left by the gold miners of 1896-97.

Finally, we reached the Scales. That is the spot where the gold miners had all of their loads re-weighed and charged per pound to use the tram up to the summit. No tram exists today. From here we got a look at the infamous Golden Stairs in the distance. They are neither gold or master crafted stairs but a steadily steep climb that kept the early gold miners in a single file line inching their way toward the summit and then on to the Klondike gold. At this point Reinet, my 39 year old daughter-in-law, took my food bag and Hans, my 39 year old son, took my Therm-a-rest Pad and added these things to their loads. I insisted that I could carry them but they wouldn't let me. They were trying to lighten the load in my pack to ease the strain on my body. I hated that they were adding to their load.

Reinet started out ahead of us to lead the way through the snow up the Stairs. She kick stepped into the snowy mountain when necessary to create stair steps but mostly we followed the footprints left by others before us. Two thirds up this steep, steep slope of Stairs we ran out of snow. Here were exposed rocks...big...loose...and no trail. They wanted me to remove my pack and scale the rocks without it, saying Hans would come back down after it. No way was I going to do that to Hans. Besides, how could I go home and say I did the Chilkoot Trail if I didn't carry my pack all the way? I promised to take it off if I became too frightened or felt too insecure. Hans insisted on staying behind me and Reinet led the way through the rocks and boulders, trying to test each step for solid footing. Unfortunately, her stride was longer than mine and I couldn't always follow her. They both kept encouraging me with praise for my efforts. The hiking sticks had been put away and we were on all fours, grasping in gloved hands any rough edges these menacing huge rocks offered. We were now climbing 500 feet of almost vertical, steep, steep, loose rock and boulders. I didn't dare look down for fear it would throw me off balance.

Finally, Hans said, "Mom, if you feel you are scared or about to fall, warn me."

What ever did he have in mind–waving to me on my way down? Oh, I was scared all right, but the ranger had said they had never lost anyone on the final 1000 feet to the summit called the Golden Stairs and I kept reminding myself of that. Also, I kept saying, "God, please don't let there be an earthquake." That would have been the end to all of us. This was indeed the severest challenge I had ever had on a hiking trail. It took us an hour and a half, painfully picking our way through the rocks. They kept encouraging me with praise for each difficult move and almost every move *was* difficult in this section of the Chilkoot Trail. They were constantly concerned for my safety...perhaps even more so than I was. I was able to wear that pack all the way up and down and for that I am very proud. They were more aware of my 70 years than I was. At False Summit, we left the rocks and came onto the snow again. Here we took a rest in an area where the snow had melted away. When we took our packs off and looked back, we saw that the scenery was overwhelmingly gorgeous at this height. Our view up was of majestic white mountain tops. They seemed to survey their tall companions that were also covered with snow. Looking down into the deep valleys below the tree line, lush shades of green came into view.

I told Reinet that once we reached the summit and saw the Canadian flag, she would have to sing the Canadian anthem, since she was Canadian. Immediately, she broke out into song. It is a beautiful anthem and she sang it well. After a short break we continued to climb, climb and climb in the snow until we came to former Gov. Wally Hickel's sign on a high rock. Reinet climbed up and read it to us. It was some sort of greeting about the Trail. This was THE summit and we didn't even realize it. We squeezed through a narrow opening in the rocky terrain and continued trudging along in the footsteps Reinet and other hikers had left behind. At this point, Reinet had gone on ahead and was waiting for us on the Canadian side to take our picture. When we saw the Canadian flag flying on top of the Chilkoot Pass Warden's Station, we danced for joy. Our exhilaration exploded at the sight of this long awaited accomplishment. There was lots of snow, but also lots and lots of sunshine and not much wind. We did a group hug and they both told me they were proud of me and I thanked them for bringing me along as a birthday present for my 70th year. We were exhausted but the victory of making the summit built up quite a bit of adrenalin. Inside the cooking cabin we ate some hot noodles and then enjoyed the luxury of an outhouse. Before leaving we took a photo of the Canadian flag waving in the wind, and yes, Reinet had sung the Canadian national anthem. We had reached summit at 5 p.m. after starting out at 8 a.m.

Hiking through the snow down to Happy Camp was slow, sluggish and tiresome. However, the scenery was fantastic. Snow as far as the eye could see in a Cinerama view of high Canadian mountains against a bright blue sky. Even the lakes below were still covered with snow in this midsummer season. I struggled through the snow. Weary, weary, weary. Tromping through it seemed endless. We finally arrived at 10 p.m. exhausted. We had made the 8.75 miles from Sheep Camp over the summit and into Happy Camp. Some young hikers we had met along the way were gathered at the cook cabin to greet us. They had worried about us and figured we must have defied the Canadian rule and spent the night at the summit cooking cabin. Because of the usually strong winds, the Canadians ask hikers to keep going after a short rest.

While we struggled through the snow those four miles from the summit to Happy Camp, I wondered why the first camp on the Canadian side was built so far away from the summit. It was SNOW! Here, near the end of June, this stretch of the trail was covered with lots of snow. We had been warned that there were only eight campsites free of snow at Happy Camp. Although we were probably the last into camp that night, we got a snow free site upon a hill because one of our new hiking friends had saved it for us. She was Paulette from Massachusetts who had parallel hiked with us for awhile but soon needed to move on, because of her faster pace.

A Canadian girl we had met at the last camp told me how frightened she was climbing the rocks on the Golden Stairs. "I kept thinking of you and how on earth you were going to handle this section. Weren't you scared?" she asked.

"Yes," I admitted, "but I kept talking myself out of it."

"Aren't you proud?!" everybody kept asking.

"Maybe later I'll feel that emotion," I said. "Right now, I am too numb and too exhausted to think at all."

I wasn't hungry but Reinet wanted me to eat. I ate what I could. Hans was sitting out on the small porch of the cook cabin and called in to see how I was doing.

Wearing my headlamp so I could see in the darkened cabin, I answered, "I'm just trying to finish the noodles. I'm not very hungry."

"If they are still hot, I'll finish them for you," he replied. It was important that we didn't leave any food behind in this wilderness cabin because of the bears. Also, we had to haul all of our trash out. Fortunately for me Hans' appetite was up to the task.

I stumbled up the hill to our campsite and went to bed. Hans and Reinet had put two hand warmers inside my silk cocoon inside my sleeping bag. My feet stayed nice and warm. I always slept in the next day's clean dry socks and of course my heavy underwear. I slept warm and cozy all night. The silk cocoon raises the temperature inside my bag 10 degrees so I often pull its hood around my face. Under those conditions my face muscles were so relaxed that my mouth was soon wide open and snoring. I was their entertainment for the night. I'm glad they found it amusing and not irritating.

We intentionally slept in until about 10:30 a.m. I crawled out of the tent and looked for a secluded place beside one of the streams coming down the slopes into the river so I could bathe. I could only find semi-privacy at a stream near the trail leading into Happy Camp. At that point on a hiker's journey the focus is on the camp ahead and not what is happening on the hillside. So I took a chance and removed all of my clothing and sat naked in that stream of cold water with snow all around in the bright warm sunshine. What joy! When hikers did turn and look up at me, they hesitantly waved and politely turned their heads back to the trail. Perhaps they, too, knew the pleasure of submerging one's body into water after strenuous hiking.

I am amazed at how fast others do this trail. I think they must focus on the 33 miles and think, "That's about 10-11 miles per day. I can do that." However, they don't take into consideration the steep terrain, the snow and the time needed to just stop and enjoy the scenery and wild flowers. All along the way, hikers were envious that we were taking six days and conceded that was the way to do it.

Two days later it felt so good to have finished this six day hike. I am so proud of myself for having done it. It was not a piece of cake. Each section had its challenges and easier parts and all were indescribably beautiful. When words fail us, we try cameras. But even they fall short of declaring the beauty Mother Nature provides on this trail.

What a lucky person I am! Can you imagine two young people

willing to take a 70 year old on such an incredible journey?! They were so pleased with my efforts that they now give me an all expense paid hiking/camping trip every birthday.

(Note: I owe the success of this hike in part to Bonnie Murphy, Athletic Director of the Anchorage Senior Center for assisting me in training. **Betty Arnett**) Excerpts from "Hiking the Chilkoot Trail" (at age 70) June 2000 © pending.

# A Very Special New Year's Eve
### Art Elliott

It was supposed to be a different New Year's Eve, a real Alaska holiday spent working in the woods. Fresh air, exercise, good companionship and doing a good deed helping a friend—what a great way to start 1965!

On New Year's weekend, my friend Howard Hanson, was going to haul a prefab cabin the 200 miles to Gulkana, with his old 1950 Dodge power wagon, then to Sourdough and over a trail to Crosswind Lake. The cabin was being put together by another teacher named Bill Johnson.

The old power wagon had been retrofitted with seventeen-inch-wide airplane tires, from an old DC-3. We got it loaded up. Bill Johnson and another friend from Gulkana, Danny Ewan, were coming along. We all offered to take turns riding on top of the load but Bill Johnson said, "No it's too far, and too cold." So he drove up in his little English car.

It took two to three hours to reach the village of Gulkana. In those days most of the houses and buildings were quite small. First we stopped at the home of Oscar Ewan, where Bill was planning to stay. Oscar was the patriarch of the village, a real nice old man. His cabin was kind of typical; there was a caribou head under the table, and a couple of rabbits and so on. Bill invited Howard and me to stay there, but Danny piped up and said we could stay at his cabin. We jumped at the chance.

It was cold; way below zero. Howard had a head bolt heater in the old Dodge, but there were only a couple of places in the village that had electricity–Oscar's cabin and Fred Ewan's store. The parking was easier at Oscar's cabin, so we left the truck there and Bill Johnson said he would take care of plugging it in.

In the morning, after a restless night (because of the missionaries who were also staying at Danny's cabin, and were trying to burn green wood) we discovered the truck was not plugged in.

Bill said, "The cord wouldn't reach, so I plugged in my car."

The truck wouldn't start. Howard had a propane bottle with a weed burner on it. We got hold of a stove pipe with an elbow, put that under the truck, and Howard started up the old flame thrower. It took a while, but it warmed the engine enough we could get it started.

We got ready to go and went into Oscar's cabin to get Bill. They were getting ready to eat, and Oscar was just going to give thanks. He started in by giving thanks for all the good years, and he started in 1936. 1936 was a good year, and we are thankful for that. 1937 was a good year... When he finally finished, we got up.

We drove north to Sourdough and got ready to start on the trail to Crosswind Lake. Bill had told Howard that there wasn't much snow, but there was a foot and a half, so we had to stop and put chains on the old truck. Danny Ewan rode in the cab with us, and Bill and another of the boys from the village rode on the back. We were back in a couple of miles, when this kid started yelling at us to stop.

The oil plug had fallen out, maybe from heating it with the propane torch. Five quarts of oil had leaked out. We followed the trail of oil back to get the plug. It had melted its way down through the snow and into the brush and we couldn't find it. Bill said they would go back to Sourdough to find an old oil plug. Since Howard had brought only five extra quarts of oil, he asked them to bring some more oil, too. They all walked back, and Howard and I waited. Finally they came back with an oil plug that fit and a two gallon GI-colored can labeled "oil." We were back in business.

When we got down the line a bit, it was 30 below and Howard suggested we stop, let the others warm up, and use the weed burner to thaw out the spare oil. He had the heat going on the GI-can when it went "Whoof." It was not oil, but floor wax! We didn't dare go on with no extra oil.

We offloaded the building supplies beside the trail, turned around and went back to Sourdough Lodge. There we found a couple of other guys from Anchorage in a broken-down truck which needed a tow down the road to the service station. Howard agreed to tow them, but first he had to help Bill get his car started. Bill had left the key turned over too far, the heater had been running all day, and the battery was dead. We hooked the chain on and pulled him. Nothing happened so I stopped the truck and I went back.

He said, "How do you start a car when you pull it?"

I said, "Put it in second gear until you get rolling, and then let the clutch out quickly, and it will start."

We pulled it some more, and it started. Then, when Howard turned the truck around to go back, he got the hind wheels, with their smooth tires, a little off the edge of the road and couldn't get up. So, we got the weed burner out again, this time to thaw out the winch.

We hadn't seen a car in all the time we were there, so I stretched the winch cable across the road to hook it onto a telephone pole. Of course, a car showed up right away. That happened three times. Anyway we got out of there and back to the Lodge, where we hooked up the broken-down truck. Bill said he would go ahead and meet us at the station. We got about two miles down the road and there sat Bill's car, not running. He had stopped and it wouldn't start again. So we had to unhook from the truck and hook onto Bill's car and pull him again while I gave him a few words of encouragement. I told him, "Now if you stop this car again Howard won't stop for you. We'll just leave you." So we got him going and told him to keep going. We went back, hooked up, and hauled the other guys.

What else happened? Well, next, our truck ran out of gas, so we had to put the spare gas in it. Finally, we headed back toward Anchorage.

At Glennallen, we stopped at a restaurant. The bathroom water was frozen up.

Somewhere after Eureka Lodge the truck started acting up. We would get it running and it would quit. A big tanker truck came by and gave us a pull. The truck ran for a little bit and quit again. Finally, we pulled over, parked, and got our stuff out. We got a ride to Palmer, where we stayed at the hotel over night. Sunday morning a Valley homesteading friend of ours, Doyle McCombs, picked us up and gave us a ride to Anchorage. When Howard got his truck, he found out the coil was bad.

What a way to start a New Year.

# Beach Balls
## Lois Hermansen

Somewhere in our attic is a crate filled with small green glass balls, a reminder of my first real Alaska adventure. It was the fall of 1973 following our move that summer from Nebraska to Dillingham, Alaska. My husband, Lloyd, had accepted a job as Service Unit Director at Kanakanak Hospital, a Bureau of Indian Health Service area that served 29 villages in addition to Dillingham. This required some travel in small aircraft, which he enjoyed.

My own experience was for the most part vicarious so I was excited when a group of four other women invited me to fly with them on a beach combing trip to Cape Constantine. Ruby Cunningham worked in Medical Records, Sue Lowy as Assistant Director of Nurses, Sharon Walker was the wife of one of the doctors, and Jeanne Kipping was a Public Health Nurse. Most were veterans of the Bush lifestyle. We planned the trip to follow a big sea storm, hoping the wind and waves would carry the ocean's bounty of glass fishing floats to the beaches.

The timing was right on an overcast, cool day. We dressed in rain gear, brought sack lunches, plastic garbage bags to carry our loot, and climbed into a chartered Cessna 207 owned by Krause Air Service. We were not a petite bunch so our pilot, Bob Cummings, loaded us according to size and weight and we took off for the Cape. We flew south and west from Dillingham, skirted the Togiak National Wildlife Refuge, across boggy tundra with lots of little tundra lakes, down to the beach at the tip of the Nushagak Peninsula. Ruby was retiring soon and was hoping to find some special memento to take with her when she returned to Oklahoma, so there was excitement when someone spotted a walrus skull on the beach at Cape Constantine.

Our pilot made his approach and planned to land near the skull, but doing so brought the plane into an area of soft sand causing it to nose down with a thud, bending one of the propeller blades in the process. I had visions of being stuck out there with no way to get home.

Bob surveyed the damage, found a couple of large rocks and roughly straightened the bent prop blade by pounding it between the rocks. The beach provided gifts from the sea—two fairly-long boards which he placed in front of each wheel. He climbed into the plane, revved up the motor, and as we all pushed on the wings, moved forward the length of the boards. He repeated this procedure several times until he was able to position the plane on firm sand nearer the water line. There he gained enough momentum to take off.

Cape Constantine is a barren area with no mountains nearby but with uninterrupted views of the vast Pacific Ocean. The women with prior experience gave advice about the best places to search, high tide areas where little bits of vegetation held sand, seaweed and the Japanese glass floats blown in from the ocean. Soon we were filling our plastic bags with these treasures. It was especially rewarding to find a ball with the cord netting still attached, or one that was larger than the usual softball-sized float. A fox watched us but kept his distance, lending a sense of being in a wild and remote place. We combed the beach, ate our lunches and hoped our pilot had made it back to Dillingham safely. Intermittent light rain dampened our clothing but not our spirits.

Before 4 p.m., our scheduled pickup time, we decided we had found every glass ball in the area. We had also eaten all of our food, and wondered if we should have kept some in reserve. The wind picked up a bit and we began to feel the fall chill. Some thoughtful soul remembered to bring matches so we gathered driftwood and started a fire. We tried to position ourselves near its warmth but out of the range of drifting smoke as we watched for our return flight. Daylight began to fade.

Finally we spotted a speck in the sky that turned out to be our plane. We were elated when it landed down near the water. We doused and buried our campfire and dragged our glass ball filled bags down to the plane. This time it was a smaller Cessna, a 185, piloted by George Krause himself. He did not have much to say as we squeezed ourselves and our bags aboard, and took off quickly. We were a solid mass of bodies and balls and I felt some trepidation as our glass filled bags pressed against us, picturing potential mutilation if we crashed. Nevertheless, there was no way that we were going to leave those treasures behind.

The flight back to Dillingham was uneventful and subdued. As we landed, George made the only comment we heard from him about the mishap. Spotting Bob Cummings near the airstrip, George muttered, "There's your hotshot pilot."

A new propeller for a Cessna 207 was pricey even in 1973, and I'm afraid Krause Air Service made no profit on our beachcombing charter.

# White Water River Rafting
## Betty Russell

I was in my early sixties when, while visiting my daughter in Alaska, I was invited to go white-water river rafting with her and some friends. I thought it was some type of "Disney" type ride on a rail. Boy was I in for a surprise! Furthermore, the day we were to leave, someone mentioned that they noticed in the paper that two photographers for National Geographic, who had been standing up in a raft taking pictures, were thrown overboard and drowned. Well, I'm definitely not much of a daredevil, so I wanted to give my ticket away, but my daughter wasn't about to let me off the hook.

We drove to the staging area, where we joined the rest of the party on a truck which drove us down a gravel road to the river. The boat crew put raincoats and life vests on everyone. They pushed me onto the raft and announced the swells that day were rated about a four (on a scale with the highest a five.) To say that I was a reluctant passenger was putting it mildly.

With my heart pounding, I held on to my seat as the raft swirled down the rapids, water sloshing over the sides, splashing over us. Everyone except for me was bailing the water out as fast as it came in. All I could do was to hang on for dear life and scream!

Finally, we landed and they handed me out. I would have been happier about the blessed dry ground if it was the end, but it was only half-way and this was just a lunch and potty break. I was surprisingly hungry, and ate most of my sack lunch; then it was back to the raft. If there was any other transportation, I would have taken it.

To my surprise, the water began to calm down and I began to enjoy the magnificent scenery. I was the oldest person on the raft and our guide let me use the paddle for a while. I managed to steer us around in circles. The guide referred to me as "Mom." We drifted lazily, enjoying the day and the conversation, until, too soon, we came to the landing place.

That evening when I had time to reflect on what an exciting adventure it had been, I decided it had been one of the most exhilarating days of my life.

# Overflow on the Susitna River
## Jan Boylan

I had wanted to make this snow machine trip for several years, and the first year my hubby and I were invited, I couldn't go. The second year I was called out of state on family business. Then in 2003 I was able to make the trip without mishap. We had such a good time; I eagerly looked forward to once again trying to keep up with the guys.

The trip began on the first weekend in March, 2004. After meeting Friday morning for breakfast and pictures in front of Eureka Lodge (about 125 miles east of Anchorage on the Glenn Highway) loading up with extra gas, sleeping bag, and clothes for three more days, fifteen of us took off early Friday on our snow machines.

We headed north across the rolling hills and canyons behind Eureka Lodge en route to the Gracious House about ninety miles from Cantwell on the Denali Highway, about 126 miles away by snow machine. I had studied a map of the area and had some idea where we were most of the time, but sometimes I was completely lost, and depended on the guys to make sure I got where I was going. Jon, Ken, and Dave knew nearly every hill and valley, and I knew they knew where they were going. The faster riders led the way, and a few of us slow pokes brought up the rear. My hubby was the "sweeper" and always came last to make sure nobody got separated from the crowd. Every so often the leaders would stop to make sure we were still all together, and then we would catch up and they would take off again. If they came to a really tough spot in the trail they would all wait to make sure we all made it through safely. There would be plenty of help in case of mishap.

Shortly after we started up the Susitna River, traveling on the snow atop the ice-covered river, we saw an airplane fly close overhead and land on a nearby sand bar. We rode over to talk to the pilot. He told us there was a lot of overflow on the river up near the bridge on the Denali Highway, and we should find an alternate route. From then on we stuck close to the side of the river where we could jump out on the bank in case of problems, and we found them soon enough.

Dave Miranda ran into overflow, but was able to ride to the river bank and not get wet. Others followed him onto the shore. The rest of us followed cautiously, but stopped on the river very near the bank where the ice held firm, as the leaders had stopped and blocked the path. Jon Kolbeck stopped ahead of us, in the mouth of a creek. He was staying on top of the ice just fine until he tried to move again. Then the back of his sled (snow machine) went down through the ice and the track was pushing water when it spun. Fortunately, the skis held on to firmer ice pack, preventing the machine from sinking in the deep river. A couple of the men grabbed a ski each and tried to pull the machine ahead out of the hole in the ice, but when Jon tried to help it along by giving it gas, the water from the spinning track doused them good. They immediately went to rolling in the snow to dry off before the water could penetrate their clothing. It was cold, and nobody wanted to get chilled and hypothermic, as we were still quite a distance from our destination.

Dale Rosenbaum put a rope on Jon's sled to tow the snow machine out, but as soon as he put a little pressure on the rope, he, too, found himself with his track underwater and the skis hanging on. Jim Fimple had a wide track, so he came to the rescue. He had started to back up to Dale's sled to pull it out, when we noticed there was a patch of grass sticking up through the snow a little to the right. Better to pull him up on land instead of up the creek. Dale's sled was successfully pulled to safe harbor, and then Jon.

Again we were on our way. This time we were on land with no trail to follow. Don, my hubby, knew the area and he told us there was an old tractor trail to the highway, which we should try to find. We were all running low on fuel, and we didn't relish the idea of spending a night out, while someone went for fuel. We wanted to find that trail. So, off we went.

The year before we had arrived at the Gracious House after a great but uneventful ride, at about 4 p.m. This trip we were on the trail until after 6 p.m. Butch, our host was watching for us, and was glad to hear us coming. He was waiting along the trail to lead us in the final five miles of our trip, or to send out a search party if we didn't arrive soon. We arrived at the lodge very hungry, and quickly put the ovens to use warming up the lasagna we had sent in frozen the week before. After dinner we all dropped into our sleeping bags on the cots provided in the warm lodge, and had a well-deserved rest.

The weekend was spectacular for riding snow machines. Our party broke up into smaller groups and went in search of Mr. Snow and more adventure. The weather was clear, the snow was a soft deep powder, and everybody came in to dinner with a great story to tell. A few had break-downs and one had to be towed home. His riding was over for the weekend. Some told "I really got stuck" stories, easy to do in the deep powder. Some even had "the light turned flat" stories. It is no fun to ride in flat light when you can't tell if the ground goes up or down, and it is possible to run into a snow bank dead ahead without ever seeing the rise in the ground, or to fall into a hole you can't see because of the light. Still, a good time was had by all, and everyone was eager to go back out the next day for more riding.

Sunday a couple of the guys went in search of a better trail to get back down the river past the overflow, and came in that evening having scouted out a trail for our trip home. We would need to travel along the river bank for about ten miles, before we could again ride the river where going was much easier. It is not uncommon in the Alaska winter for rivers to have overflow. Water comes from springs and if there is no place to travel, it simply follows gravity and lies on top of the river ice, creating overflow. It then freezes over, and another layer of ice is formed in the cold. Sometimes the water flows from beneath the ice, and causes empty layers to form, depending on the particular river, springs, lay of the land, etc. This phenomenon usually presents a challenge, but being aware of the problem helps give someone a chance to prevent trouble.

Monday morning we were up early, ate breakfast, loaded our gear on the back of our snow machines, filled the gas tanks and cans, and started off for the trail back to Eureka Lodge. We stayed on land until the leaders felt it was safe to get back on the river. We were making good time, crisscrossing to find the best part of the river for travel. Unfortunately, the overflow had traveled much farther down river during the night and the leaders were having trouble staying out of the water. It wasn't deep, but there was a layer of frigid water under the thin ice, and on top of the much deeper ice which had frozen over the river earlier in the winter, and which was still solid.

I was oblivious, thinking they were men and knew what they were doing. They had never gotten me in any trouble, and trusting soul, fearless rider, silly woman, I just followed wherever they would lead. All went well until we came to a slight bend in the river. Part of the group branched off for the shore, but I didn't see them until I was already going the other way, after the daredevils. I knew immediately that was a mistake. The ice had no snow cover at that spot and was too slick for me to handle a quick turn, so I just kept going until I felt it would be safe to turn to the shore. Unfortunately I never got the chance because the snow machine started to swap ends and turn circles on ice I knew wasn't very thick. I got it straightened out once, and was on my way again, when it decided to make another turn without any encouragement from me. Suddenly one ski broke through the thin top layer of ice, and the snow machine threw me and landed on its side in about a foot of overflow. It didn't take me all day to stand up on the thick river ice, so I didn't get wet, except for my lower pant legs. The bunny boots[1] I was wearing were barely high enough to keep the water from my feet. Here I was, standing in the water, trying to figure out what to do next. I tugged and tugged, without success trying to flip the stubborn Polaris snow machine back up on its track, but my backpack and sleeping bag, which were tied to the back of my snow machine were soaking up the water, and there was no way.

My hubby was swimming his snow machine around me, checking out my dilemma and throwing up a wake so the cold water crawled over the top of my boots. Finally after learning that his snow machine really could swim circles around me, Don parked on shore and started to wade out to me.

The guys on shore were trying to figure out a way to help without getting wet. I saw no sense in anybody else getting wet and kept yelling at them to stay out of the water; two people were easier to dry out than fifteen.

Help was on the way so I waited for Don, and together we were finally able to turn the sled over. While Don tried to get the snow machine started after its bath, I waded to shore, breaking about an inch of ice on top as I went. It just wouldn't hold me, but the ice below the overflow was very solid.

By now, there was a long rope ready, so I took the end of it and waded back to the machine about seventy-five feet out in the middle of the river. Don had been able to get the machine started, but we couldn't get any traction in the water. Between us we were able to get the rope around the spindle of the snow machine so the men on shore could pull us in without getting wet. Don helped push and guide the machine while I tried to walk along beside and handle the throttle and the handlebar.

After only about forty-five minutes, which seemed like hours, we finally got safely to shore, cooled off a bit from the exertion, and we were ready to start off again. Fortunately neither Don nor I were wet except for our feet and hands. Our body heat soon warmed the water in our well-insulated bunny boots, so our feet weren't cold, and the heated handle grips on the snow machine would quickly dry our gloves when we got moving.

We started out again. The leaders broke trail and kept us on the bank of the river. Our only concern was that we would run low on fuel, but we decided if that happened we could build a fire to stay warm, and siphon gas from some of the machines into others, so someone could go fill the gas cans. We never felt like we were in any real danger.

After another several miles we could safely travel on the river again, and made good time getting back to the Glenn Highway and a wonderful meal furnished by Jim and Darla Fimple of the Eureka Roadhouse. At dinner that night I lamented the fact that I had caused so much trouble, when Ken Bodensteiner informed me that it was a great day. "Now the rest of these guys have somebody to talk about besides me."

[1]*Bunny boots. A special flight boot made for use by the air force during WWII for high altitude flying. They keep your feet warm, even if your feet get wet and are commonly used in Alaska during the winter by outdoor enthusiasts.*

# My Ride to Where?

## Louise Gallop

The year was 1960. I was an innocent tourist from New York, ignorant of Alaska's strange ways.

Going from Fairbanks to Anchorage by bus seemed simple enough in the bus office when I bought my ticket. I'd go from Fairbanks to Tok (wherever that was), spend the night, then continue on to Anchorage the next day. I asked about a reservation for the night. "No need," I was told, "there's always space." Fine. Workers at the bus depot would surely know.

Everything went well until we got to Tok and I learned I was the only one getting off. But then—help—there wasn't a room to be had. Some big event was taking place (yes really, in Tok!) Every bed in the one hotel was taken. Every single one! It was the same at a tiny motel, the only other lodging nearby.

I wasn't the only one stranded, it seemed. Two bus drivers were also left without lodging. I will call them Driver A (for Anchorage) and Driver F (for Fairbanks). They found that their permanent rooms had been commandeered. I gathered they needed other rooms, too, for people arriving later from the South.

As I wondered what to do, the hotel manager offered me a cozy spot to spend the night–under the pool table in the lounge after everything closed up. Right then it was 2 p.m. But the bus drivers came with news. They had located beds for all of us at Northway, further along the road. That sure beat the floor in Tok, and I'd love to ride some more. Gratefully, I got back on the bus.

We drove and drove. At Northway, Driver F said, "Why not go the rest of the route with us? There's nothing in Northway to do, and we'll come back here."

Great–a chance for more sightseeing. At the motel, I ran to the office, left my suitcase and called, "Don't rent my room, I'll be back with the bus." I settled down in my seat again.

We traveled on and on–further than from Tok to Northway–and suddenly... No! I couldn't believe the sign. We'd crossed into Canada!

Something, somehow, I'd misunderstood. I couldn't remember a word about coming to Canada. I was in a foreign land, my luggage was hours and miles behind, and we kept on–another ten miles or more. Then we stopped nowhere at all. Out of that nowhere, a man appeared–the Customs Agent. He came aboard and was handed a very official list–the names of my fellow passengers. One by one he checked us off, until he got to me. He couldn't find my name, of course.

"I'm not going to Canada," I said. It wasn't quite the truth; I was already there.

He looked at me, nodded, and moved on. So—I wasn't headed for jail. Where was I headed? I still didn't know–not until we reached Beaver Creek.

A Canadian bus met us. The buses traded passengers so they could continue their journey–some to Whitehorse, some to Alaska.

We hit Northway very late at night. There wasn't a sign of light or life. Driver F and Driver A made coffee for us in the café. They found our keys and sent us to bed.

Since we really should have been in Tok, we had to make an early start so Driver A could collect his bus there, and get started toward Anchorage on time.

Compared to the day before, that leg of the trip was tame. I do remember two things, though. A few of the passengers were tinged with the strange smells of dried salmon and home-cured hides. Somewhere along the Richardson, Driver A hauled me (the only tourist) to the roof of the bus for a shot of a scenic view better than I could get from my seat.

The next summer, with a teaching job secure, I came back to Alaska to stay. I'm pretty sure my unorthodox trip was a big part of the reason I decided to return.

# Crash!! Surviving the 1976 Mt. McKinley Hang Gliding Expedition

## Mason Wade

### June 2, 1976

It was so unbelievable that we really had made the summit. After twenty-six days of glider grunting, we stood on North America's highest peak: 20,230 feet above sea level! Mt. McKinley rises right up out of the tundra with a vertical rise of 18,000 feet. Fourteen years of living in Alaska, I had dreamed of this moment, and the three other pilots were beaming with the same anticipation. Already, Ed, Bob, Kent and I fantasized about doing full circle turns around Mount Hunter, then flying over Wonder Lake and thermaling for miles from the warmth 18,000 feet below!

Our flight path had been decided months earlier. We had ascended via the West Buttress route, which was the least difficult way to drag, carry or push the gliders. The McKinley National Park Service refused us permission to land in park territory. We had no choice but to land at the Kahiltna International, a runway on the Kahiltna Glacier. This is a common starting point for West Buttress expeditions, and is located at 7,000 feet elevation, just outside the park's boundary near the western base of Mt. Hunter.

Oddly enough, we were not alone at the top. From the other side of the summit, two women appeared, carrying no water or gear, and heavily fatigued. They were members of the Denali '76 All-Women Expedition. They explained that two of their party were severely injured on the South Buttress and were waiting for help at around 19,000 feet. Rodger, our cinematographer, manned the radio to reach the chief ranger, and the girls tried to rest and regroup. Our operation was delayed in a rescue situation.

Getting the gliders to the summit was no piece of cake. Originally, we had intended to make our base camp as close to the launch area as possible in case inclement weather, not at all unusual for McKinley, forced us to reschedule our take-off. Two days earlier we started to dig in at 19,000 feet until Jim was warned by radio that a jet stream with 100 m.p.h. winds would make that altitude unsafe for us. Back down to 17,000 feet we went, passing our cached gliders at 18,000 feet, weary from the necessary extra effort and disappointed at another day's delay. Once we established camp, we were able to grunt the gliders up to 19,000 feet the following day.

Weak from weeks of high altitudes and dwindling food supplies, the last grueling 1,230 feet of the haul seemed endless. I would drag my glider two feet, then have to force in five large lungfuls of thin air to get enough oxygen to move on. We may have been worn, but we were all ready to fly! We were hoping to be airborne by 6 p.m. Already the time was well past 7 p.m. We unsnapped the glider covers.

It was eerie. The air was so still that foot-launching to the north may have caused problems getting around the summit and its plateau at 19,000 feet. We might not have been able to get enough altitude to head south for the landing site. We all agreed on a launch from the South Face. However, hidden from our vantage point was a treacherous finger of cornice snow protruding from the face.

At 20,000 feet and as far north as we were, light was no problem. Twilight, the subarctic night condition, wasn't due until 11 p.m. Despite the clearness of the day so far, pressure was building, and storm clouds were slowly moving in from the northeast. Far below, clouds blanketed the earth like fluffy cotton. We were being warned to hurry.

The setup area was just waiting for us: a flat spot a few feet below the summit afforded us plenty of room for our wings. The direct sun was warm on our faces, and with the strange windless condition we were able to use bare hands on our safety clips. The view was incredibly breathtaking. All around us snow- capped peaks drained into rivers of ice flowing to the green lowlands of spring. Far in the distance, thousands of small lakes reflected the evening sun.

Bob won the toss and was to be the first to fly. The rest of us would stagger our launches within seconds of each other. The idea was to fly in formation for the filming. We couldn't help remembering this had never been done before.

I had a hard time getting my harness over five layers of clothing.

Not knowing exactly what to expect temperature-wise, we wore all of our expedition Polarguard clothing. I felt prepared to sky out at 40,000 feet. I had a 35 mm wide-angle motor-driven camera at the tail of my glider, and to counterbalance that weight, a lead nose plate. With my glider cover stuffed under my bulky jacket, I wasn't feeling all that light and agile.

Everybody was ready and waiting, but the filming helicopter was late in arriving. We fidgeted and grumbled a bit, annoyed with yet another stall, and did not relish the colder night air creeping in on us. Still no sound of the chopper. Rodger got on the two-way radio to find that his cameramen had been forced back to Talkeetna, some 75 miles away, to refuel. Minutes turned into hours. We began to talk about scrapping the film and taking off without the chopper.

Bob checked his batteries one more time. Since the 15,000 foot mark, Bob had broadcasted our progress to listening ham radio jocks over half the state of Alaska. He planned to transmit during flight, with the radio strapped to his lower arm. KANC, the "top or rock" radio station, was one of our expedition sponsors. They agreed to broadcast his live in-flight transmission. Bob moved his radio under his jacket, since severe cold shortens battery lifespan rapidly.

It must have been 10 p.m. when we saw the helicopter nearing us. We all clicked into action mode, and watched as Bob clipped in for a final harness check. It would be only a few running steps, then a drop of 10,000 feet over the South Face. He began his launch, running and then off. Suddenly, he sank from sight. Ed and Kent were horror stricken. In a few seconds that seemed like eons, Bob rocketed into view and away from us, traveling pretty fast, probably more than 30 m.p.h.. From my starting position I couldn't see exactly what went down, and assumed that at the outset he hadn't attained enough airspeed, and had barely recovered from a mushing stall. As I surveyed Bob's footprints in the snow left for me to follow, I wondered what his first words to our waiting public were.

Amazingly, I called my mother on ham radio at 20,320 feet just before takeoff. She spent the night praying.

A final harness check from Gene, our backup pilot, another couple of deep breaths, and I was trucking down the snow ramp, and then off into the air. I proned out a little early, but kept up my speed. Just as I was starting to feel the majesty of the scene around me, my left wing hit the southern cornice. The impact and the hard whip to the left forced the left corner of my control bar to smash into the hard packed snow. I jolted through the bar like a ragdoll, and realized I was becoming a rock instead of a bird. As my right wing dropped under me, I went over the edge. A yawing motion had rotated me

180° in the harness. I could see the faces of my friends on the summit contorted with terror. They watched as I fell to certain death. My speed was increasing as I dropped quietly. Time had stopped for me. It was now a matter of exploding apart on the rocks or freezing to death in a crevasse 10,000 feet below.

Well, it really happens like they say in near-death experiences. Incidents in my life sped through my head. Three years of fantastic flying, my twenty-first birthday dinner party at 10,000 feet, my girl-friend, my family and lifelong buddies ... I didn't want to leave now. Could I stop my fall somehow? It would be foolish for anyone to look for my remains. Soon it would snow and I would disappear under a white blanket. Slowly the glacier would take care of my body in its own way.

It reverberated through me again and again. I was hitting the mountain like a stone bouncing down a cliff. My mind was still churning when I stopped with one final thud. I was breathing hard, and tried to focus my eyes on the sky to get my bearings. I was in control again and evaluating my present situation. I began to hear yells above me. I checked for broken bones and concentrated on relaxing myself. Miraculously, about 800 feet from the summit my mangled control bar had pinned me to a large, steep slab of snow.

My first impulse was to remain stationary for fear that any movement at all would start me sliding again. Looking around, I found myself spread-eagle on the top side of the glider sail. I was tangled in the cables which were severed by the many collisions with sharp mountain rock. I slowly unwound and unhooked. Bracing against the broken glider tubes, I was able to pull myself uphill.

The first big problem was over. I was no longer attached to the wreckage. The glider was twisted pretzel-fashion, and the wingtips were missing. Only the kingpost was intact.

My partner, Ed, was shouting down to me, pleading with me to move around and show some signs of life. After a self-inspection, I shouted back that I was okay even though a few of my ribs stabbed at my lungs every time I took a breath. I was in total survival mode, and ran down a list of several important things in my head. I cautioned myself not to lose my wits and go into shock. I started testing my footing, digging my toes in against the hard snow to make footholds. After the first few steps, I realized I would need crampons to make it. Funny, I hadn't packed them in my flying gear. I used my kingpost as an ice axe, and edged a few more feet from the wrecked glider. It was too steep to go much further without a rope around my waist.

The gang at the crest was trying to decide how to rescue me. All the climbing equipment had been left in camp at 17,000 feet. Even at that, the ropes were too short to reach me. If a traverse rescue from a lower point on the summit ridge was attempted, the risk of an avalanche would be extremely high. We urgently shouted back and forth, and decided that the only one of our party qualified to lead the rescue was Gary, our co-leader. Unfortunately, due to so many unforeseen delays, Gary had remained resting at 17,000 feet, exhausted by the stress of the climb. It must have been midnight by the time Kent left to get him.

Bivouacking for the night without tent or supplies wasn't my idea of a good time. I wasn't sure how long I would have to wait for Kent to return with Gary, but I estimated it would be a good six hours. If the wind started to blow, the temperature would drop enough to claim my toes and fingers. I had to build some sort of shelter while I was still able to move.

Where I was situated was as good a place as any. First I stomped out a level platform. Now, except for me, everything around was vertical. Straight up and down. Using the kingpost, I started breaking snow away from the top of the slab. I made a niche barely large enough to house my body in a tight curl. This would help in conserving body heat. And with any more scraping, the soft snow-ceiling of the cave might have collapsed. I gingerly approached the glider once more, found the camera in one piece , and removed it. Hopefully a few shots were triggered off. Grabbing a handful of broken battens, I left the aircraft for the last time. At the edge of my platform, I made a fence with the battens. This would prevent me from rolling off if I passed out from shock. I used my glider cover to insulate me from the cold floor and crawled into my shelter to wait.

I was still wearing my harness and helmet, and the foam padding in my UP cloud harness was a definite plus in keeping me warm. The night was so quiet. The glistening peaks mesmerized me. I began to drift off a bit in my front row seat, then quickly alerted myself, remembering how important it was for me to stay awake. And alive.

The crew moved further down the summit ridge to better view my predicament. They set up emergency rescue camp at 19,700 feet; luckily someone had brought a tent. Gene and Ed alternated shifts to keep me talking. I heard Gene singing with his strong, resonant voice, and joined in. Staring at Gene's silhouette against the night sky, I was comforted by the closeness which passes between friends of many years. I forgot how cold my toes were. Maybe it was 3 a.m.

### Daybreak June 3, 1976

Groggy, and positive it would stay dark forever, I was overjoyed to see a sheet of light gradually moving westward. Ed ordered me to move around to get my circulation going. I looked out to greet the dawn at what must have been 4:30 a.m. I was hoarse from yelling. Getting any energy up was impossible. I crawled to a stand and glanced down at an avalanche billowing on a distant face. Fear electrified me once more. I was located in the middle of one huge chute. For a moment I thought I could see the rescue party only minutes away. I waited–tense, exhausted, drained and praying to see Gary soon. I went crazy as I watched the figures turn away from the summit. To save heat, I crawled back into my slot, wondering what would become of me. Ages later, I heard Gary calling to me.

The party that turned away was yet another expedition with a gravely sick member. I was glad to see Gary, well prepared with rope, water and enough Dexadrine to get everybody back on their toes. He took the direct route down the shoot to reach me. With Gene as anchor man, Gary descended to the end of his fixed line. It was no easy feat. The last half of the distance he had to free descend to my shelter. There he was, draped with camera, jumars, crampons and ice axes, looking like Spiderman. I leaned over to put on my crampons, and realized how burnt out I was as Gary handed me the water and the Dexadrine.

Buzzing by us every minute or so, a Lear jet encircled the mountain. It must have been the search party for the missing Denali women. The noise of the engine threatened to trigger a sizeable avalanche directly over our heads. We quickly began our ascent.

This was the steepest part of the climb I had encountered the entire trip. I was hoping the Dexadrine would kick in some power soon, and after a few delays, I started tuning in to the enjoyment of climbing. Nearing the narrow shoot to the ridge, we were both startled by a mammoth Air Force HC-130 roaring over the summit. My buddies had placed a call for emergency rope and supplies, and the drop was made short of the ridge. Fortunately, we were almost home free, as long as the plane didn't precipitate a snow slide.

A large cloud engulfed the summit bringing with it light winds just as we pulled ourselves over. I was glad to be on top. Waiting in my little hole would have been sheer terror now, with winds that might have dropped the temperature severely or blown me off the face.

The cloud began to disperse by the time we descended to the rescue tent. There, I blinked my eyes in disbelief. Buddy Woods was trying to land his hotrod turbine helicopter next to the tent! Buddy had been flying our teams to the top of great mountains for the past two years, and is one of Alaska's super bush pilots. He must have been scouting for the two injured women, for he made another pass and flew off.

My strength was ebbing. I was roped to Gene, and we were already lagging behind the others. I was able to persevere because of

Gene's constant encouragement and ignored the pain all over me. All of a sudden Buddy returned, and promptly landed at 19,000 feet. Prior to this it was amazing that a helicopter could make a rescue attempt at 14,000 feet! Buddy spoke quickly with those ahead of us for information about the Denali women, and then was up as quickly as if he had taken off at sea level. Within a turn, he was above and over the summit. I knew he would find the expeditioners.

The sun was low in the sky, and the camp was in shadows as we approached 17,000 feet. Movement was excruciatingly slow. Gene was patient and understanding, even though the others were a good hour ahead of us. The trail was well used, but we had to descend carefully and stay roped. Denali Pass teased us with its 1,000 foot vertical face. Below us the crevasses gaped. The drugs had worn off completely long before I reached camp, and I was delirious with fatigue. By the time I recognized my tent, I could only stagger to bed, armed with the extra sleeping bags left behind by our one successful flier. It was pure heaven to sleep.

### June 4, 1976

Because of the drain of the past two days, everyone slept late this morning. The weather was perfect for flying. Ed and Kent hurried to the summit and their stashed gliders to take a birthday soar for Kent. I had slept well, but still ached. Camped next to us was, yes, another expedition which had brought a physician along. He gave me the once over and told me all I needed was plenty of rest. This, after having plummeted 800 feet down the side of the tallest peak in North America!

As it drew near their estimated launch time, all expeditioners made their way to the ridge to watch for the gliders. Gene spotted Ed first, and the crowd became quietly transfixed. Everybody's face was skyward. Ed was looking good, so small, just slowly moving in the sky.

The cameras were clicking, and then Kent popped into sight. Soon they were tiny specks in the virtually cloudless heights. Gene and I watched the Kahiltna for almost an hour, trying to spot their landings. We spent the time talking up another McKinley flight, and how we'd organize it. Then we turned back to the tents for some serious card playing.

*This account is one chapter of a multifaceted experience. It is dedicated to the memory of Gene Maakestad, who died some two months later in a hang glider accident. It is Mason Wade's story. Reprinted with permission from the book, "Crash!! Surviving the 1976 Mt. McKinley Hang Gliding Expedition" by Mason Wade, published by Northbooks, Eagle River, Alaska.*

# Memorable Happenings

# The Snow Shoe Race
## Dorothy H. Kruger

In 1992, long time friend, Dolores Roguszka, and I entered the snowshoe race sponsored by the Anchorage Senior Center. This was a new addition to the festivities for the annual Fur Rendezvous event. It had been 25 years since Dolores had been on a pair of snowshoes, and I had never used a pair. But we were game. After all, all those entering would be seniors too, so we felt we could hold our own.

Just before we were to line up for the race, an old moose walked through the area, leaving deep holes in one portion of the course before he could be driven off. From the starting line we could see those monster holes but were not concerned about them. We should have been.

We lined up, and an old sourdough looked us over and said, "I'll take the skinny one." Well! How rude! Dolores and I immediately decided we didn't want to be that old fart's partner anyway. At the same time, this quite attractive, and *skinny* black lady stepped forward to take her place beside him. Somewhat affronted by his insolent remark, Dolores and I were still undaunted and more than ready to go.

Dolores was the first one off. She was making good time as she rounded the curve heading toward the moose holes. She was safely by the first one, and then the second one, when the third one got her. Down she went. Didn't she see it? My niece Myrna would have said, "Of course she saw it! She hit it didn't she?"

Dolores's legs are short. The moose's legs were long. Dolores couldn't get out of the moose hole. The more she struggled, the deeper she went. Things couldn't get worse. But of course they did. Sitting half in and half out of the moose hole, Dolores had an asthma attack! Round the course went that nasty old sourdough and his *skinny* partner! And then again! Dolores coughs and struggles. And coughs and struggles. Unable to get to her the crowd calls out encouragement. Finally, red faced with exertion, Dolores is able to pull herself out of that moose hole and gamely tries to make up lost time.

Then it's my turn. I thought I was flying around that course, but I was probably going at a snail's pace. Naturally the old sourdough and his *skinny* partner won the race, but in spite of it all, Dolores and I did come in second! (The fact that there were only two teams entered in this race is nothing we need to bring up, of course.)

Two years later, Vivian's husband Don MacInnes, my husband Paul and I enter the race again. This time there must have been about 16 people entered. Determined to win this time, I held back and watched to see just who was on each relay team. Then I chose the team with the most men on it. As soon as I stepped in line with my carefully chosen team mates, the man in charge pulls an 81-year-old lady out from the line of the opposing team and puts her in front of our line. Oh, dear. Was I to be foiled again? Or maybe, just maybe, this little lady would turn out to be the Champion Snow Shoe Racer of all Alaska and I would go home with my blue ribbon after all.

Soon the "Official with the Whistle" gave a toot and away we went. Two members of the opposing team made it around the course in the same amount of time it took our diminutive 81-year-old team-mate to make it around once. But my momentary disappointment was soon lost in the excitement of the race. Never have I seen such determination! We all cheered her on at the top of our lungs. She might have been going so slowly she seemed to be going back-wards, but she completed the entire course without even stopping to catch her breath. Or was it that she wasn't moving fast enough to have even lost her breath? I don't know. But I do know, that like the trooper she obviously was, she gritted her teeth, put her head down, and placed one foot in front of the other until she'd finished her turn around. We all gave her a standing ovation.

Because we were so far behind, every man on our team attacked the course at a *run* trying to make up time. Naturally every man on our team *lost* time by falling down. So it was second best again. Oh, well, it was worth it and there's always another race. Someday I'll try again. I'd still like to come in on the winning team.

# New Arrival
## Pauline Lee Titus

Having newly arrived in Alaska in 1962, I was determined to see as much of the state as I possibly could. I joined the Alaska Prospector's Society, whose motto is, "To see and know Alaska."

My very first trip with them was to Kennicott Copper Mine on a chartered Cordova Airlines DC3. As we approached May Creek, the pilot circled round and round. All I could see was green everywhere. Then I spotted a "band aid" among the trees.

"Yipes, is that where we're going to land?"

My traveling companion said, "That's it."

But the scariest part of the trip was going from the May Creek landing strip to Kennicott. A Model A flatbed truck with seats on each side of the back met us and took us up the Mizina Canyon wall to Kennicott.

There had been a landslide earlier, and the road had been graded just wide enough for one vehicle to pass through. We went over the slide area with the sheer wall on one side and a steep drop on the other.

At McCarthy, we walked among the empty, closed houses of what was then a ghost town. They told us there had been dishes left on tables, glasses on the bar, and other abandoned belongings everywhere. The mine owners had suddenly arrived in town, told the people the mine was closed and that the last train would leave in a few hours.

We had lunch at the lodge and toured the mine. We were not allowed to enter the buildings, but we drove between the glacier and the towering old buildings.

Then we flew to Cordova, where we had an all-you-can-eat crab dinner, cracking crab on plates made of freshly sawed log rounds. After dinner, we were taken to the historic Windsor Hotel, a rambling collection of rooms that backed on the mountain, so that you could climb two or three flights from the lobby to your room and find yourself looking out the window at ground level.

The next morning, we were picked up by a school bus, given box lunches and taken to see the Million Dollar Bridge. It was intact then. You could walk across it, although we didn't. It partly fell down during the 1964 earthquake, and is no longer as impressive.

We ate our lunch on a sunny bank overlooking Child Glacier, which was calving regularly. One berg that broke off was so large it sloshed and splashed on us clear across the river. After lunch, we visited a salmon tender and then flew back to Anchorage, where it felt like we had stepped out of the past into the present.

# The Leaky Tent
## Jon Kolbeck

In the spring of 1963, after spending the winter in Florida, my buddy and I decided to come to Alaska. Jobs were kind of short. We looked for work from April until June, and then went to Cordova because George Atkinson, of A and G Construction, had a job there and he wouldn't take us because, he said, they were going to "hire local."

We stayed in a leaky tent outside of town. After a day or two, we walked downtown and saw George at the gas station. He asked, "What are you doing here?"

We said, "Well you said you were going to hire local. We are about as local as we can get."

He said it would be a few days. So we waited a few days, until June 9th, which was my birthday. Here we were, it was my birthday and we were about broke, lying around in a tent that leaked and leaked. I went down and actually spent the night in the lobby of the Northern Hotel, where George was staying. The next morning I went to his room and banged on his door. I said, "When are we going to go to work?"

He said, "It will be a couple of days, what room are you staying in?"

I told him, "I'm not staying in a room; I'm staying in a leaky tent."

"Oh, well you go get your stuff, and come on down. We are hauling the kitchen out there today."

So we got our stuff and rode out fifty two miles across the "Million Dollar Bridge," and started setting up camp, and I slept in a real building that night.

We were building the road from the bridge to Chitina. We worked until October, when we got froze out. Before the next season, the 1964 earthquake wiped out the bridge and ended the road project. But by then I had a little money and didn't need to sleep in a leaky tent.

# Steaming Duck Farts
## (Ice Bowling)
### Dorothy H. Kruger

On the outskirts of Anchorage, Alaska, on the highway to Seward, is a bar called The Peanut Farm. This is a large, handsome, log building with a small pond in the back where ducks congregate to raise their families in the summer time. But in the winter, the pond freezes over and the ducks fly south. This leaves the frozen water to the human populace who hold their annual Ice Bowling Contest during Fur Rendezvous every February.

For this sport, real bowling balls and pins are used, and lines are painted on the ice to form the lanes. Bales of hay are brought in to make a safe box for the bowling balls to roll into at the end of each painted "alley." Young boys are hired to act as pin setters and an outside bar is set up which features the special, and widely acclaimed drink of this social event. This novel drink uses hot coffee as a base, a jigger of Crown Royal is then added, topped with a little Kahlua, and finished off with a dab of good old Baileys Cream. This unique drink is called "Steaming Duck Farts," and is well known from one end of Alaska to the other.

Ice bowling can be a serious business for some of the more dedicated bowlers in Anchorage, but for some of us it's a time of happy camaraderie and good clean fun. Not to mention an opportunity to enjoy the featured drink of the season. Bowling on ice that has been rippled and grooved by the strong winds coming in off Cook Inlet, with temperatures hovering around the zero mark, is a challenge for the best of bowlers. For me, a non-bowler, it goes far beyond the word "challenge."

In 1995, the young pin setter I had was new to the game, particularly the way I played it. But with promises of dollar bills floating before his eyes, he was willing to learn. The Peanut Farm paid each pin setter a certain amount for the work they performed, but I explained to my young accomplice that I was no bowler, and each time he helped me knock down the pins I'd give him a dollar. The first couple of times my bowling ball went wobbling down the ice to end up either in some one else's alley or off the ice completely, my young friend (with much urging on my part) dutifully pushed over the pins my ball hadn't touched. He did this by remaining seated on a bale of hay and reaching out with one booted foot to inconspicuously knock over as many of the pins as he could reach without getting up. As promised, each time he "helped" me I gave him a dollar bill.

As his pockets began to bulge with those pictures of George Washington, he became more and more adept at his job as "helper." By the time we left for the day, he had learned to literally slide off his bale of hay and onto the ice scattering bowling pins in every which direction. He had so many dollar bills sticking out of his pockets when he went home he looked like a young bank robber. I've often wondered what explanation he gave his mother for his new found wealth.

Could it be that I started this young man off on a life long path of corruption? Probably not. Our rooting section on the side lines showed him our antics on this outside bowling alley was just our own special way of enjoying this part of the Rondy celebration.

And though a prize was offered for the bowler with the highest score, which I had of course, I did not accept it. I left that for someone who had earned it honestly.

# Just One Year
## Margaret "Peggy" Hicklin

It all began in the 1930s when my two older brothers came to Alaska for two summers to work on fish traps out of Ketchikan. Twenty years later, in the summer, a friend and I rode to Seward on an Alaska Steamship to spend six weeks in Anchorage. We worked in Emard's Cannery and spent any free time visiting nearby sights. It was the year Mt. Spur erupted which made our summer that much more exciting.[1]

One year later Jean Leeburg and I drove up the Alcan to spend a year in Anchorage. That road trip was a challenging experience and further fueled our taste to see the "real" north.

Fort Nelson, where we stopped one night, was mainly a sawmill and a lodge/store. Before heading out the next morning we took a brief walk back in off the road. Down in a hollow a short way we saw a camp; a tent, a crude clothes line and an open fire going. A swarthy young man was moving about. When he saw us he asked if we'd like a cup of coffee. We smiled at each other in agreement and accepted the logs he offered for chairs. He retreated into the tent for a couple of mugs with no handles (and no cream or sugar). Settling down we traded stories. We learned he was a trapper and dealt in furs. When conversation slowed, he offered to get a few fish for our dinner if we had half an hour. Here's the "real thing" we thought and followed him over a knoll to a small pond. He'd picked up a willow pole with hook and line attached. Standing on the edge of the water we watched him slap a fly on his vest and attach it to the hook. I watched anxiously, so hoping he'd catch a fish so we could be impressed. I needn't have worried; in short order he had four nice sized grayling. He proceeded to clean and wrap them in a couple of large leaves, and we took them gratefully and went on our way.

About five o'clock that evening found us on the shore of a lovely lake further up the road roasting those tender morsels for our supper. No fish I've tasted since has ever compared with those, and no experience has seemed so completely "north."

As for Anchorage, both Jean and I have stretched that year to over fifty and we're still here...so much for "one" year.

[1]*Editor's note: 1953. It made an awful mess in Anchorage.*

# My First Year in Alaska
## Millie Renkert

In 1945 while working as a secretary at the FBI Field Office in Grand Rapids, Michigan I was offered a one-year assignment to the Anchorage Field Office because I had previously expressed an interest in Alaska. Was it coincidence or destiny that the FBI office in Grand Rapids was closing just as there were openings in Alaska and I was ready for adventure?

I was 23 and eager to see Alaska as I had read about it and attended a slide presentation by Father Bernard Hubbard, S.J. Luckily for me, I had the option of coming by air or Alaska Steamship's 'S.S. Alaska'. Naturally I chose the latter which afforded the opportunity of stops in Ketchikan, Juneau, Valdez, and Seward as well as the trip on the Alaska Railroad from Seward to Anchorage.

Sadly my year was nearly over before I got to see much of Alaska except for the Matanuska Valley, Curry, Copper Center, and, briefly, Kenai. The trip to Kenai was by air (there were no roads in 1946.) Shortly after we arrived a small child was scalded by falling into a tub of hot water and we had to return immediately to transport him to the hospital in Anchorage.

Finally, a fellow I had been dating, who knew I wanted to see more of Alaska, made arrangements with a bush pilot to fly us to McGrath where we had friends. When we arrived, the pilot was asked to fly a bride to Ophir, a mining community, where her husband was working. The pilot agreed he could take one of us to Ophir if the bride's luggage was not too heavy. So, off I went, leaving my friend in Mc-Grath. Once in Ophir it was too late to make a return trip to McGrath, so I got to see all the miners coming in from the "creeks." There was a big party for the newly weds, and I had a great visit with the locals.

The next morning the weather was "socked in" and people told the pilot not to fly. Eventually he decided to take off and what a ride! He was watching the mountains so he wouldn't hit them, while I was watching the river so we wouldn't get lost. (The pilot later told me he really needed my help). Over the Takotna Mountain the plane was like a kite with updrafts and downdrafts. The pilot's reassuring words were "If we get over this mountain, we'll be okay." I was so happy when we landed safely in McGrath I could have kissed the ground. I decided I'd had enough of small planes, and not wishing to miss my scheduled trip back to the States the next day, I returned to Anchorage by commercial air leaving my friend (and the bush-pilot) in McGrath to make his way back anyway he could.

After a vacation in the States I signed on for another year and have been in Alaska ever since.

Oh, yes, and I married that friend in 1947.

# The X-Madam
## Dorothy H. Kruger

Located at the foot of Mt. Marathon on the edge of Resurrection Bay is William Seward's namesake. Surrounded on three sides by snow-capped mountains, Seward, Alaska is a small seaport community, and before the Good Friday earthquake in 1964 it was the farthest north year round open seaport in all of Alaska. Many ocean-going vessels visited the port, passenger ships as well as freighters, and here freighters unloaded all manner of supplies and foodstuffs for the interior of Alaska. Seward is the southern terminus for the Alaska Rail Road, the northern terminus is Fairbanks, and until the mid 1960s freight and passengers would be carried north by rail from this busy little town on the bay.

Because of the number of seamen and stevedores coming into Seward on such a regular basis, the "Line Girls" from Alley B were an accepted and necessary part of the community. Worthy matrons of the little town might have ignored them by refusing to speak to them, but they knew the presence of the girls kept them all safer, particularly at night when the ships were in.

The Line Girls kept to themselves and were not allowed on the streets of Seward between the hours of 7 and 9 a.m. in the morning, and 4 and 6 p.m. in the afternoon. These were the hours when the "respectable" women of the town might be going to and from work. The Girls from the Line were a somewhat noisy bunch of women, but beautifully groomed and all wore fabulous Alaska jewelry, jewelry encrusted in gold nuggets, diamonds and jade.

Irene Neusbaum, alias Helen Williams, had been a madam on the Line for many years. She eventually left Alley B and started a more respectable business of her own called the *Third Avenue Home Laundry*. One of her customers at the laundry was my father, who took sheets and pillowcases etc. into her each week from his lodge on the Kenai at Cooper Landing. My father always called her Helen, though the name she used at the laundry was Irene. Undoubtedly he knew her before her respectability, but I never questioned him about her. Because my father called her Helen, I did too.

In 1952, my first husband, Bob, was drafted into the army and sent to Fort Richardson in Anchorage for his basic training. This meant I had to give up our apartment and find smaller accommodations—accommodations that would also allow my cat and dog to continue to live with me. Somehow, my father arranged for me to move in with Helen, at her home laundry. Helen agreed to my cat and dog, so I rented her front room from her and we all moved in.

Life with Helen at the *Third Avenue Home Laundry* was generally pretty quiet and almost boring. I'd work all day in Frances O'Brien's gift shop, then come home at night and Helen and I would play canasta and drink tea until midnight before going to bed. Both of us were happy to stay up late, and happy to have each other's company. Helen had an irascible personality, though she treated me with kindness and never complained about my animals. The whites of her eyes were a sickly yellow with fine red lines present, and her ever-present cigarette stained her fingers brown. Her low-pitched, foghorn voiced recalled the appropriate quote, "A prostitute's whisper." This is not to be confused with another quote called "A prostitute's *whisker*," which is something entirely different, and probably doesn't require explanation either. Helen never spoke of her previous occupation, and though I was fairly overcome with curiosity, my mother's constant admonishment of, "Dorothy, *always* be a lady!" still rang in my youthful ears forbidding me to ask such a personal question.

Once in a while, some of the "girls" would visit with Helen and still be there when I'd get home from the gift shop. I'd hurry in to join them around the kitchen table, all big eyed and Dumbo eared, ready to learn anything I could about these infamous women. My curiosity was so great, I probably quivered like a puppy begging for attention. But within seconds of my arrival they all excused themselves and went home. And I never learned a darn thing! (Eventually I did learn that the head girl was named Gypsy, and one of the youngest girls was called Dyna-Flo, but I never learned that at Helen's house.

Gypsy was tall, auburn haired and stately, Dyna-Flo was short, blond and bubbly.)

In order to keep their doors open, the girls from Alley B paid a regular fee to city officials in both Seward and in Anchorage. Periodically they revolted against the money they had to pay to those in Anchorage, 130 miles away. On those occasions when they quit sending the money in, their businesses would be shut down and padlocks put on the doors of their "houses." Then the girls would have to find some place else to stay until things quieted down once more, which probably meant they agreed to send money up to Anchorage again.

This situation occurred once while I was living with Helen. I came home from work one evening to find every flat surface in Helen's home draped in all those fabulous clothes. But I never saw THE girls. I would come home from work to see that articles of clothing had been moved around so I knew the girls had been there, but I never saw hide nor hair of them. I really expected them to move in with us, and was eagerly and apprehensively looking forward to their arrival. Thwarted again. They never arrived.

After I'd been with Helen a couple of months, she took in another roomer. A lady named Sammy who rented Helen's dining room as her sleeping room. The night of the day that Sammy moved in something unusual happened to Helen. She didn't want to play cards very long that evening, saying she didn't feel all that good. Helen's demeanor was always kind of gruff anyhow, and that night she was even more so, particularly with Sammy.

Even though it was relatively early, we all went to bed. Or at least, Sammy and I went to bed. Helen went to her room and "rummaged." Helen's bedroom was right off the dining room, the room Sammy was renting as a sleeping room. For about an hour Sammy and I could hear Helen rooting around in her bedroom, slamming doors and dresser drawers over and over again. And the air was turning blue with the profanities issuing forth from that room. Sammy would call out to me, wanting to know what was going on, and if this was a nightly occurrence, and should we call the police? I could only assure her it had never happened before, and that I didn't have the faintest idea as to what was going on. A couple of times I got up and walked into the dining room to talk with Sammy, and found her wide eyed with fear with the covers pulled up tight around her chin. Although Sammy was probably 20 years older than I, she obviously was going to leave everything up to me to take care of. And naturally I didn't have the faintest idea how to take care of anything going on in that house that night.

Finally, Helen left her bedroom and went into the kitchen. She was still muttering to herself, still swearing a blue streak, and bumping into, and falling over, everything in her path. Then we heard her in the bathroom. Ohhh boy.

To keep my cat from using the shower stall as a potty box, Helen always kept the removable, slatted, wooden, shower floor in an upright position at the entrance to the shower itself. Helen had obviously fallen against that slatted floor and sent it crashing down into the metal shower stall, creating a noise that could have awakened the dead. Again I went into Sammy's room. Again Sammy was lying in her bed with her eyes as big as saucers, and the bedclothes tucked in tight all the way up to her ears. This just couldn't go on like this, so this time I decided to gather what courage I could and confront Helen. I went into the bathroom and there sat Helen in the middle of the floor with her head in the toilet bowl and retching her insides outside. I asked her what was wrong with her and could we do something for her? Even as I said it, I knew the WE was going to be ME...Sammy was going to be absolutely useless. Helen ordered me to "get old Doc Sheldon down here." I called him and he came immediately. Sammy and I huddled in the dining room behind the closed door trying to hear what Old Doc Sheldon and Helen were talking about. The most we got out of it was Helen trying to convince the doctor it was her "old ticker," and the doctor insisting her problem had nothing whatsoever to do with her old ticker.

The next time I saw my father I stood toe to toe with that big man and demanded to know what he knew about Irene Neusbaum alias Helen Williams. With reluctance, he told me a little bit about her, not much. But enough for me to know I'd just had my first experience with an old alcoholic who would occasionally throw in a few potent little pills for an additional boost into oblivion.

Helen could have been right after all...with what she might have consumed that night, her "old ticker" could have been rocking around the clock!

# My Rewarding Summer
## Micki Nelson McGhuey

My family has a cabin on Big Lake. We have no boat, jet ski or other toys to distract us, so we enjoy watching nature in all its glory. The cabin is situated six feet from the water's edge so we sit on the porch listening and waiting to see what critters will entertain us tonight. During summer we see a variety of birds, including loons and mallard ducks, salmon and trout At night we see beaver and muskrat swimming by.

Early spring we had many birds stop by on their way north. We saw a family of beavers, two adults and two babies swimming by. A mother Mallard came by and brought her five brand-new babies for their first visit to the cabin.

Thursday Rick came up and as we were sitting on the porch the mother Mallard came by with her babies again. We fed them duck pellets on the grass in front of the porch. Then the babies came up onto the porch and ate by our feet. Each time they came we could see how much they had grown since the last visit. We are always pleased and excited when the whole family is together. We count each duckling as they swim around the tree in front of us.

Our mommy duck is amazing. We were feeding the ducklings when suddenly the mom made a quick sound or a wing flap signaling an alarm that only the babies recognized. The babies were immediately in the water and swimming by the shore under a tree. Rick looked to the left under the tree to see why they departed so quickly. I heard a noise and looked up. Six feet above me was the full body of an eagle. Wings spread wide and in full swoop I could see the outline of every feather. The eagle flew to a tree and lunch was lost for that day. Mother Mallard took her babies under the dock and maybe every fifteen minutes she would come out, look, and then take her young back under the dock. We looked and saw nothing but she knew or saw something we didn't.

Next day the duck family came back. We were feeding them and suddenly the mother made a noise or moved a certain way and all the babies were again in the water. Just then a big, red dog came around the corner of the cabin sniffing where the ducklings had been. I had never seen this dog before nor since.

The next week when BJ and Jacob were getting ready to go swimming the ducks came by so the boys came onto the porch to feed them. We quietly walked on the porch. The babies came onto the lawn and porch to feed at the boys' feet. Mother Mallard moved and all but one of the babies flew into the water. That one lay with its head under the porch instead of moving into the water like the rest. I stepped down and grabbed hold of its body and tried to pull it out, but the silly bird kept pulling to go under the porch. I was surprised when I grabbed hold of the bird that it didn't fight me. I wanted to pull it out so it could go the other direction into the water. I pulled on the body and its neck was bloody. I thought, "Oh, no, it is caught on a nail and it's cutting itself." I dropped the bird and it pushed itself back under. I'm 65 and thinking, "How can I jack up the porch to get the bird out." "Oh, why doesn't a boat come by or someone to help," but I was on my own. So I pulled hard again trying to free it. It came out followed by a brown head and two black, beady eyes looking at me. I flipped it out on the lawn while the boys watched and didn't understand any more than I what was happening. We thought maybe the duck was in shock and maybe would come out of it and hop back into the lake with the rest of his family. The boys went back to their swimming. I thought the duck was dead so I grabbed a black bag, picked it up to get it out of the kids' sight, but it was alive like I had hoped and thrashed its way out of the bag. I let it lie there not knowing how to help it. I watched it for a while and could do nothing for it. Mother duck and siblings came by often calling for it, but nothing happened. I went into the cabin to fix dinner and let the duck rest. I came out a little later to check on it. It was gone. It may have been dinner for a weasel or mink. That is nature's way, but we like to think it went back into the water and joined its family.

I still don't know how the mother Mallard knew there was danger to her babies.

At the end of summer we saw a pair of loons and two babies.

Early in September I was privileged to see two big, fat beavers. It was 9:30 at night, just before dark when I walked out on the porch and there was a beaver just climbing out of the water onto the shore eating clover. I watched for about five minutes being very quiet when I noticed that there was another big beaver a little further down the shore. I had never seen them before up on the shore like that eating clover. They then waddled into the water and swam off, one following the other. That evening I also saw two baby muskrats playing in the water.

That was the end of my wonderful summer!

Poetry

# Seldovia, 1974
## Cathy J. Kincaid

I had a cottage on the slough and I was happy there;
bald eagles circling overhead and sea salt in the air.
My cottage was a pretty sight tucked in among the trees,
it's dark orange wood and deep red trim contrasting with the leaves.
The trees were birch and cottonwood and spruce so tall and spare
with mossy trunks set off by red cranberries everywhere.
The window box matched the trim of doors and sills and eaves.
Forget-me-nots came tumbling out competing for the bees.
All round the house there grew, profuse and intertwined,
the monkey blue geraniums and honeyed columbine.
The poppies opened with a shot like corks from bottled wine.
The ferns unwound beneath a stump where Jacob's Ladder climbed.
Coral tinged, the clouds set sail, across the sky toward night
from midnight sun that never fails, a sailor's true delight.
Then, in the fall, when colors turned, the ducks and geese took flight.
The wind blew cold, the snowflakes fell, the moon shone full and bright.
The cottage stayed so warm and snug, the old oil stove held heat.
I'd keep a soup warm on the back while baking bread and meat.
I had a cottage on the slough, all ship shape, tight and neat
and I was safe and happy there, and life was warm and sweet.

# Morning
## Marv Fuhs

We top this rise
and the windshield fills
McKinley and Foraker hold hands
under blankets of snow
the early morning scene
shapes the day
we hold to each other
by feeling across the seat.
We sense it;
we are infinite and small.
The black top road
ever bringing us closer
climbs another rise and closer still.
The windshield further fills
with solemn majesty;
we are in the valleys
that look up
to mountains that fill our life.

# Comes an Alaska Autumn Night
Renee Pagel

The north wind breezes nip the air
The sky is fair and clear
I hear the Ravens calling
Winter is getting near.
The geese are soaring southward
The colorful leaves have come and gone
The flowers are all withered
From cold, clear, frosty mornings.
I stop to rest myself
On a hill side that is steep
I go to dreaming of my past
And I slowly fall asleep.
My heart is lingering lonely
For my loved ones way back home.
I see my mother waiting
Inside the farm house door.
With the smell of kitchen odor
Of fresh baked new breads
The family's evening supper
With folded hands,

And bowed heads.
And then I slowly listen,
I hear the trickling streams
And that I'm only waking
From another lonely dream
The magpies flying in the willows
Flying high from limb to limb,
The camp robber birds are busy,
Eating from an early moose kill.
The grizzly high in the mountains
Feeding on the lone hill side.
The flies, and mosquitoes are gone,
I hear an eagle cry.
The still of the evening cooling,
The fog on the lakes near by,
The swans go swimming in
Silence, the loon makes it cry.
The smell of my evening fire
The evening shadow light
The sun goes down on the horizon.
There comes an Alaska Autumn Night.

# Why Alaska?

Christy Everett

Alaska is more than a political controversy
stamped on a ruggedly beautiful face,
more than oil spills in the pockets of politicians,
more than Uncle Sam's secret playground,
more than a place where animals, besides humans, can kill you.

Because I drove here for an adventure that turned
into a love affair I now call home.
Because contrary to popular opinion, Alaska is not an island by Hawaii,
the road is paved with potholes and hole-in-the-wall diners
where loggers and tree huggers eat the same potatoes
and talk about the same storm that keeps them here.

Because I can't remember the sky before
I met the Chugach Mountain Range,
the anticipation of awe incarnate, Aurora Borealis,
and our sun --who stays up long past bedtime,
who tells me: "Go on, don't go to sleep…
there's still so much to see."

Because Alaska is summer on steroids with a long winter nap.
Snow a backyard treasure chest filled with danger and glee.
Because it's more likely I'll be caught in an avalanche than gridlock—

traffic is waiting at the same light twice
or getting stuck behind a line of RVs
who unlike the rest of us been-there-done-that Alaskans still gawk
at the mother moose, who nuzzles her newborn child,
on the side of the road.

Because I've watched a lynx glide through
two feet of snow in my backyard,
the same snow I shuffled through moments before
and not one but two black bears, one on the porch,
one on the roof, woke me up,
one morning, as I lay naked in bed and in both happenings—
the lynx, the bears—
I momentarily understood how small I really am.

Because the storied wolf still lives in the woods
with more than three bears
and Goldilocks doesn't wear dresses as she walks down the trail
but a backpack filled with all she needs to survive.
Because I can be the star of my own survival show.

I can pee outside in the daytime as I stand on my front porch.
Yes, I pee standing up.
Just hang my bare butt over the side then do a little dance to drip dry.

Because the mountains I climb aren't metaphors.
I bottle my own glacial water or cup it in my hands and drink it
straight from the source.

Because the breadcrumbs left in my wake got buried
by beauty, by company, by moments of bliss.

Some people in the Lower 48 believe we live in igloos, in isolation,
and so they watch us on the Discovery Channel from their living room
they stopped living in when they turned that thing on
and they may take a cruise up here someday
but they never plan to God forbid move way up north past Canada
to this land of God forsaken snow and ice and if only they knew
God... lives up here too, a wise old wonderer,
wearing all names, no dogmas, who appears
in the pale pink light of dusk.

But they don't know this and they don't come. They don't travel
north on the great Alaska highway, to the last great land,
and that too, is why Alaska.

# Robert Ferrin Gilmore

An Alaskan since 1962, Gilmore has been painting and illustrating most of his life. He was born in Texas in 1928, but grew up in Sand Springs, Oklahoma. He attended Oklahoma State University for two years - his studies were in English and geology. His art training comes from correspondence courses in commercial art and years of practice. For many years, he was an illustrator in the oil and aerospace industries. During the 60s he did free-lance design and illustrations for the Anchorage telephone book, Anchorage Daily News, Alaska Industry Magazine, Concrete Association of Alaska, and various advertising agencies. In 1978 he illustrated and published a calendar of his paintings of Alaska. He has had several successful one-man shows and has exhibited in galleries in Anchorage and Juneau.

A Gilmore painting can be recognized by the brilliant colors he employs and by his realistic interpretations of present and past lifestyles, the various peoples of Alaska, its animals and landscapes. He works almost exclusively with acrylics on canvas. Although, for a change of pace he may use masonite panel or pen and ink on paper with watercolors for dramatic effect.

From 1966 to 1991, he was a scientific illustrator for the U.S. Geological Survey in Anchorage.

# Jean Paal

Jean and her husband, Victor, arrived in Anchorage, newly-wed, from New York in 1945. Within a few years they had a house, in which she still lives, and three daughters. She worked in the airline industry for thirty years. During that time she earned a degree in Computer Science from Anchorage Community College. After retiring from Western Airlines, in 1982, she became a self-employed researcher, specializing in statistical analysis of data, survey preparation and report writing.

Last year, she volunteered to help with the editing of the Senior Center's book of earthquake memoirs, *The Day Trees Bent to the Ground* which led to her involvement with *In the Light of the Night and the Dark of the Day.*

In addition to her gainful employment, Jean occasionally writes a play, serves on the board of the Opera Guild, travels, and works in her garden.

She is delighted with this book, and hopes it will spawn other collections.

# Janet Boylan

Janet was raised in southern Oregon, where she went through school. She graduated from Southern Oregon College with a degree in teaching. After working in Oregon for six years she moved to Alaska, where she taught at Campbell Elementary and Clark Junior High School, retiring in 1996, when her youngest son finished high school.

She started going to the Anchorage Senior Center in 1996 mostly to play bridge. She hadn't played tennis since high school, but found that was something she also enjoyed doing with other seniors. She gradually became interested in helping on the Board of Directors and found that it was essential to raise money for operations for the Center.

She first got interested in getting family stories on paper, and then branched out to include her classes, and getting them to write their own stories. When the Center found itself very short on funds, she decided to do a book on the Alaska Earthquake of 1964, *The Day the Trees Bent to the Ground,* which was published in 2004 and is now in a third printing.

When not compiling stories she and her husband, Don, have a cabin near Gate Creek, and they enjoy the winter sports offered in the area. "If you are going to live in Alaska you have to get out in the winter," she says. Other snowbirds leave in the winter, she leaves in the summer, if at all.

She hopes that people who read the books she helps put together enjoy the stories as much as she enjoys collecting them and getting them printed. She says, "Everybody has a story to tell."

# Index of Authors